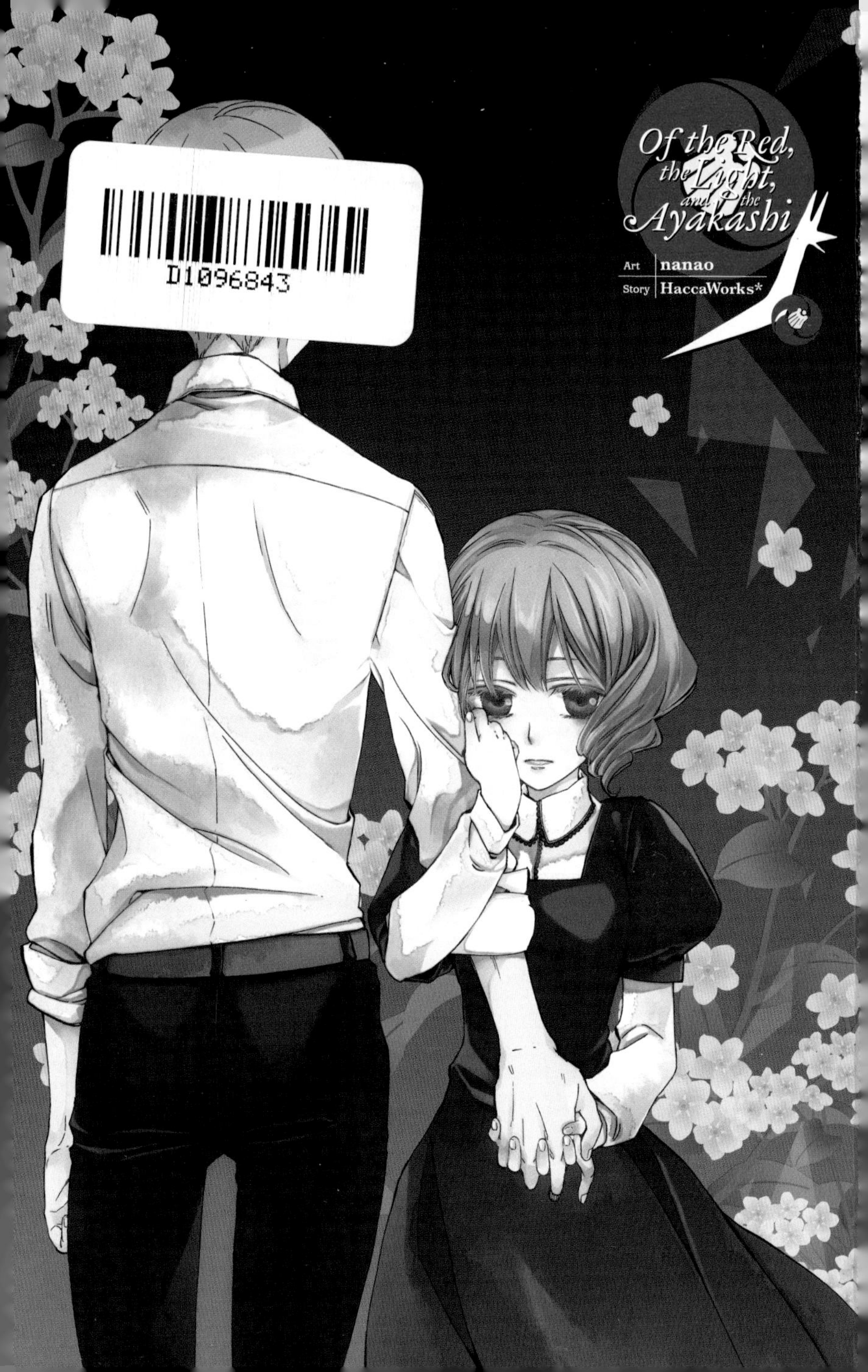
Of the Red, the Light, and the Ayakashi
Art nanao
Story HaccaWorks*

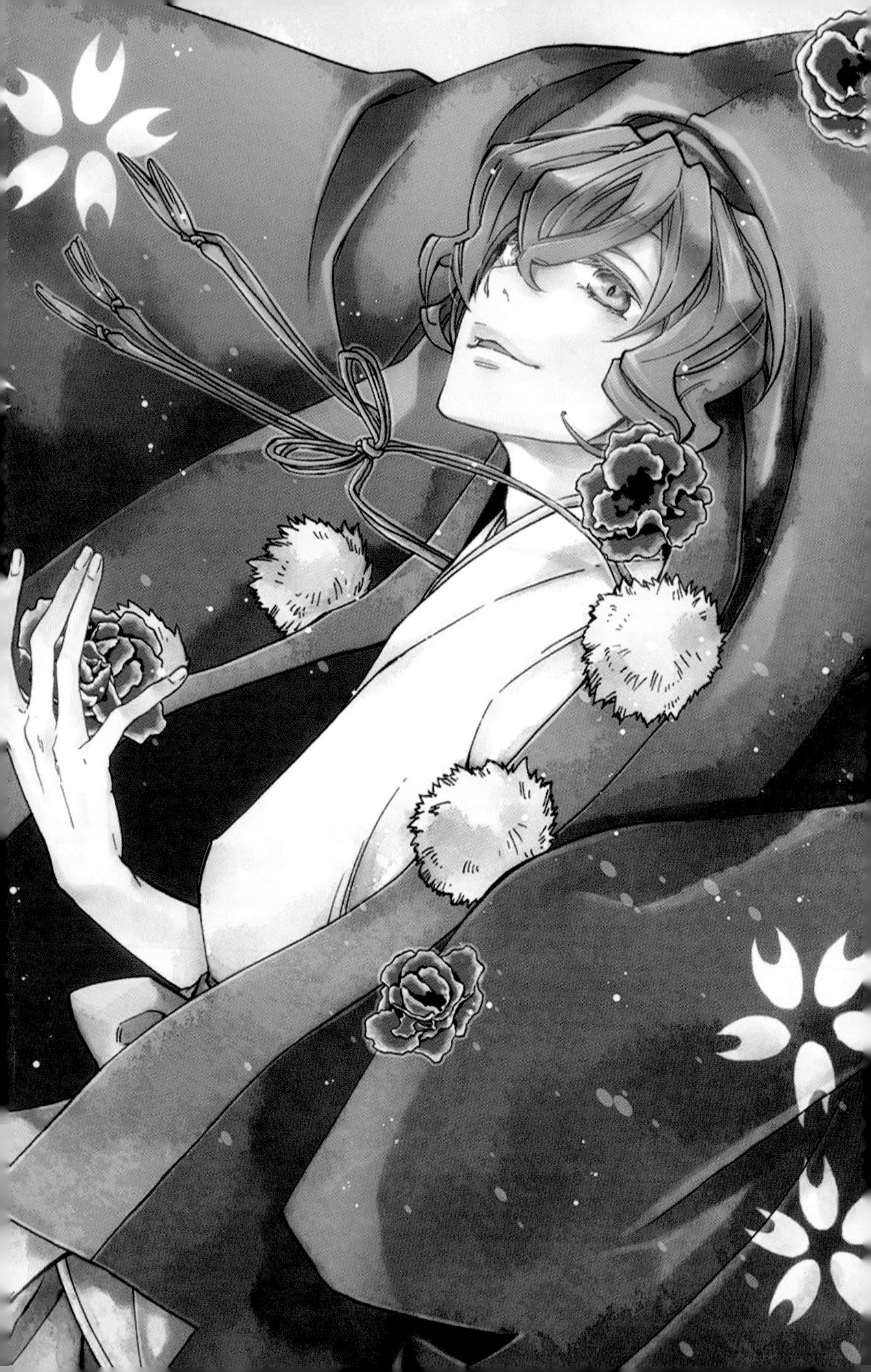

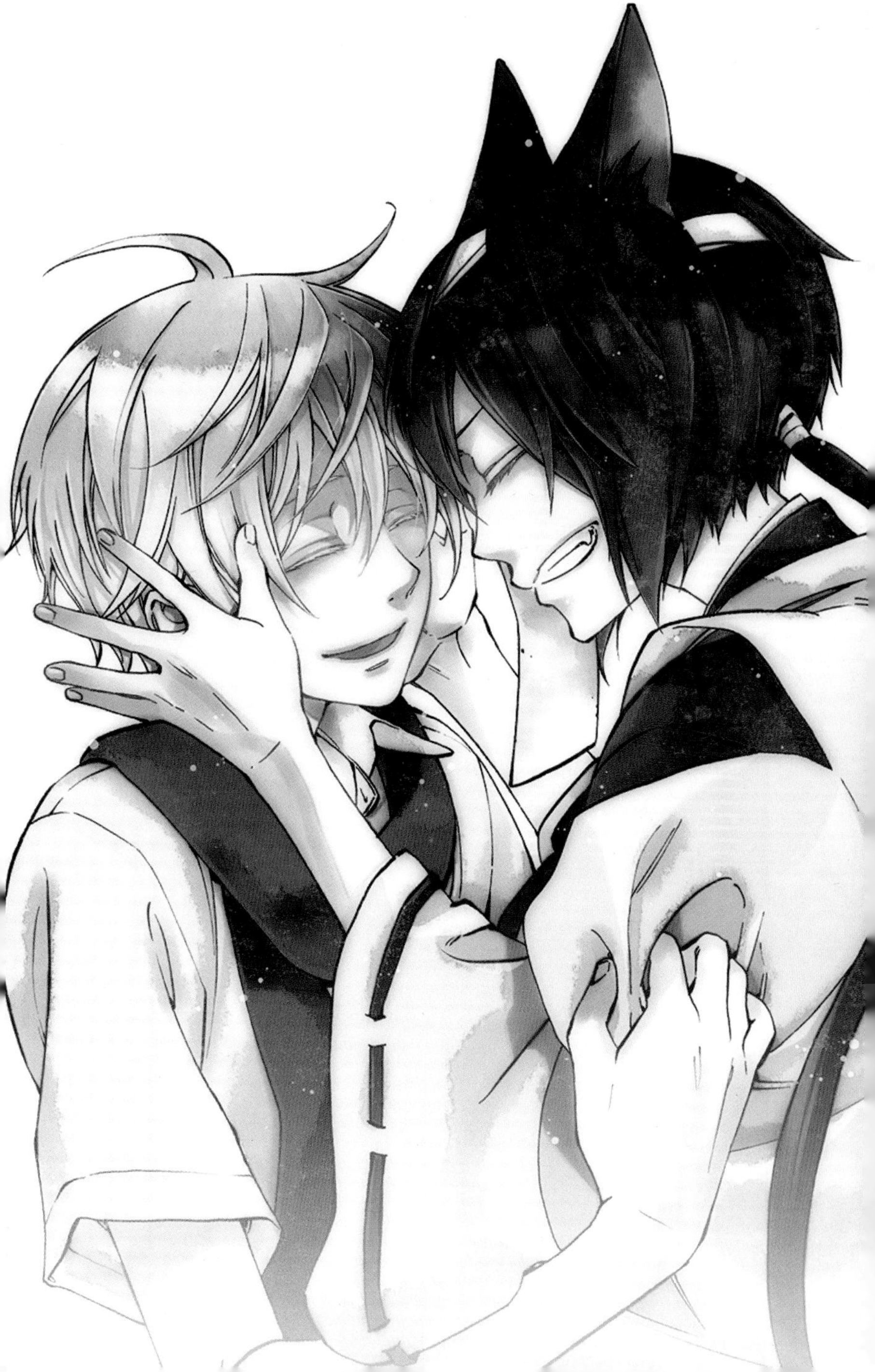

CONTENTS

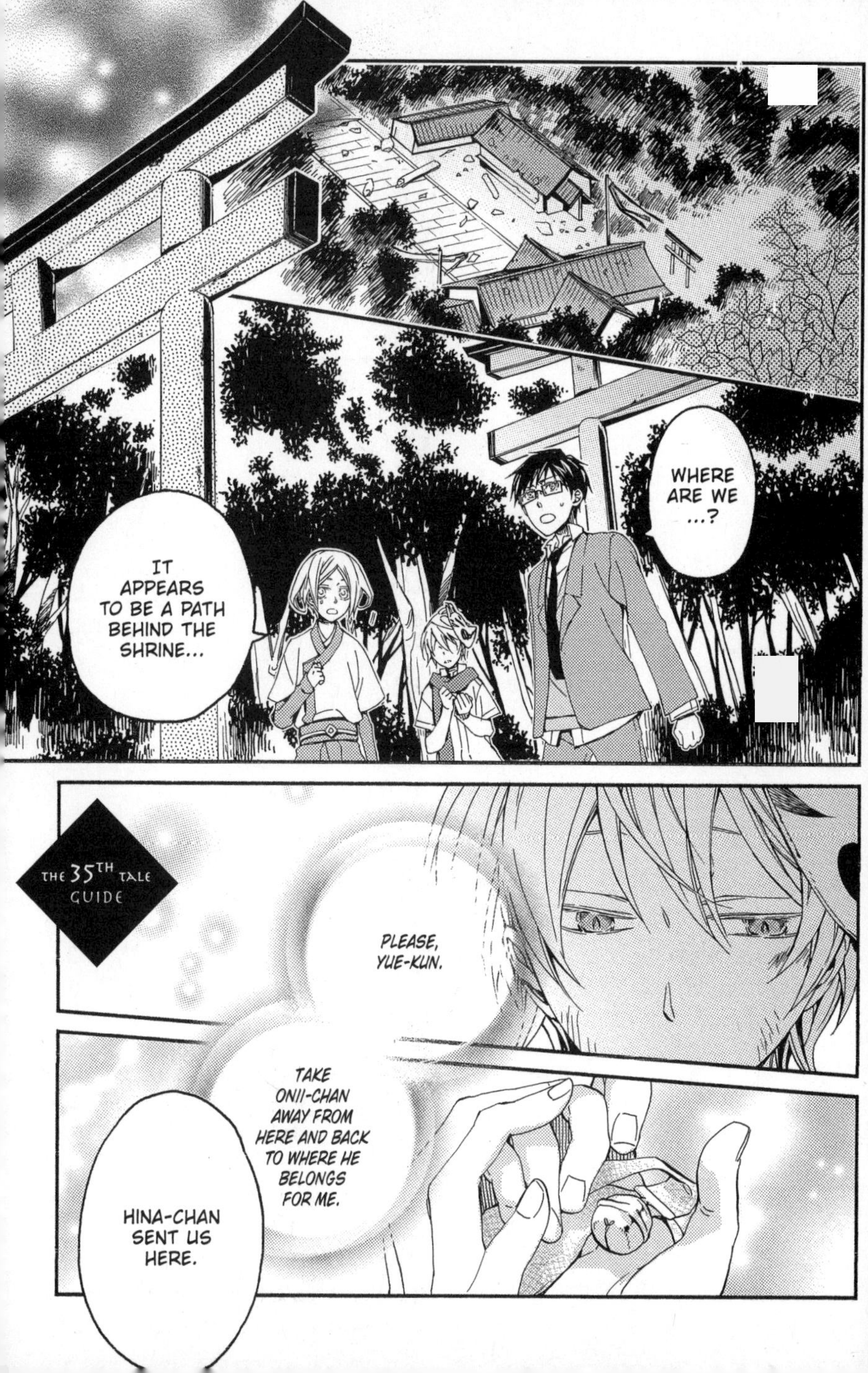
WHERE ARE WE ...?
IT APPEARS TO BE A PATH BEHIND THE SHRINE...
THE 35TH TALE GUIDE
PLEASE, YUE-KUN.
TAKE ONII-CHAN AWAY FROM HERE AND BACK TO WHERE HE BELONGS FOR ME.
HINA-CHAN SENT US HERE.

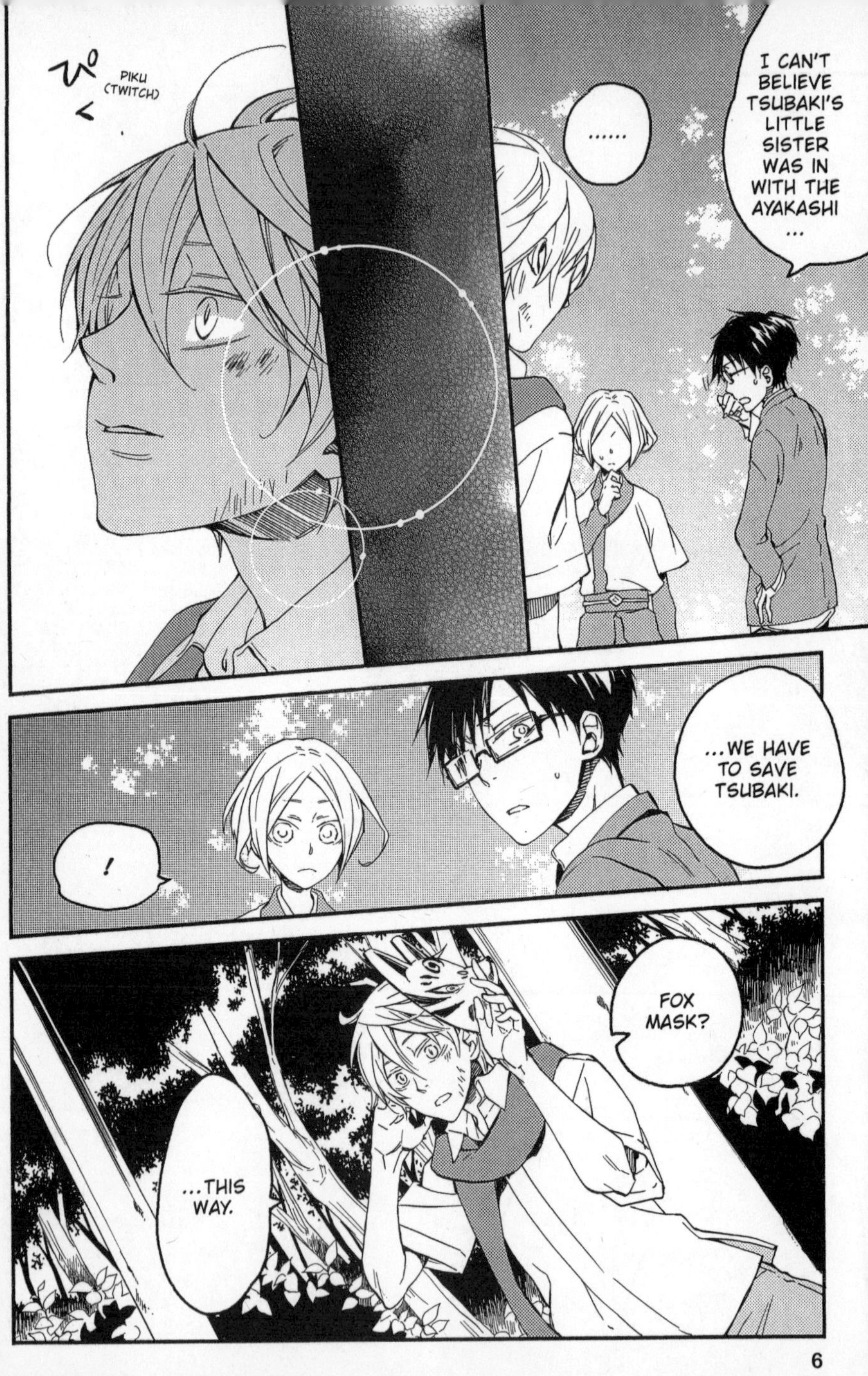
I CAN'T BELIEVE TSUBAKI'S LITTLE SISTER WAS IN WITH THE AYAKASHI ...
......
ぴく
PIKU (TWITCH)
...WE HAVE TO SAVE TSUBAKI.
!
FOX MASK?
...THIS WAY.

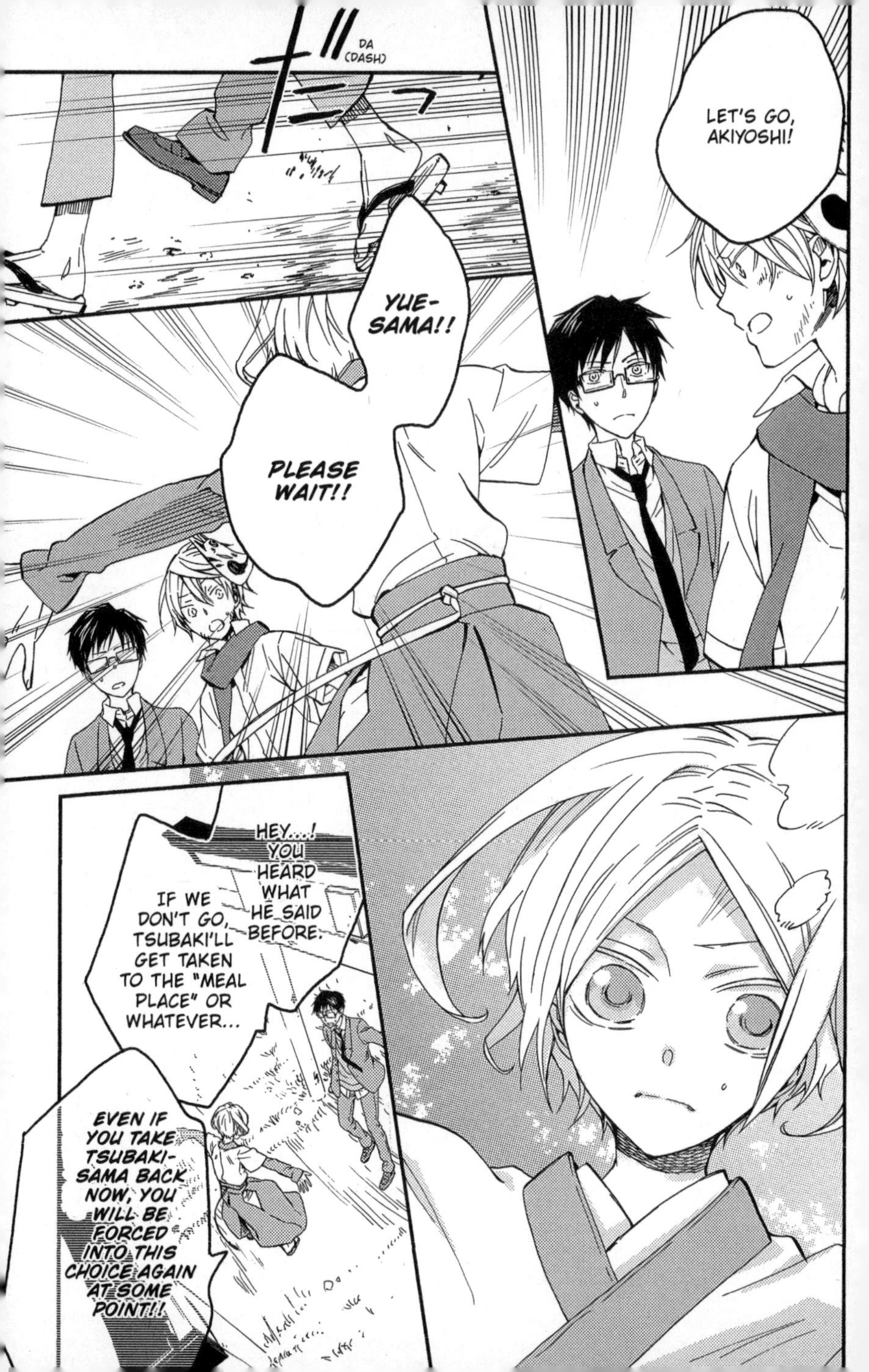
LET'S GO, AKIYOSHI!
DA (DASH)
YUE-SAMA!!
PLEASE WAIT!!
HEY...! YOU HEARD WHAT HE SAID BEFORE.
IF WE DON'T GO, TSUBAKI'LL GET TAKEN TO THE "MEAL PLACE" OR WHATEVER...
EVEN IF YOU TAKE TSUBAKI-SAMA BACK NOW, YOU WILL BE FORCED INTO THIS CHOICE AGAIN AT SOME POINT!!

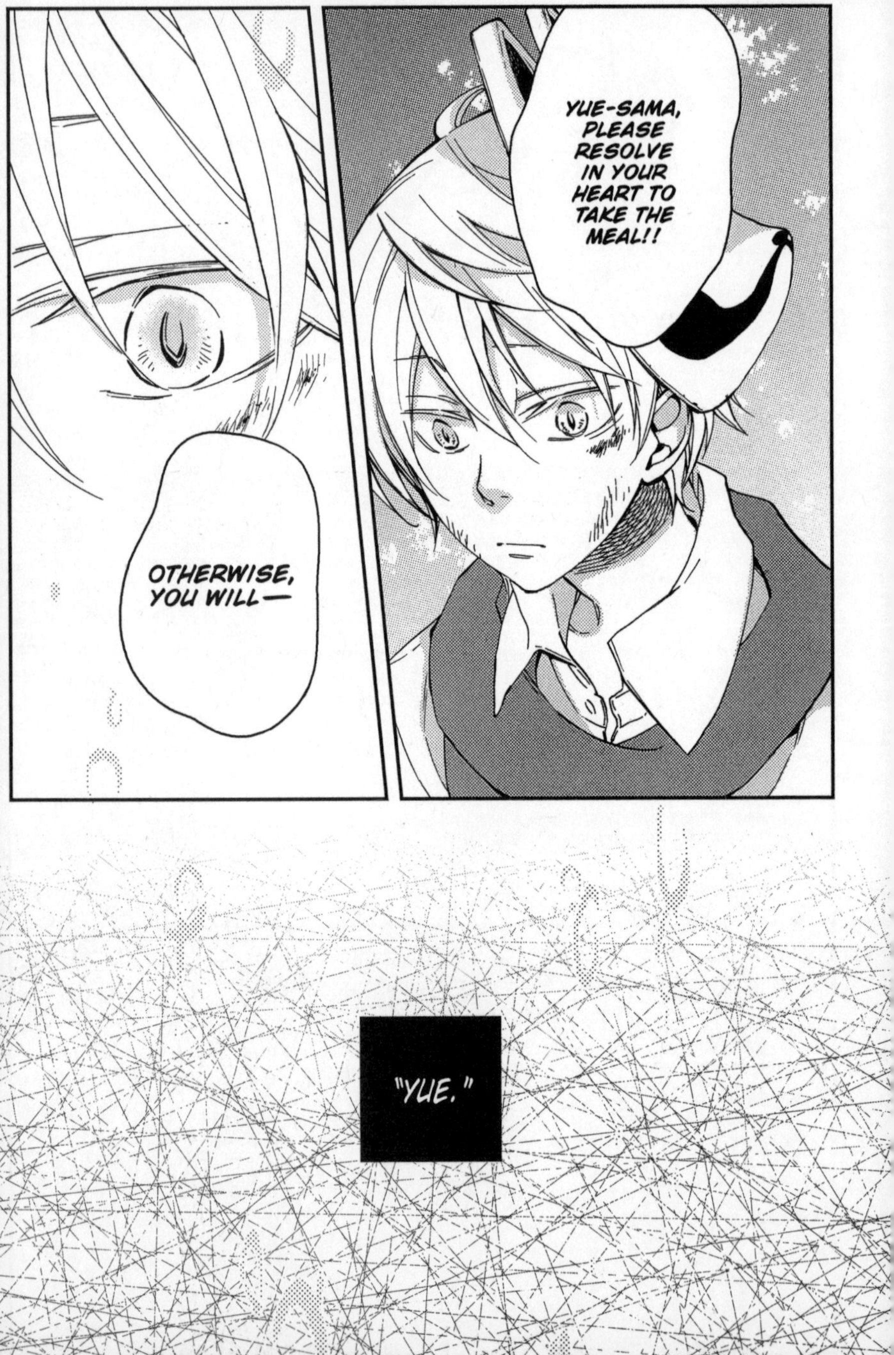
YUE-SAMA, PLEASE RESOLVE IN YOUR HEART TO TAKE THE MEAL!!
OTHERWISE, YOU WILL—
"YUE."

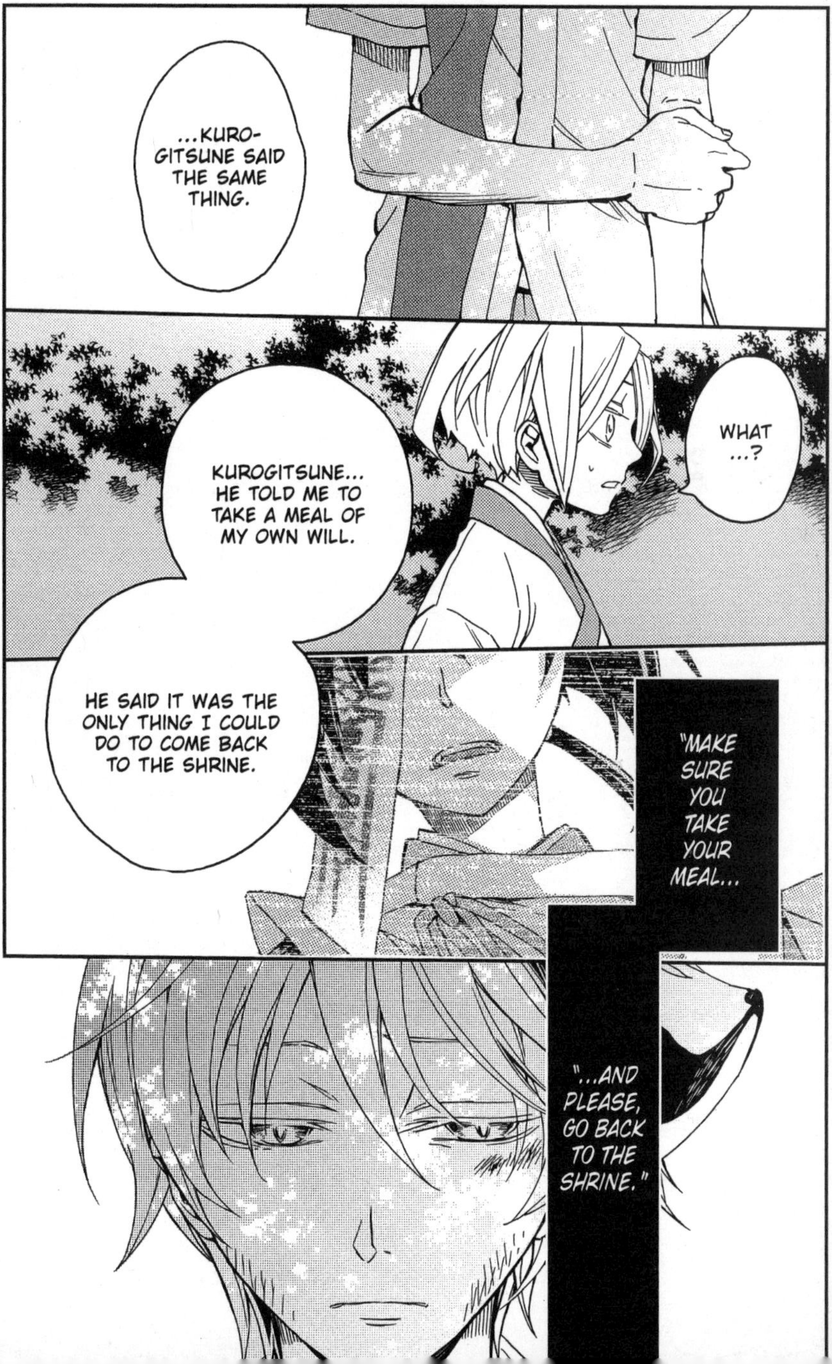
...KURO-GITSUNE SAID THE SAME THING.
WHAT ...?
KUROGITSUNE... HE TOLD ME TO TAKE A MEAL OF MY OWN WILL.
HE SAID IT WAS THE ONLY THING I COULD DO TO COME BACK TO THE SHRINE.
"MAKE SURE YOU TAKE YOUR MEAL...
"...AND PLEASE, GO BACK TO THE SHRINE."

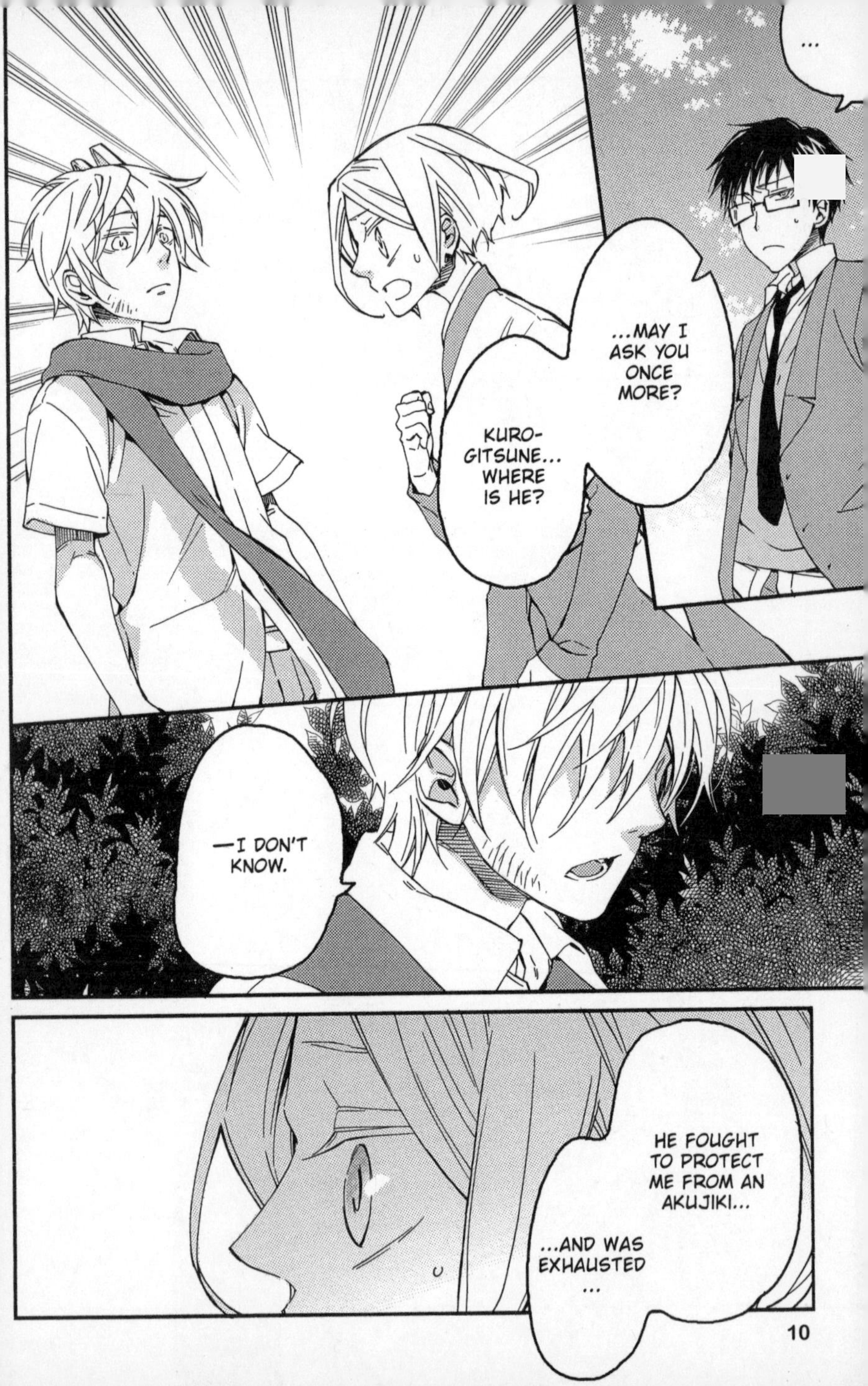
...
...MAY I ASK YOU ONCE MORE?
KURO-GITSUNE... WHERE IS HE?
—I DON'T KNOW.
HE FOUGHT TO PROTECT ME FROM AN AKUJIKI...
...AND WAS EXHAUSTED ...

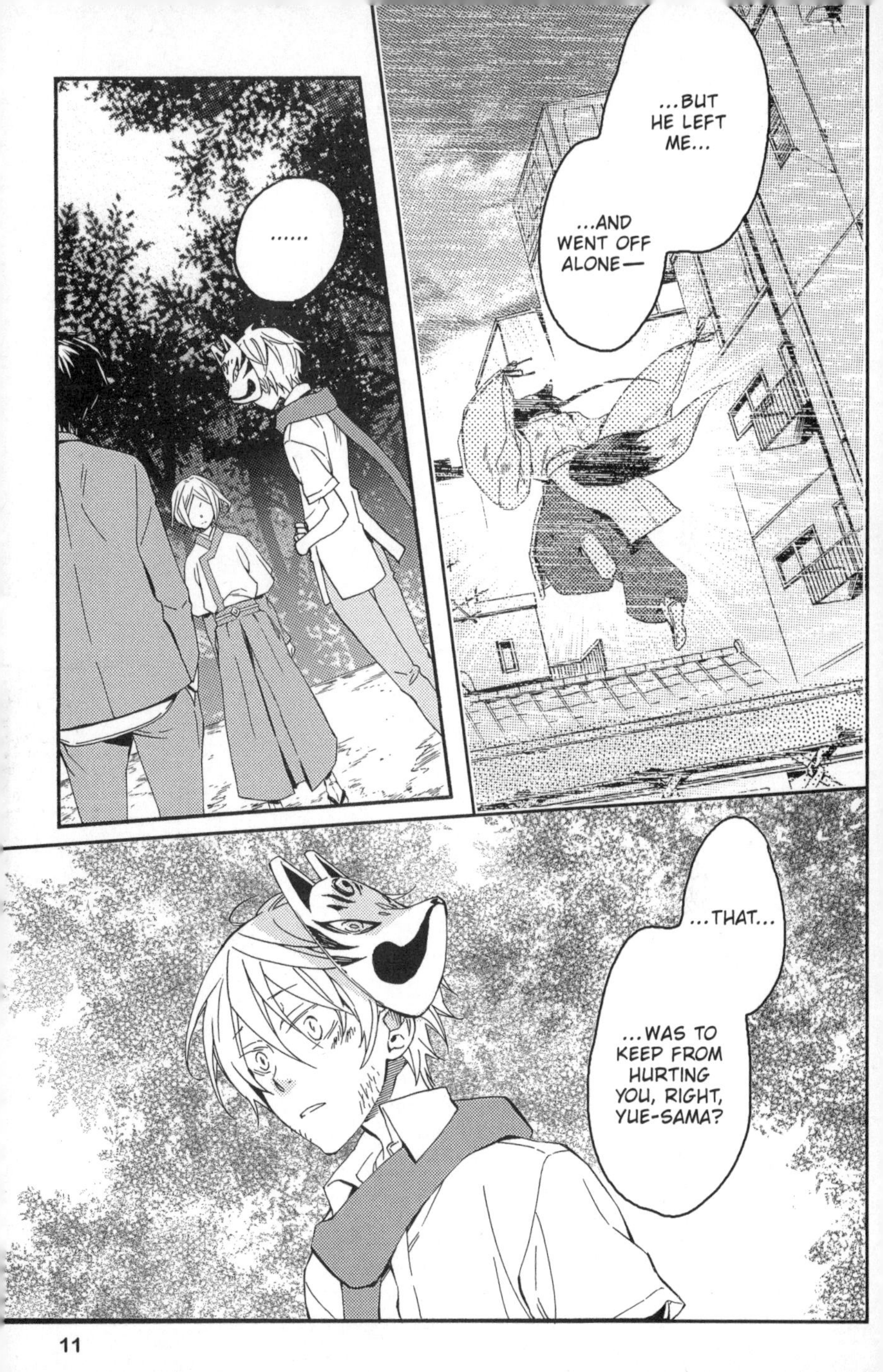
...BUT HE LEFT ME...
...AND WENT OFF ALONE—
......
...THAT...
...WAS TO KEEP FROM HURTING YOU, RIGHT, YUE-SAMA?

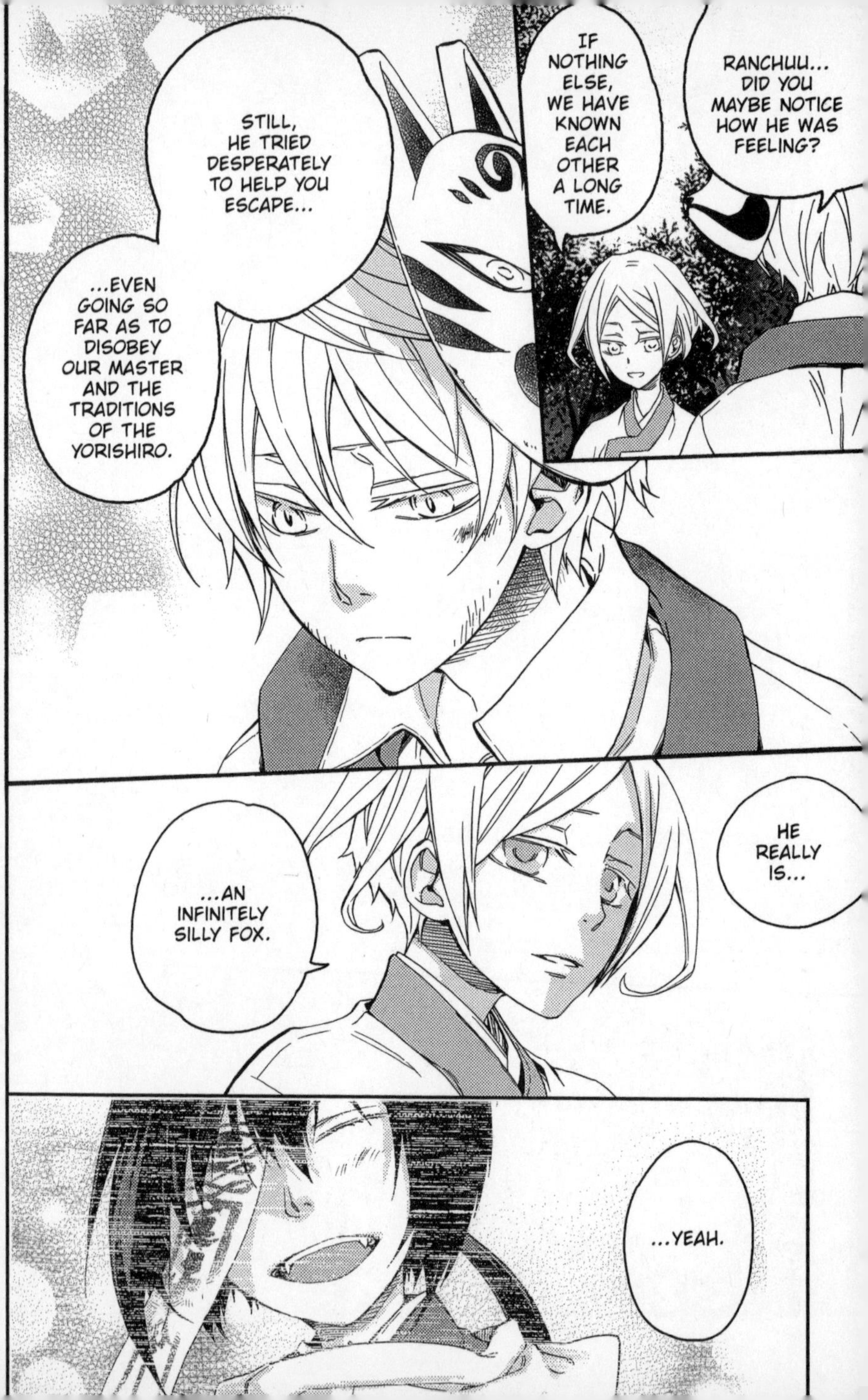
RANCHUU... DID YOU MAYBE NOTICE HOW HE WAS FEELING?
IF NOTHING ELSE, WE HAVE KNOWN EACH OTHER A LONG TIME.
STILL, HE TRIED DESPERATELY TO HELP YOU ESCAPE...
...EVEN GOING SO FAR AS TO DISOBEY OUR MASTER AND THE TRADITIONS OF THE YORISHIRO.
HE REALLY IS...
...AN INFINITELY SILLY FOX.
...YEAH.

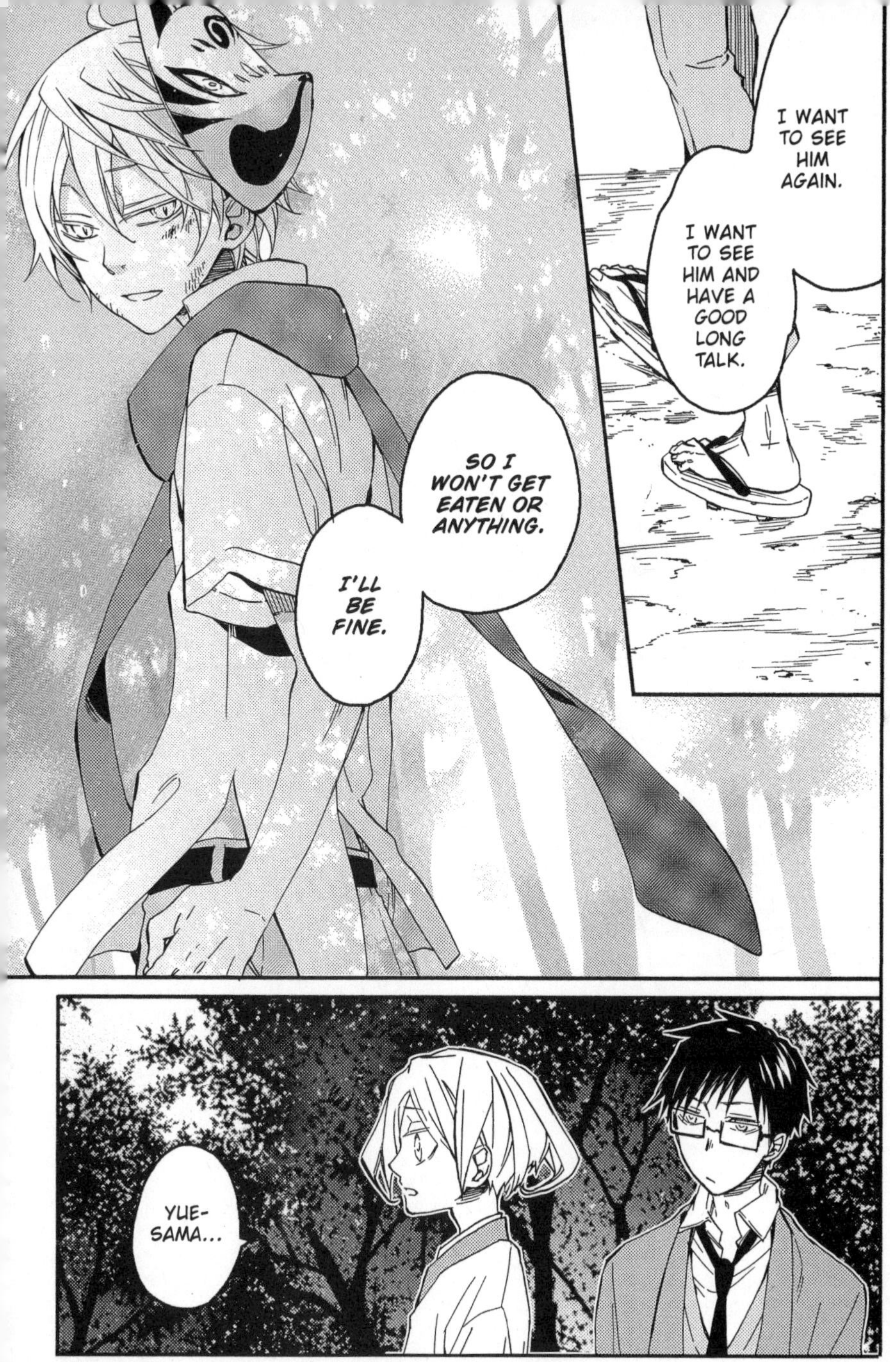
I WANT TO SEE HIM AGAIN.
I WANT TO SEE HIM AND HAVE A GOOD LONG TALK.
SO I WON'T GET EATEN OR ANYTHING.
I'LL BE FINE.
YUE-SAMA...

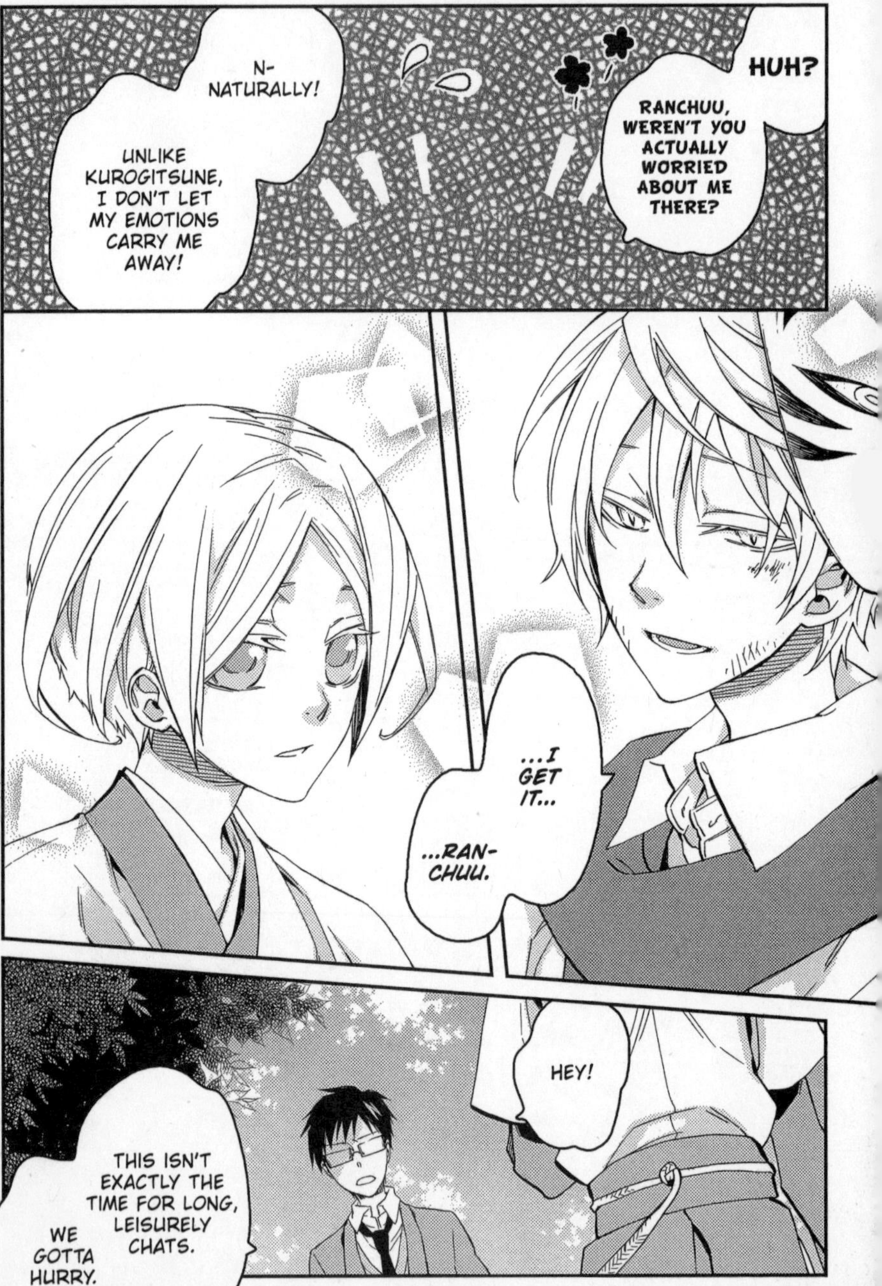
HUH?
RANCHUU, WEREN'T YOU ACTUALLY WORRIED ABOUT ME THERE?
N-NATURALLY!
UNLIKE KUROGITSUNE, I DON'T LET MY EMOTIONS CARRY ME AWAY!
...I GET IT...
...RAN-CHUU.
HEY!
THIS ISN'T EXACTLY THE TIME FOR LONG, LEISURELY CHATS.
WE GOTTA HURRY.

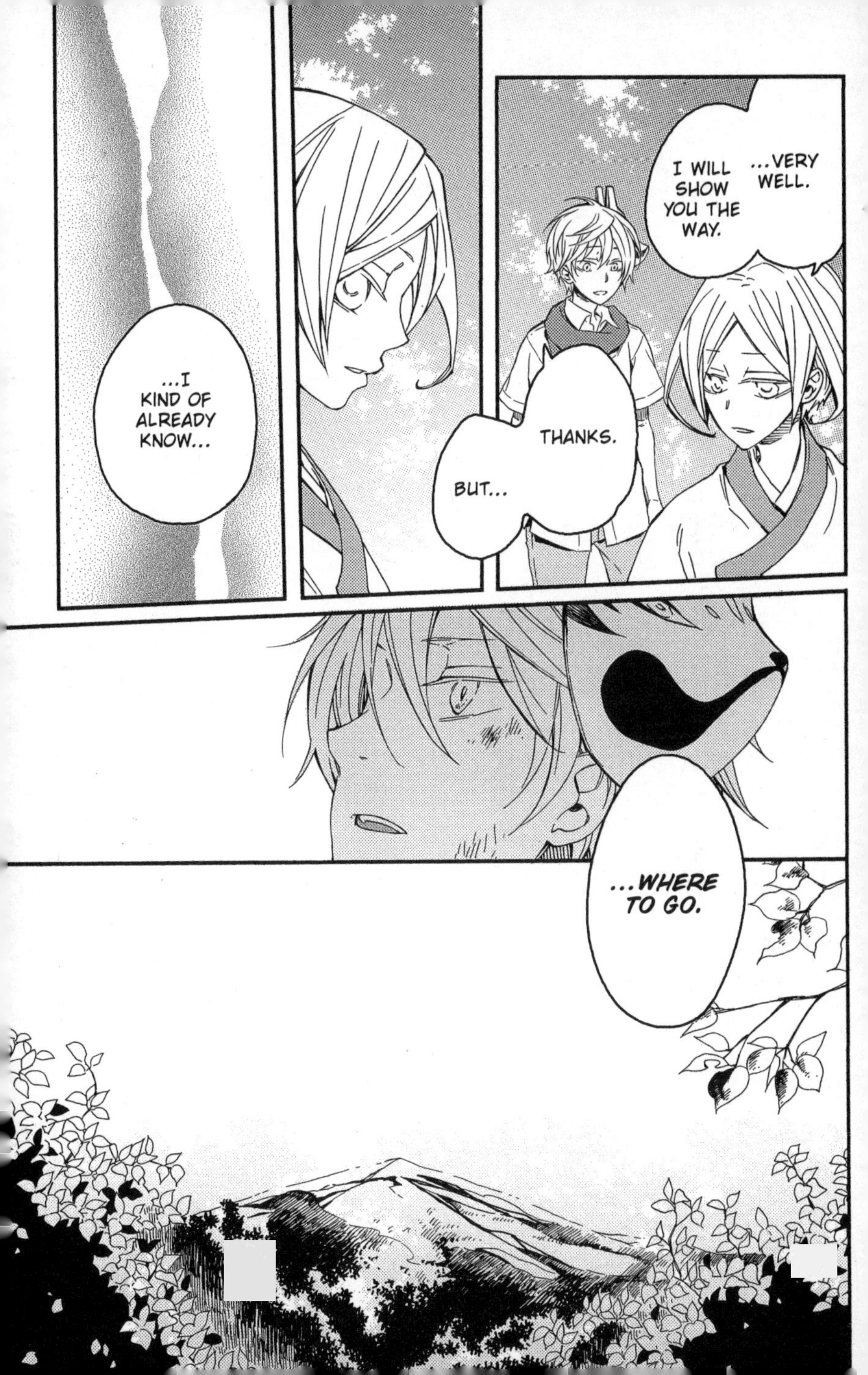
...VERY WELL.
I WILL SHOW YOU THE WAY.
THANKS.
BUT...
...I KIND OF ALREADY KNOW...
...WHERE TO GO.

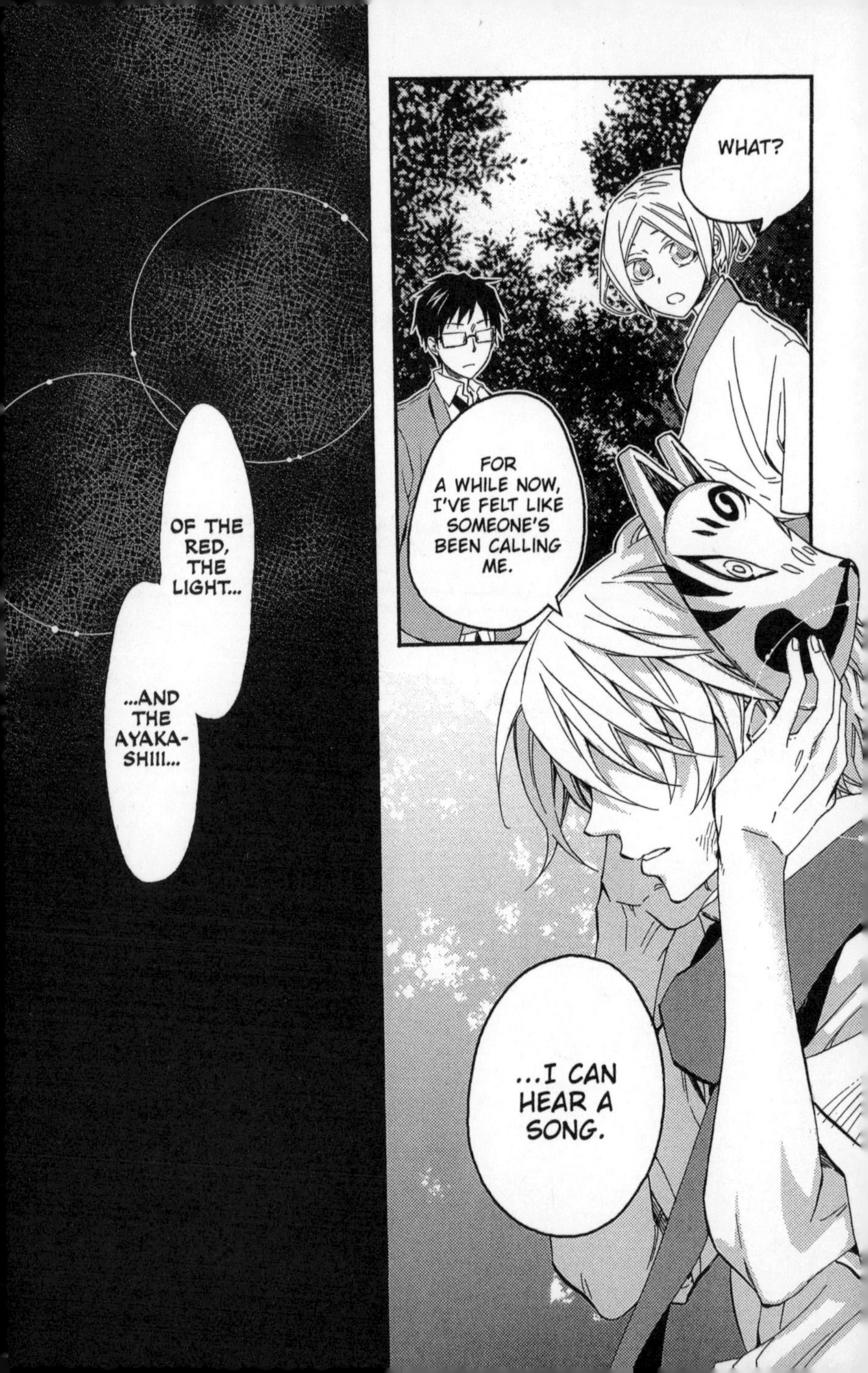
WHAT?
FOR A WHILE NOW, I'VE FELT LIKE SOMEONE'S BEEN CALLING ME.
...I CAN HEAR A SONG.
OF THE RED, THE LIGHT...
...AND THE AYAKA-SHIII...

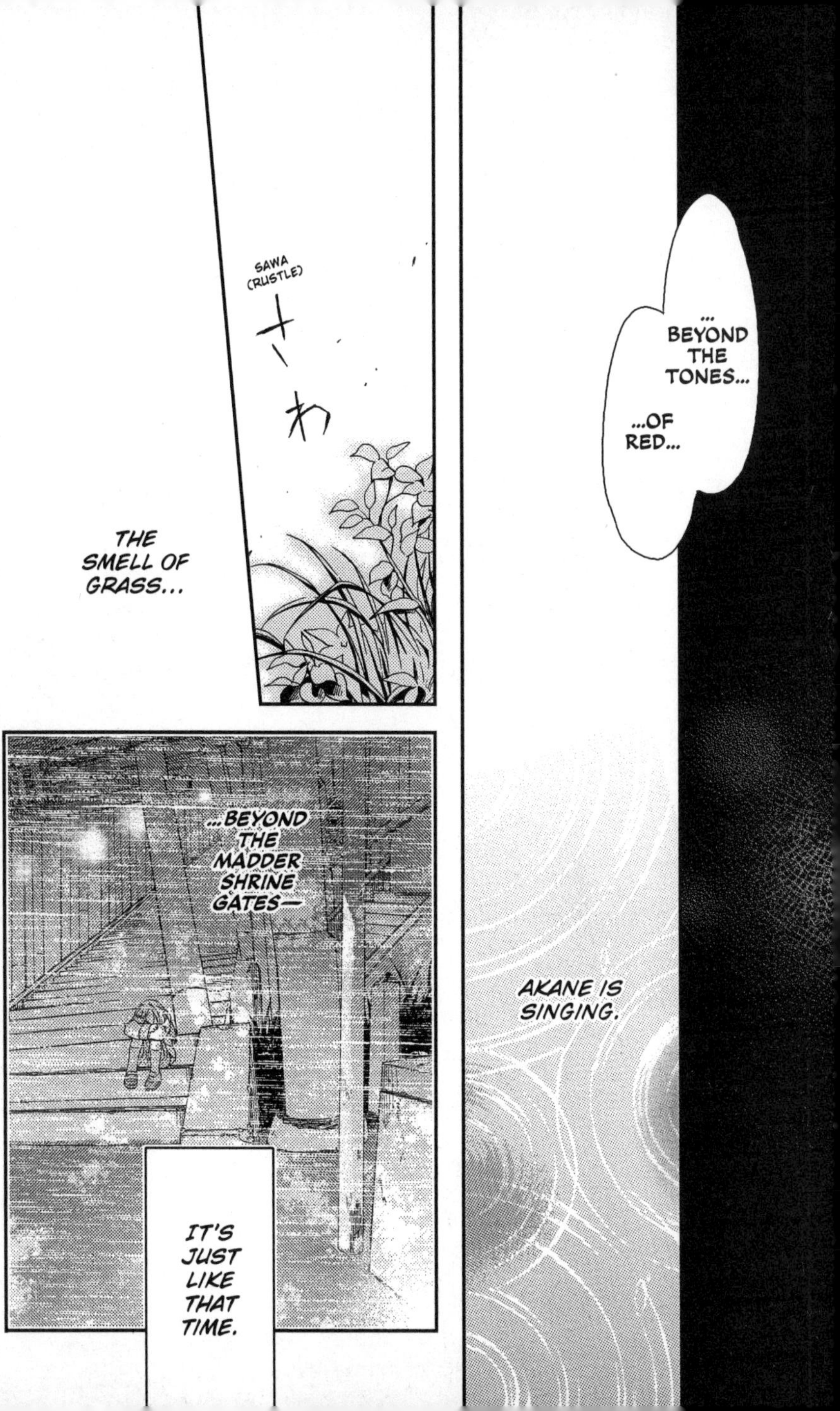
...BEYOND THE TONES...
...OF RED...
AKANE IS SINGING.
SAWA (RUSTLE)
さわ
THE SMELL OF GRASS...
...BEYOND THE MADDER SHRINE GATES—
IT'S JUST LIKE THAT TIME.

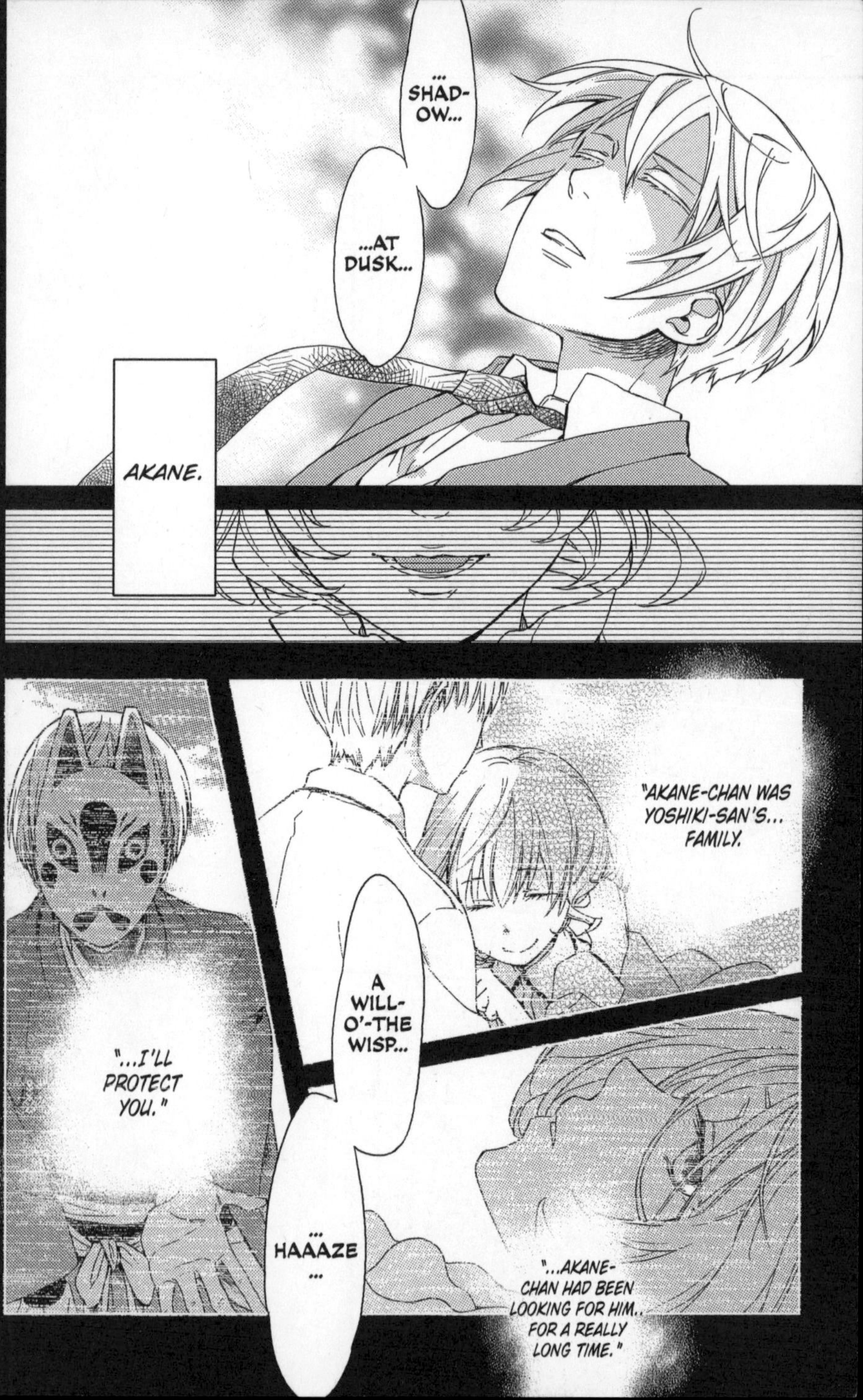
...SHADOW...
...AT DUSK...
AKANE.
"AKANE-CHAN WAS YOSHIKI-SAN'S... FAMILY.
A WILL-O'-THE WISP...
"...AKANE-CHAN HAD BEEN LOOKING FOR HIM... FOR A REALLY LONG TIME."
...HAAAZE...
"...I'LL PROTECT YOU."

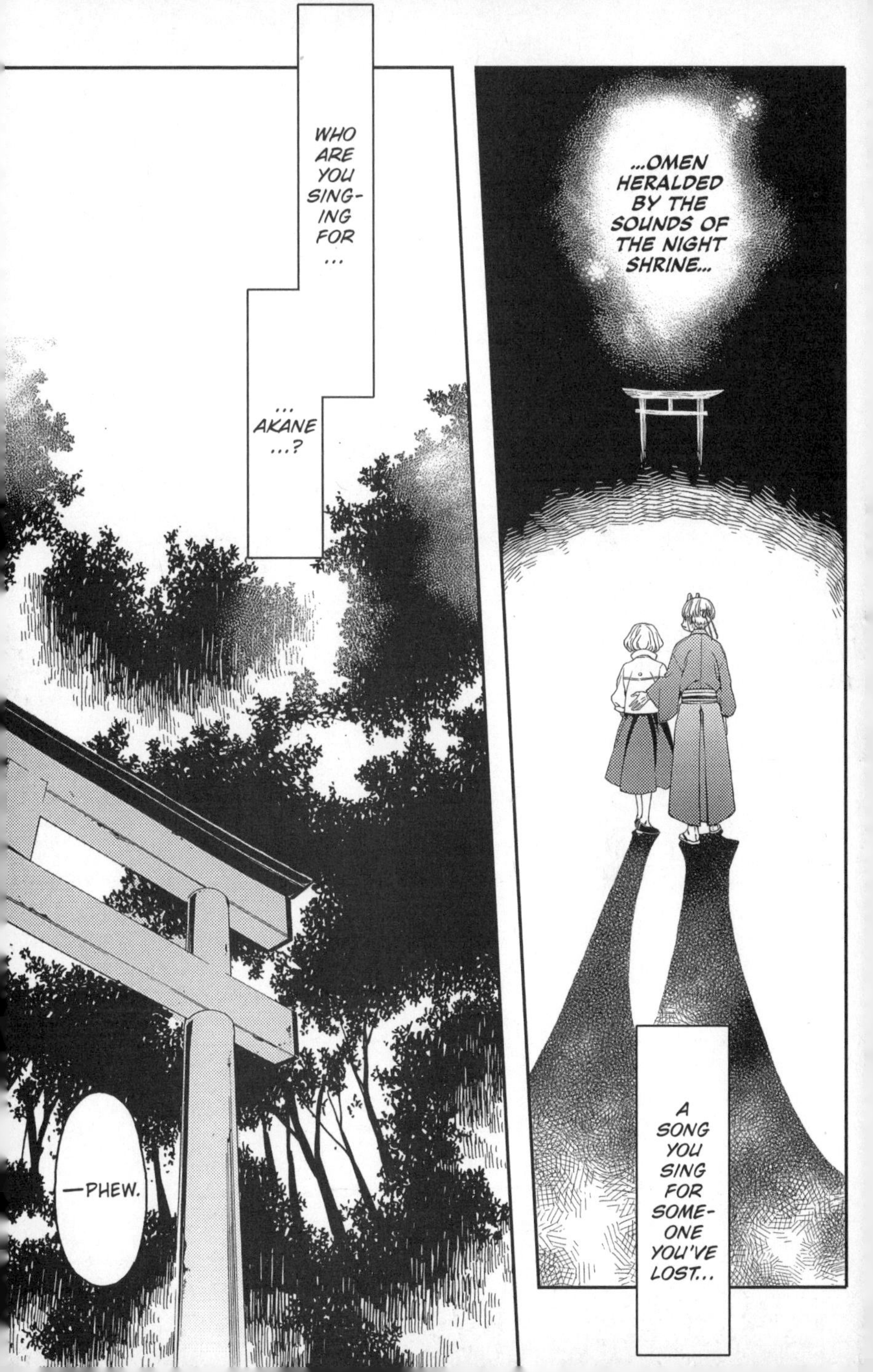
...OMEN HERALDED BY THE SOUNDS OF THE NIGHT SHRINE...
A SONG YOU SING FOR SOMEONE YOU'VE LOST...
WHO ARE YOU SINGING FOR...
...AKANE...?
—PHEW.

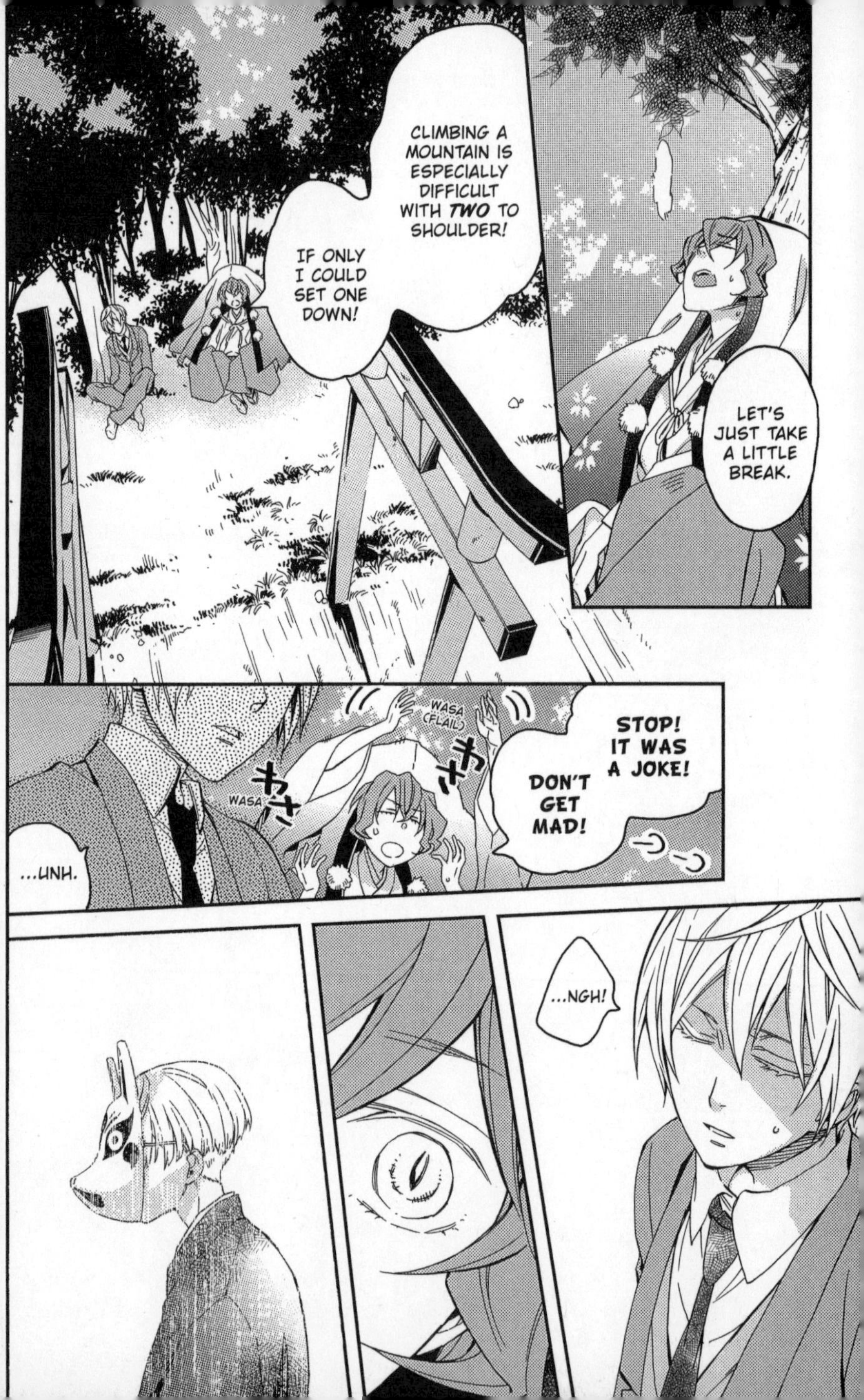
LET'S JUST TAKE A LITTLE BREAK.
CLIMBING A MOUNTAIN IS ESPECIALLY DIFFICULT WITH *TWO* TO SHOULDER!
IF ONLY I COULD SET ONE DOWN!
STOP! IT WAS A JOKE!
DON'T GET MAD!
WASA (FLAIL)
WASA
...UNH.
...NGH!

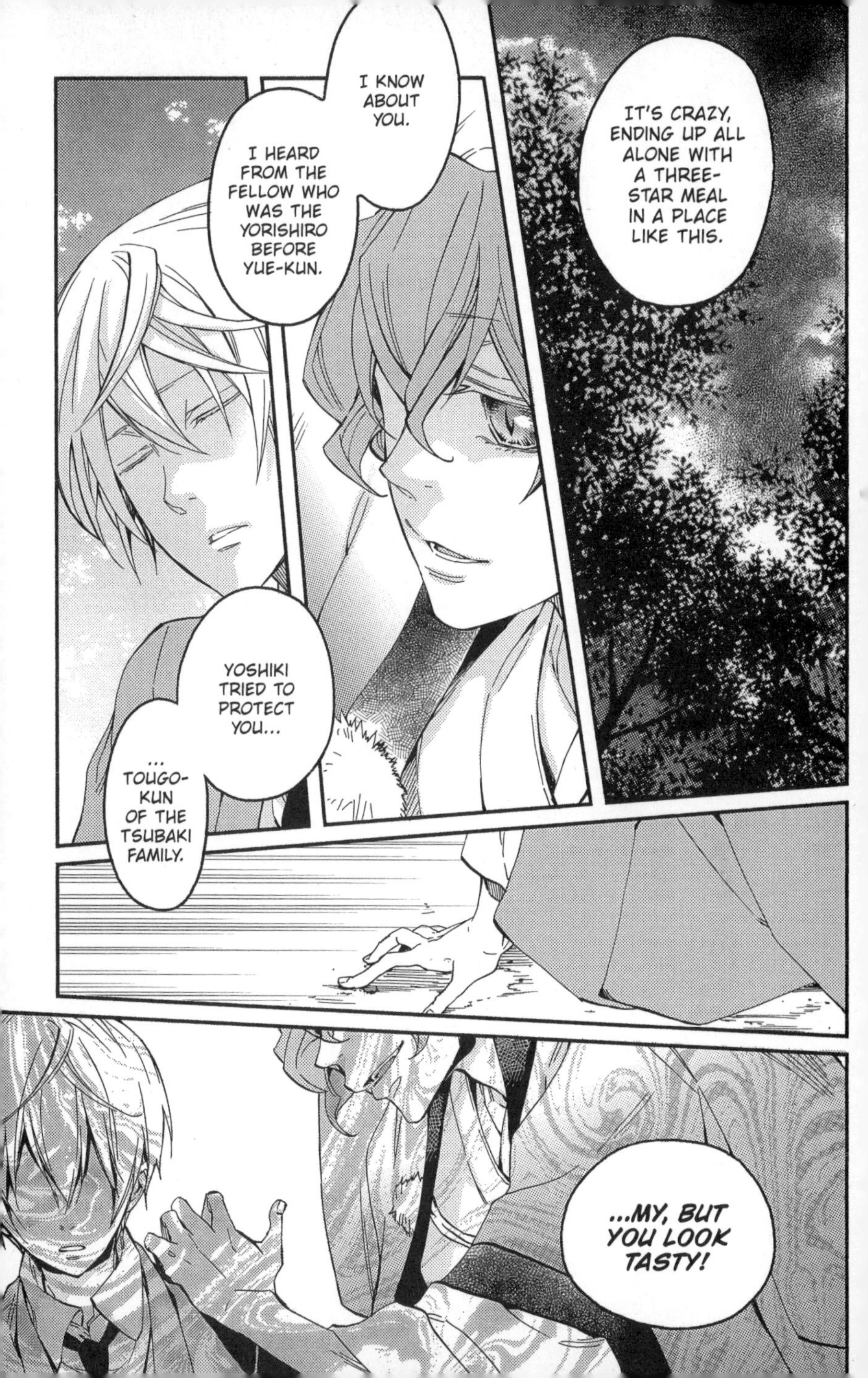
IT'S CRAZY, ENDING UP ALL ALONE WITH A THREE-STAR MEAL IN A PLACE LIKE THIS.
I KNOW ABOUT YOU.
I HEARD FROM THE FELLOW WHO WAS THE YORISHIRO BEFORE YUE-KUN.
YOSHIKI TRIED TO PROTECT YOU...
...TOUGO-KUN OF THE TSUBAKI FAMILY.
...MY, BUT YOU LOOK TASTY!

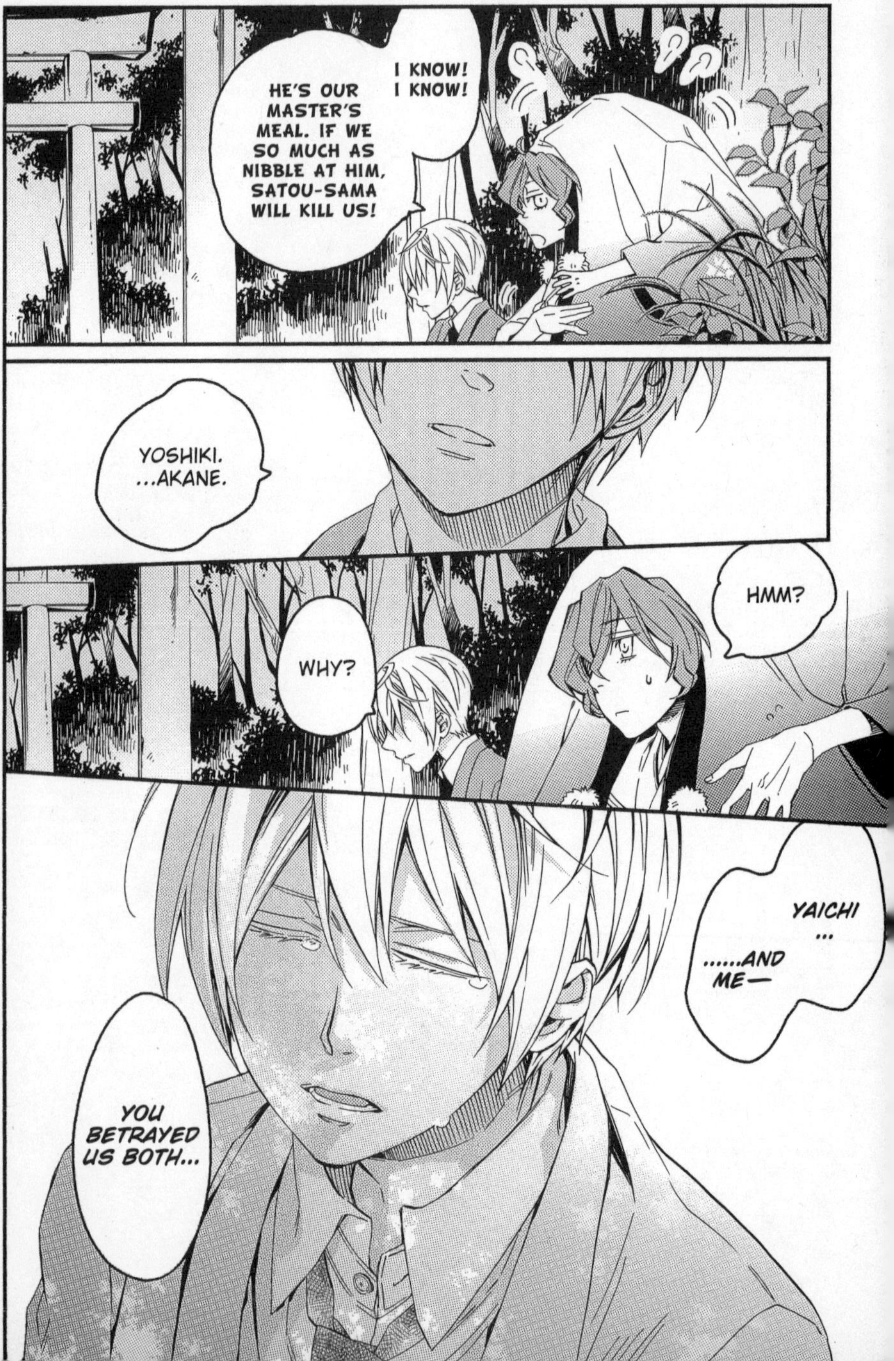
I KNOW! I KNOW!
HE'S OUR MASTER'S MEAL. IF WE SO MUCH AS NIBBLE AT HIM, SATOU-SAMA WILL KILL US!
YOSHIKI. ...AKANE.
HMM?
WHY?
YAICHI ... .AND ME—
YOU BETRAYED US BOTH...

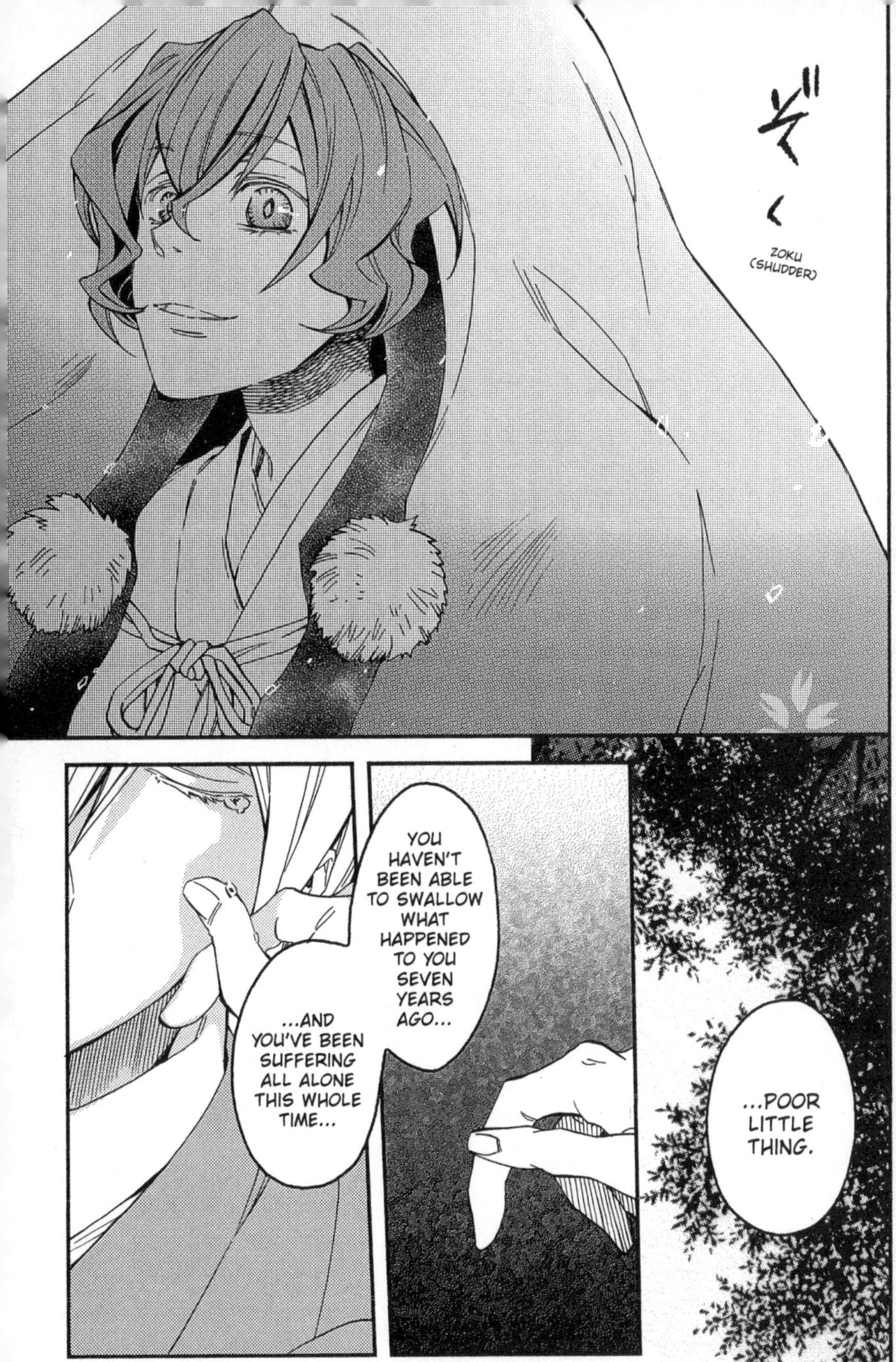
ぞく
ZOKU (SHUDDER)
YOU HAVEN'T BEEN ABLE TO SWALLOW WHAT HAPPENED TO YOU SEVEN YEARS AGO...
...AND YOU'VE BEEN SUFFERING ALL ALONE THIS WHOLE TIME...
...POOR LITTLE THING.

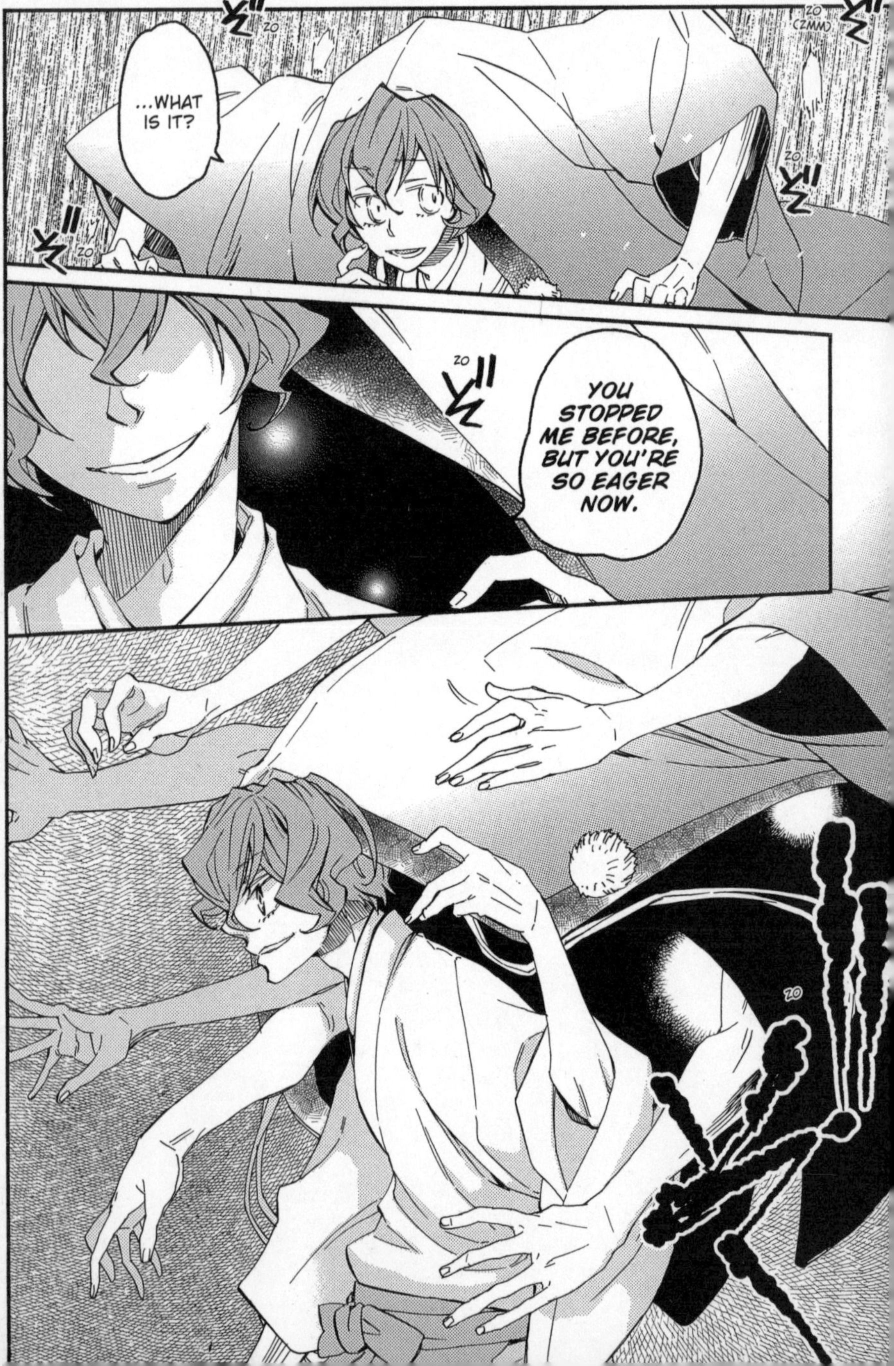
ZO (ZMM)
ZO
ZO
...WHAT IS IT?
ZO
ZO
YOU STOPPED ME BEFORE, BUT YOU'RE SO EAGER NOW.
ZO

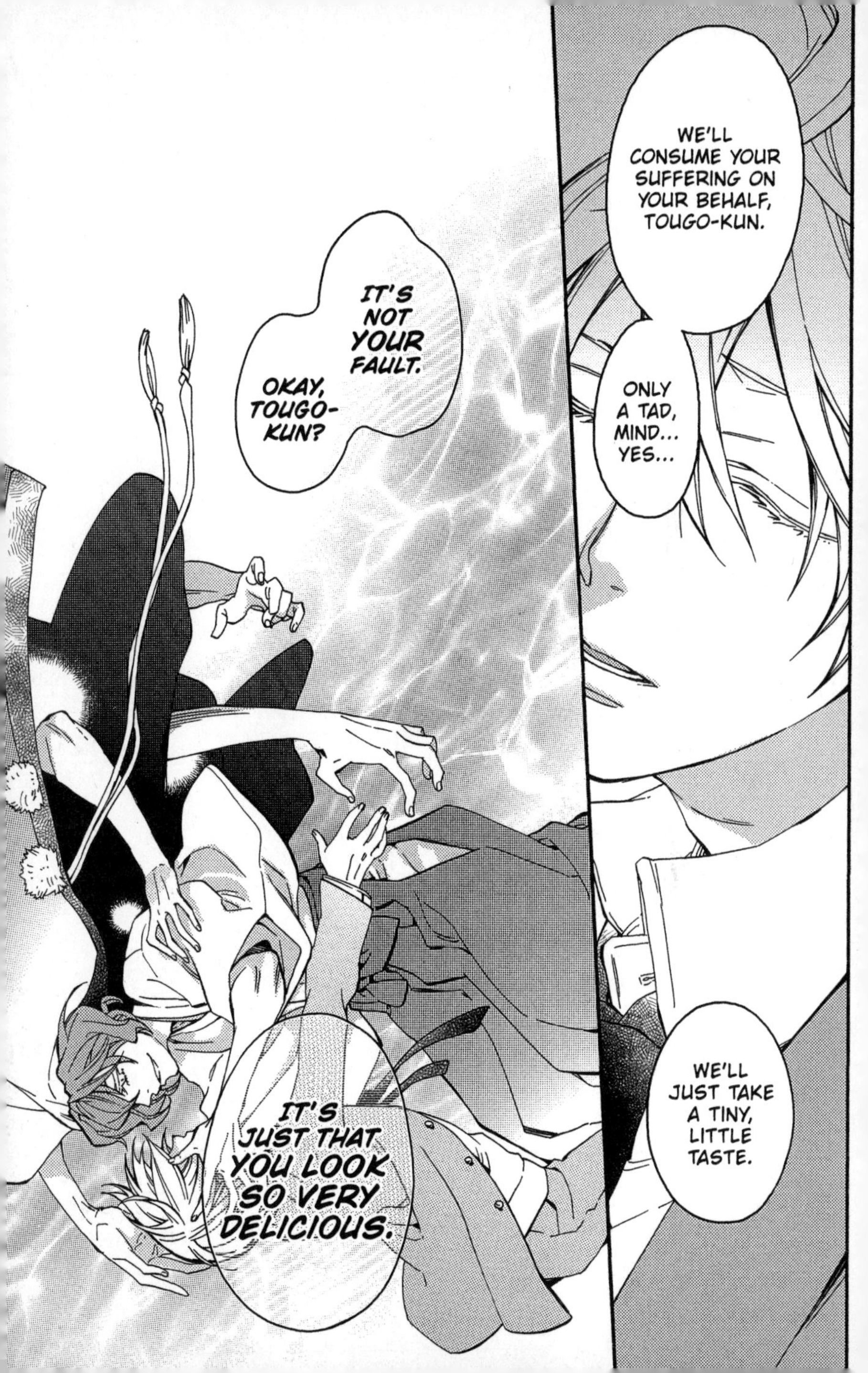
WE'LL CONSUME YOUR SUFFERING ON YOUR BEHALF, TOUGO-KUN.
ONLY A TAD, MIND... YES...
WE'LL JUST TAKE A TINY, LITTLE TASTE.
IT'S NOT YOUR FAULT.
OKAY, TOUGO-KUN?
IT'S JUST THAT YOU LOOK SO VERY DELICIOUS.

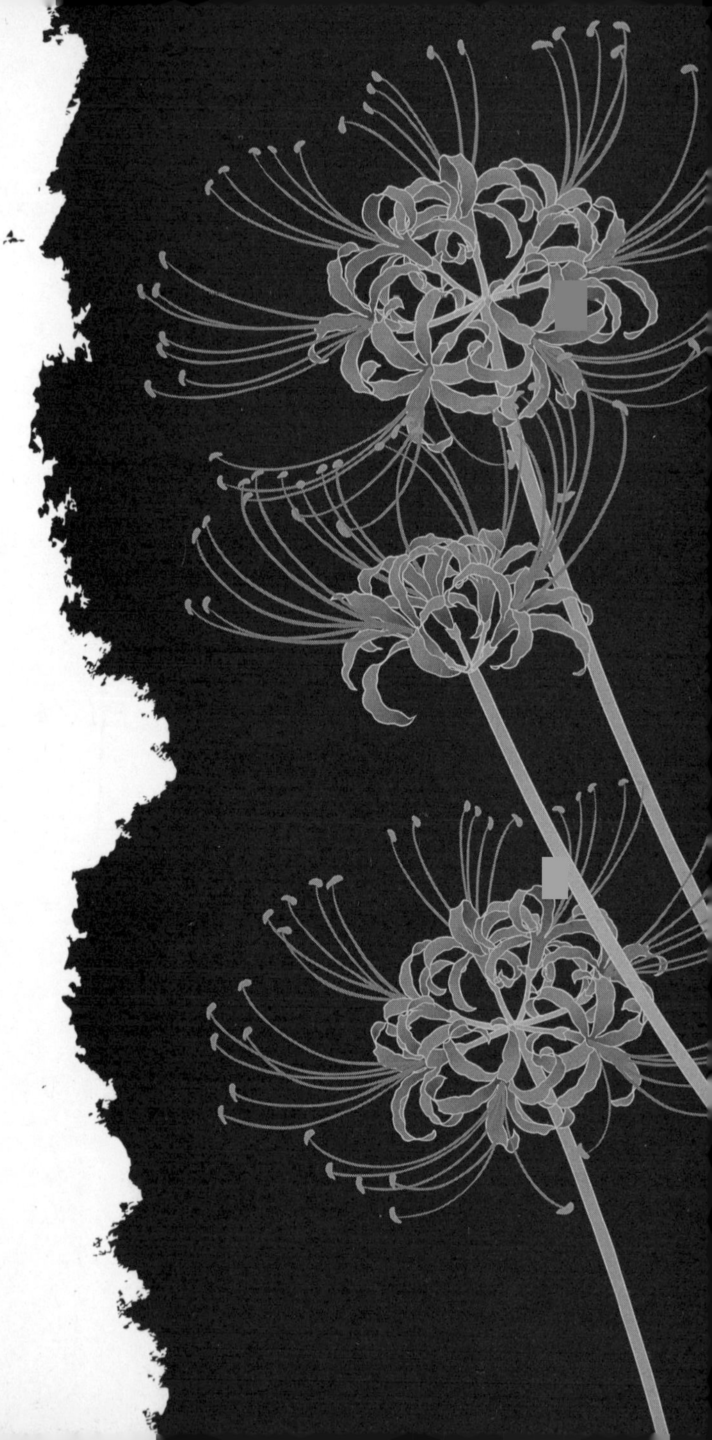

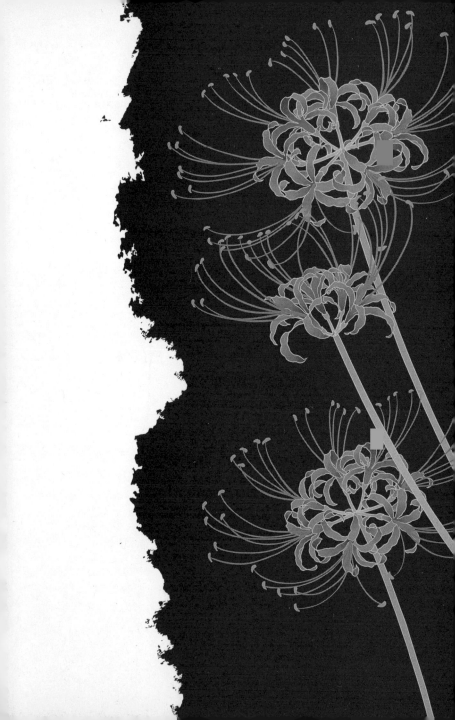

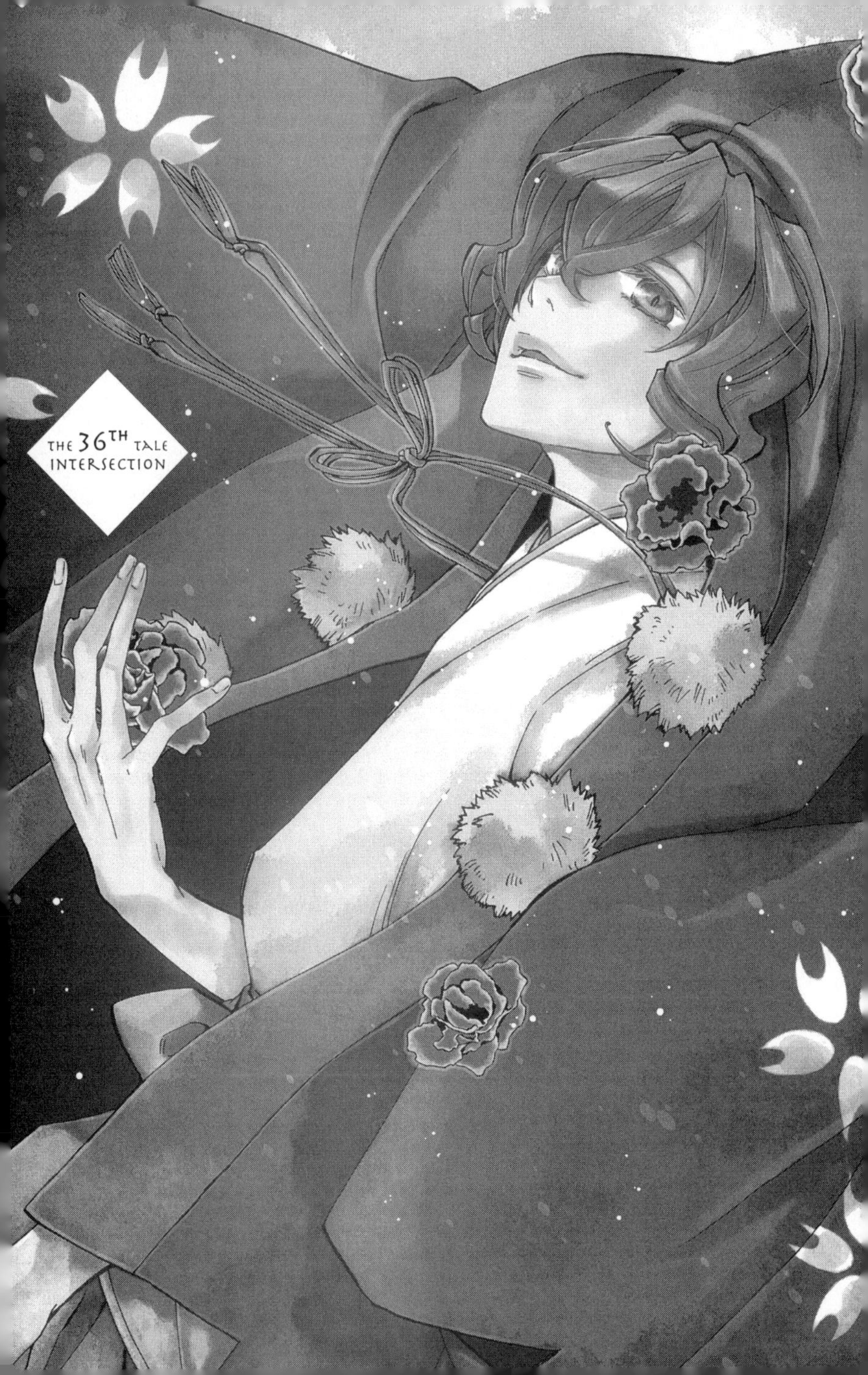
THE 36TH TALE
INTERSECTION

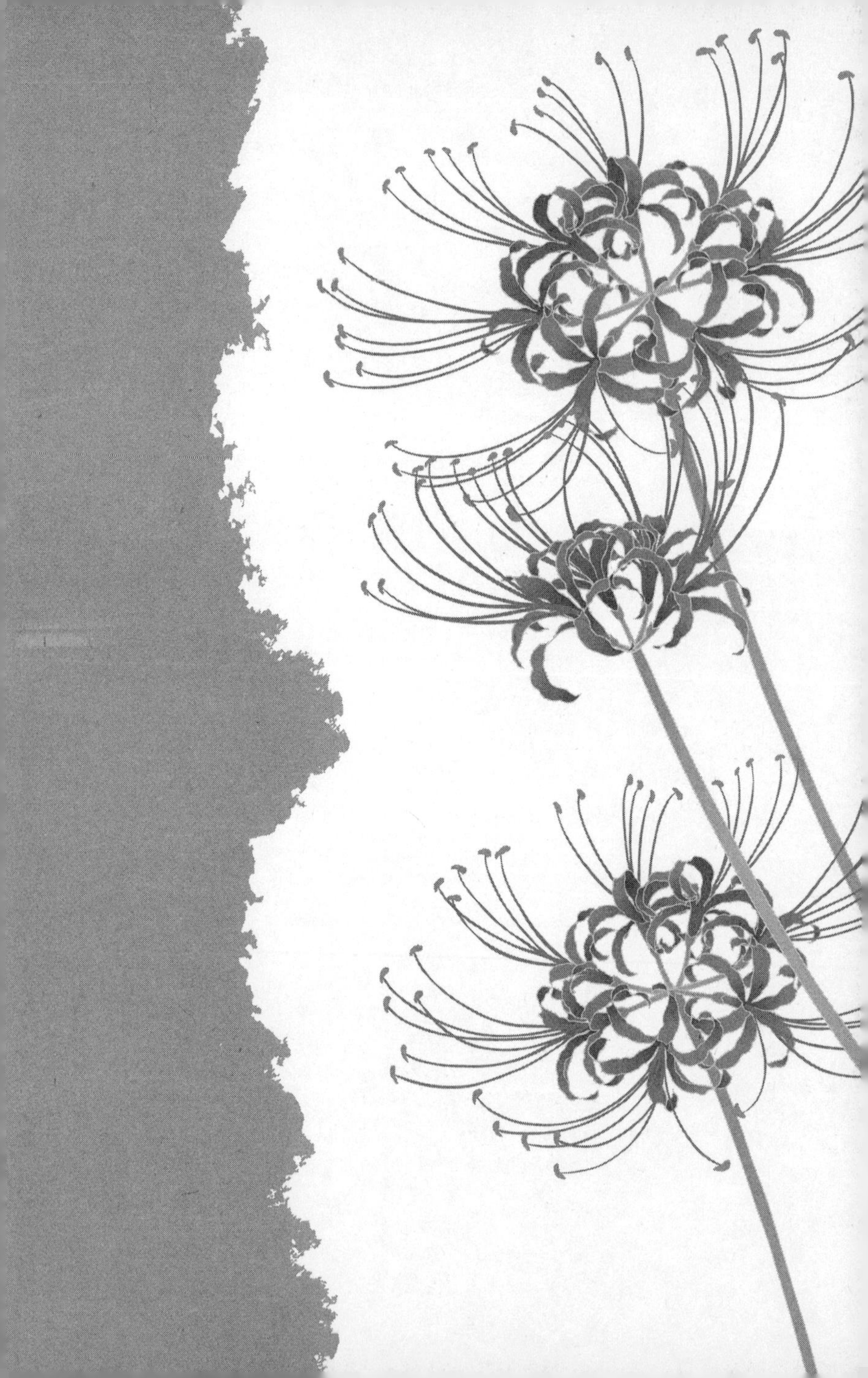

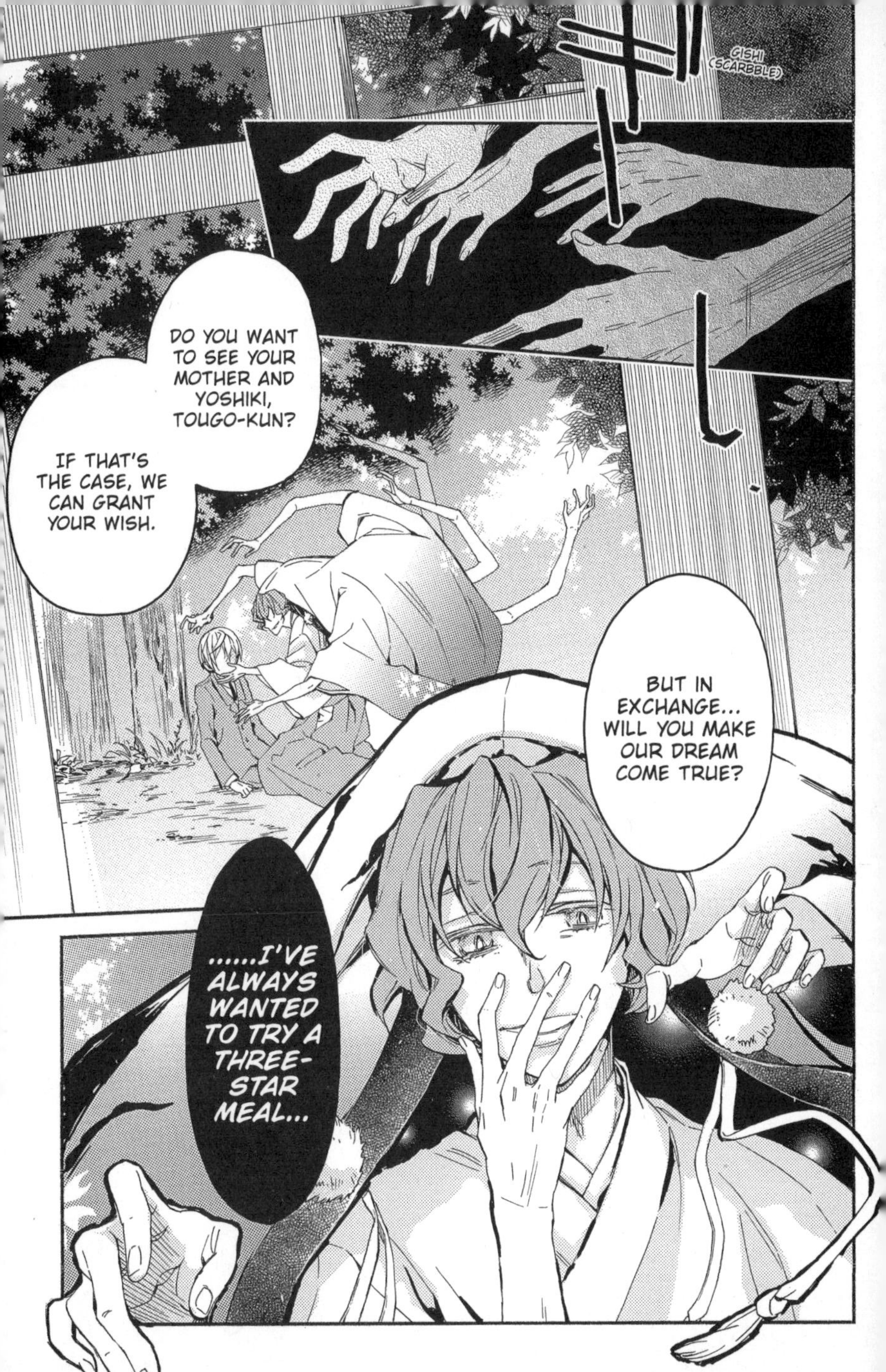
GISHI (SCARBBLE)
DO YOU WANT TO SEE YOUR MOTHER AND YOSHIKI, TOUGO-KUN?
IF THAT'S THE CASE, WE CAN GRANT YOUR WISH.
BUT IN EXCHANGE... WILL YOU MAKE OUR DREAM COME TRUE?
......I'VE ALWAYS WANTED TO TRY A THREE-STAR MEAL...

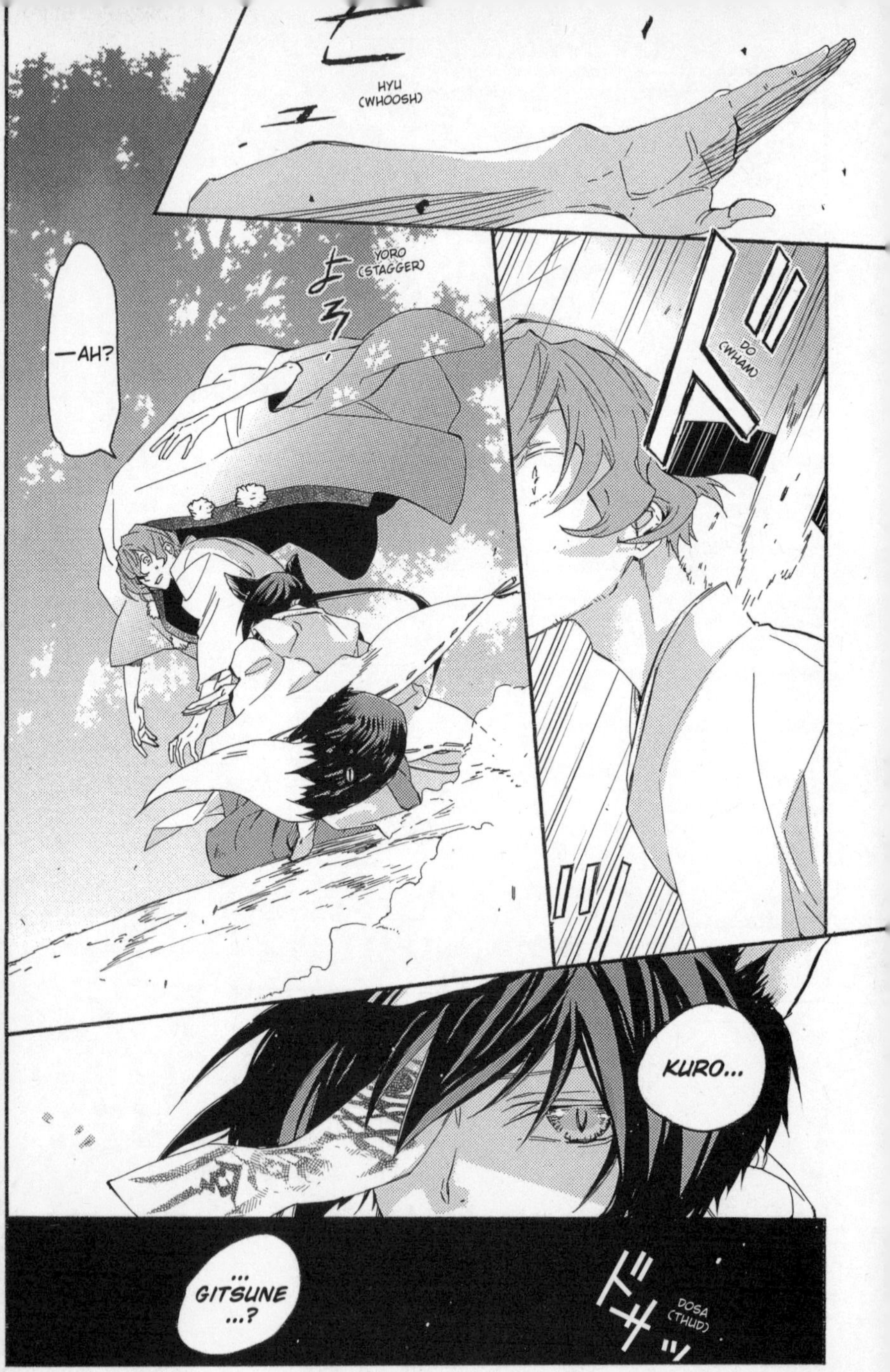
HYU (WHOOSH)
DO (WHAM)
YORO (STAGGER)
—AH?
KURO...
DOSA (THUD)
... GITSUNE ...?

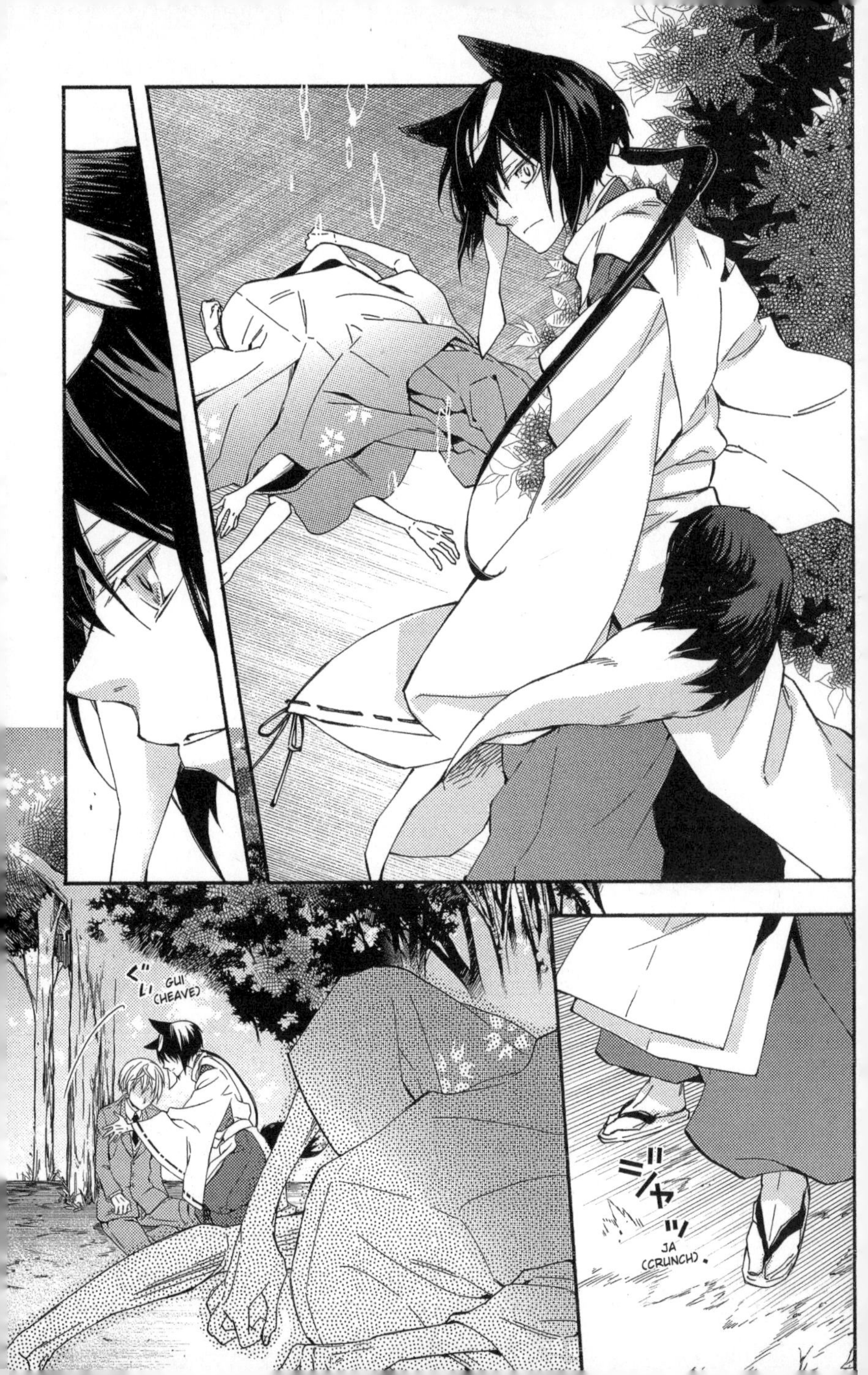
ジャッ
JA
(CRUNCH)
ぐい
GUI
(HEAVE)

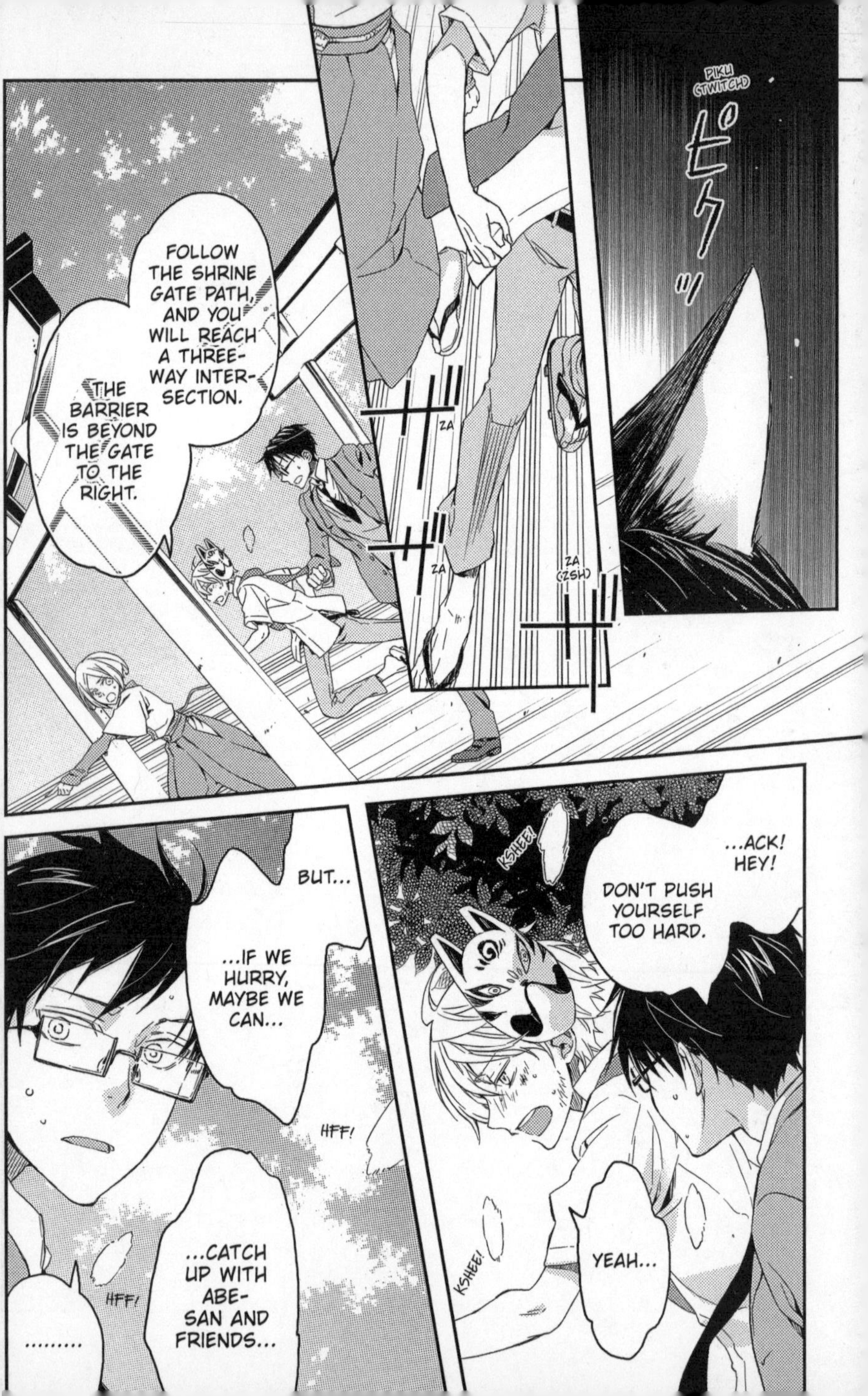
PIKU (TWITCH)
ピクッ
ZA
ZA
ZA (ZSH)
FOLLOW THE SHRINE GATE PATH, AND YOU WILL REACH A THREE-WAY INTER-SECTION.
THE BARRIER IS BEYOND THE GATE TO THE RIGHT.
...ACK! HEY!
DON'T PUSH YOURSELF TOO HARD.
KSHEE!
YEAH...
KSHEE!
BUT...
...IF WE HURRY, MAYBE WE CAN...
HFF!
...CATCH UP WITH ABE-SAN AND FRIENDS...
HFF!
....

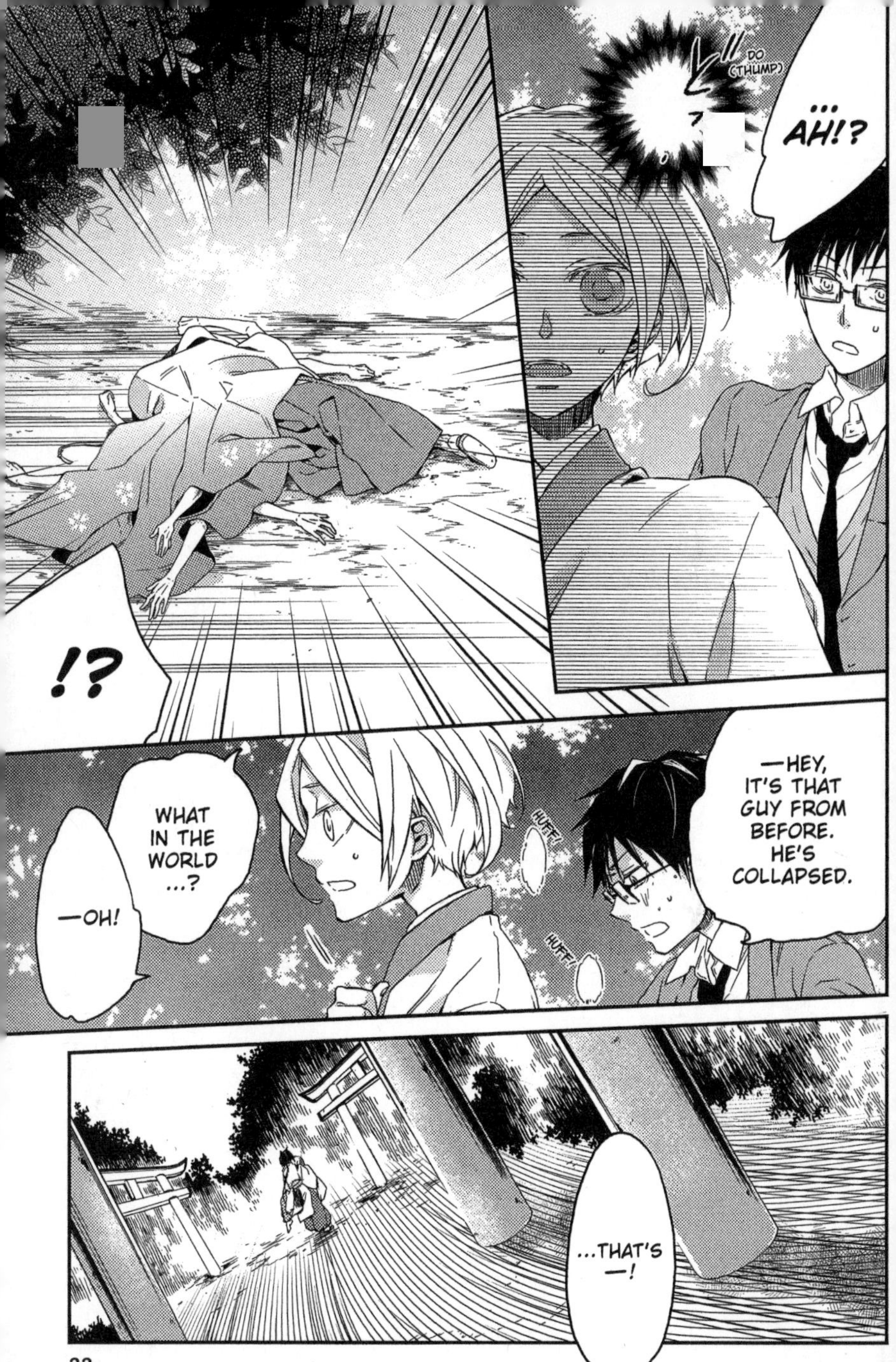
DO (THUMP)
...AH!?
!?
—HEY, IT'S THAT GUY FROM BEFORE. HE'S COLLAPSED.
HUFF!
HUFF!
WHAT IN THE WORLD ...?
—OH!
...THAT'S —!

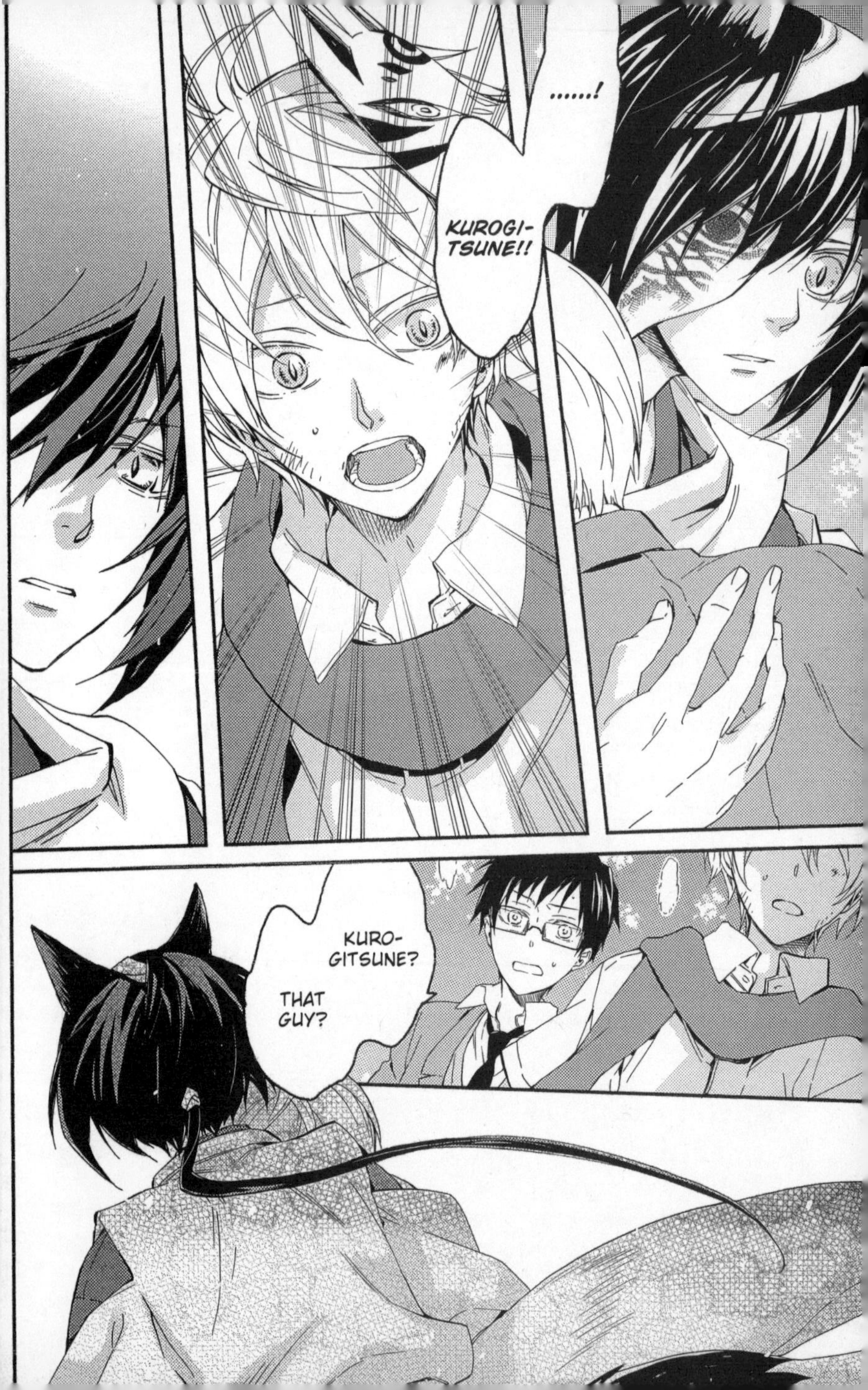
......!
KUROGI-TSUNE!!
KURO-GITSUNE?
THAT GUY?

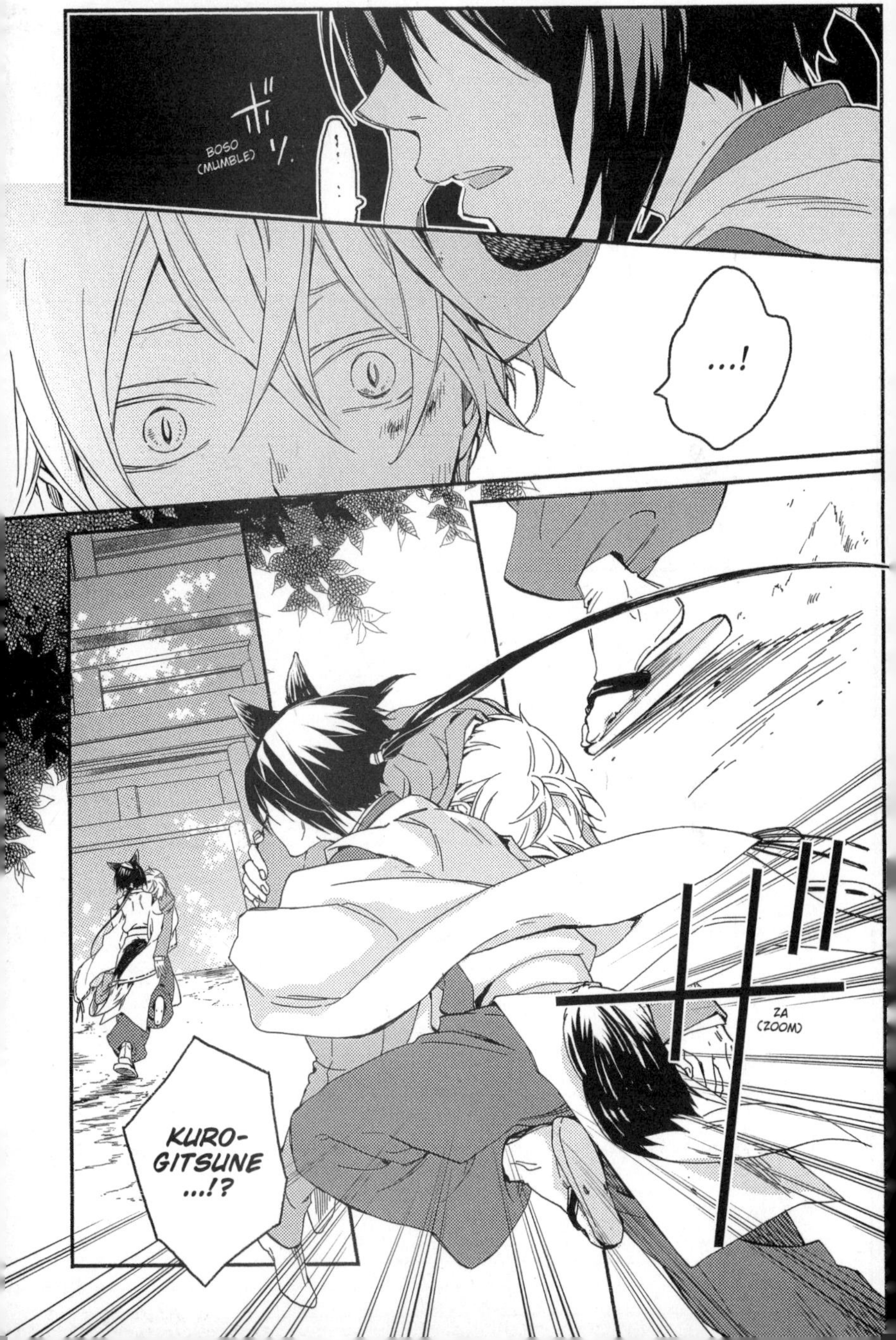
...
BOSO (MUMBLE)
...!
ZA (ZOOM)
KURO-GITSUNE ...!?

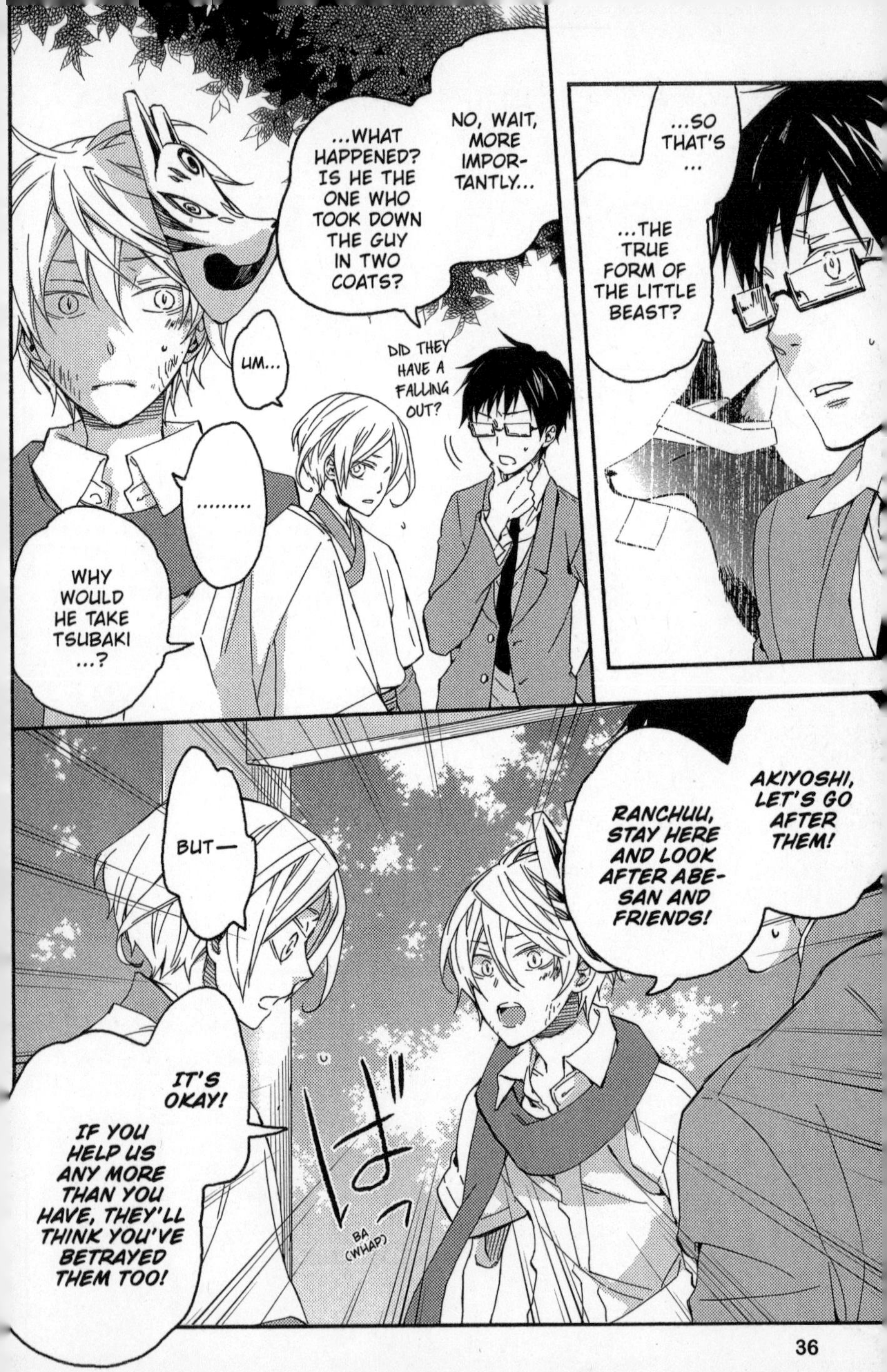
...SO THAT'S ...
...THE TRUE FORM OF THE LITTLE BEAST?
NO, WAIT, MORE IMPORTANTLY...
...WHAT HAPPENED? IS HE THE ONE WHO TOOK DOWN THE GUY IN TWO COATS?
DID THEY HAVE A FALLING OUT?
UM...
....
WHY WOULD HE TAKE TSUBAKI ...?
AKIYOSHI, LET'S GO AFTER THEM!
RANCHUU, STAY HERE AND LOOK AFTER ABE-SAN AND FRIENDS!
BUT—
BA (WHAP)
IT'S OKAY!
IF YOU HELP US ANY MORE THAN YOU HAVE, THEY'LL THINK YOU'VE BETRAYED THEM TOO!

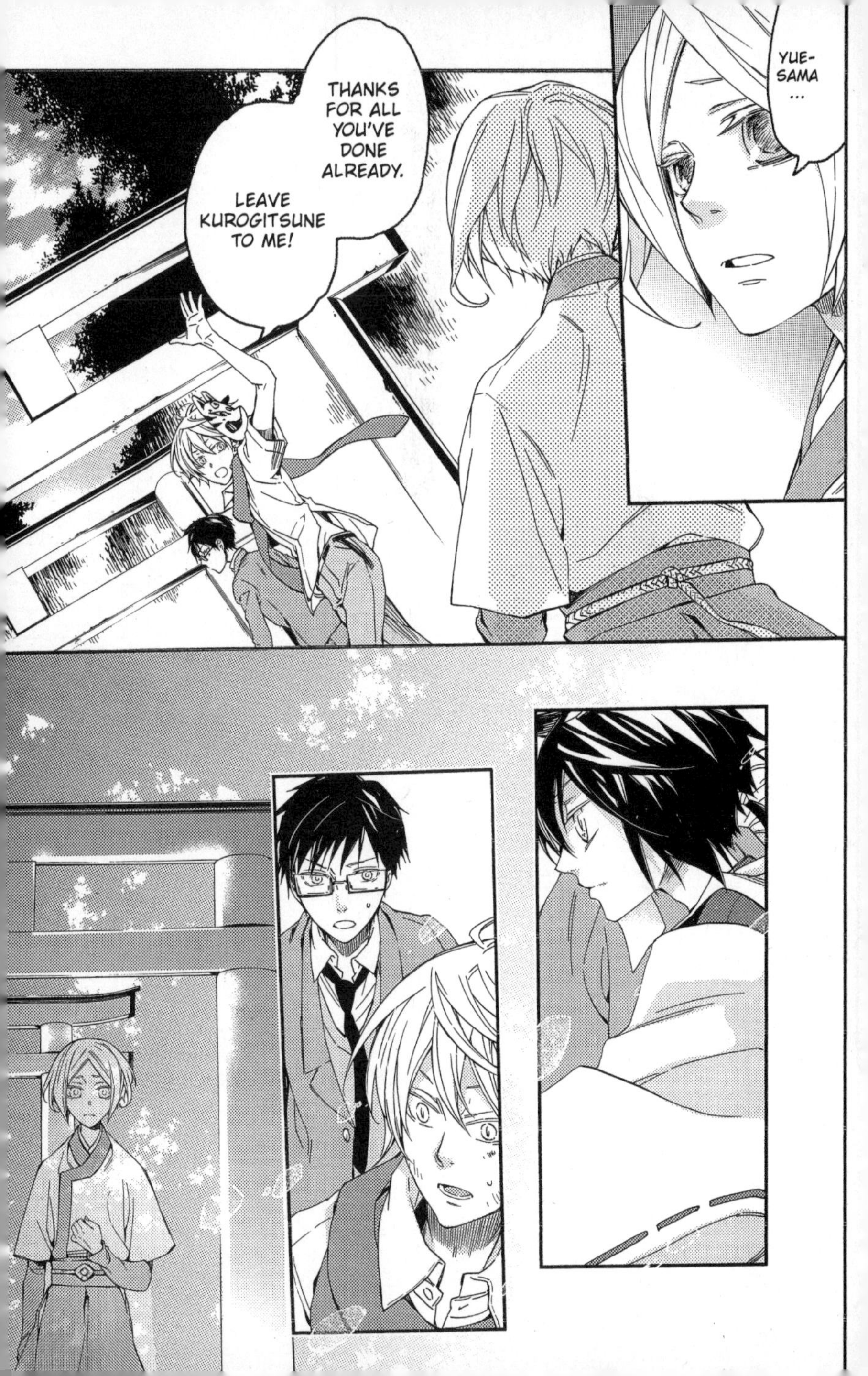
YUE-SAMA ...
THANKS FOR ALL YOU'VE DONE ALREADY.
LEAVE KUROGITSUNE TO ME!

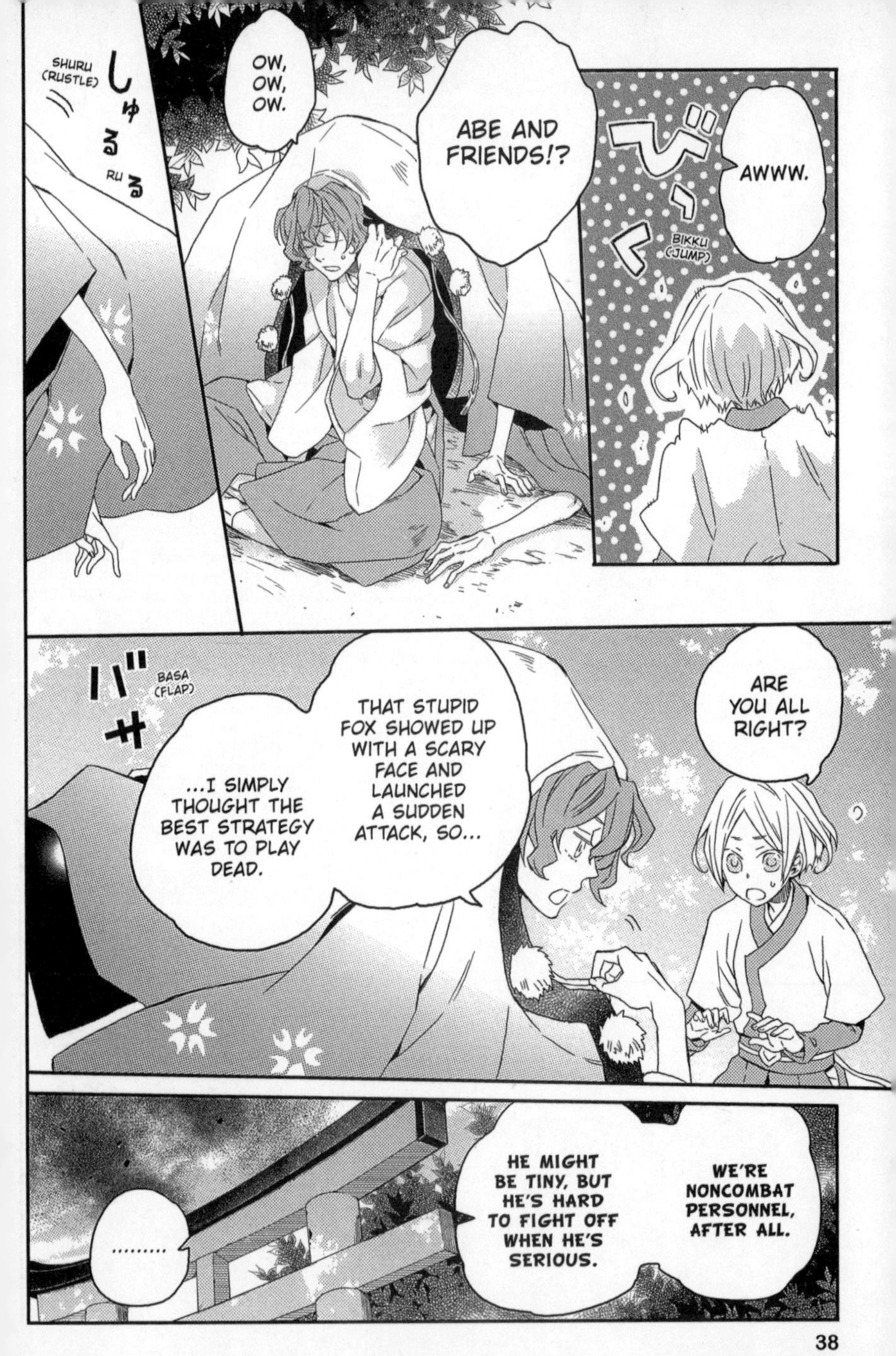

AWWW.
ビク
BIKKU (JUMP)
ABE AND FRIENDS!?
OW, OW, OW.
しゅるる
SHURU (RUSTLE) RU
ARE YOU ALL RIGHT?
THAT STUPID FOX SHOWED UP WITH A SCARY FACE AND LAUNCHED A SUDDEN ATTACK, SO...
...I SIMPLY THOUGHT THE BEST STRATEGY WAS TO PLAY DEAD.
バサ
BASA (FLAP)
WE'RE NONCOMBAT PERSONNEL, AFTER ALL.
HE MIGHT BE TINY, BUT HE'S HARD TO FIGHT OFF WHEN HE'S SERIOUS.
....

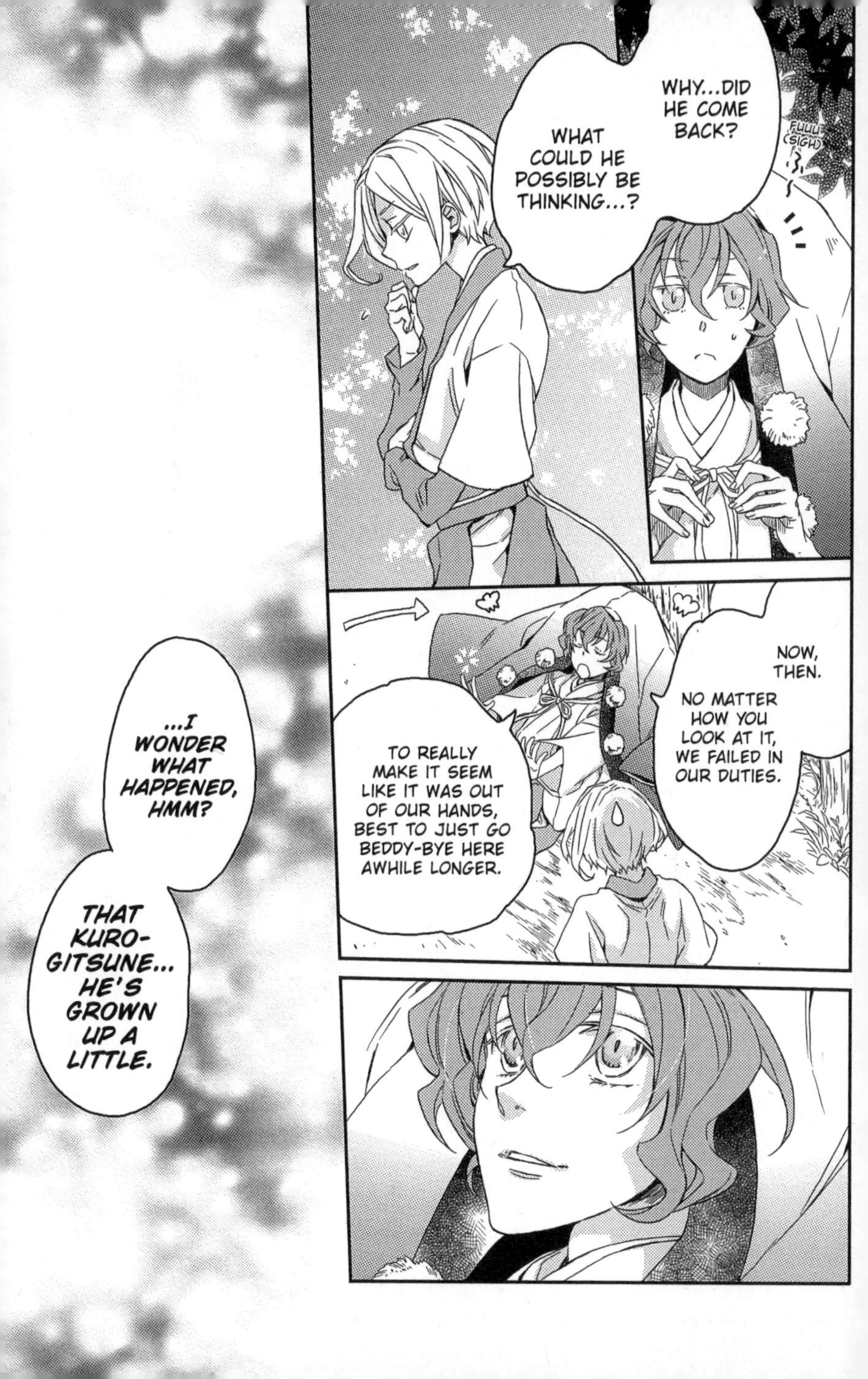
WHY...DID HE COME BACK?
WHAT COULD HE POSSIBLY BE THINKING...?
FUUU (SIGH)
NOW, THEN.
NO MATTER HOW YOU LOOK AT IT, WE FAILED IN OUR DUTIES.
TO REALLY MAKE IT SEEM LIKE IT WAS OUT OF OUR HANDS, BEST TO JUST GO BEDDY-BYE HERE AWHILE LONGER.
...I WONDER WHAT HAPPENED, HMM?
THAT KURO-GITSUNE... HE'S GROWN UP A LITTLE.

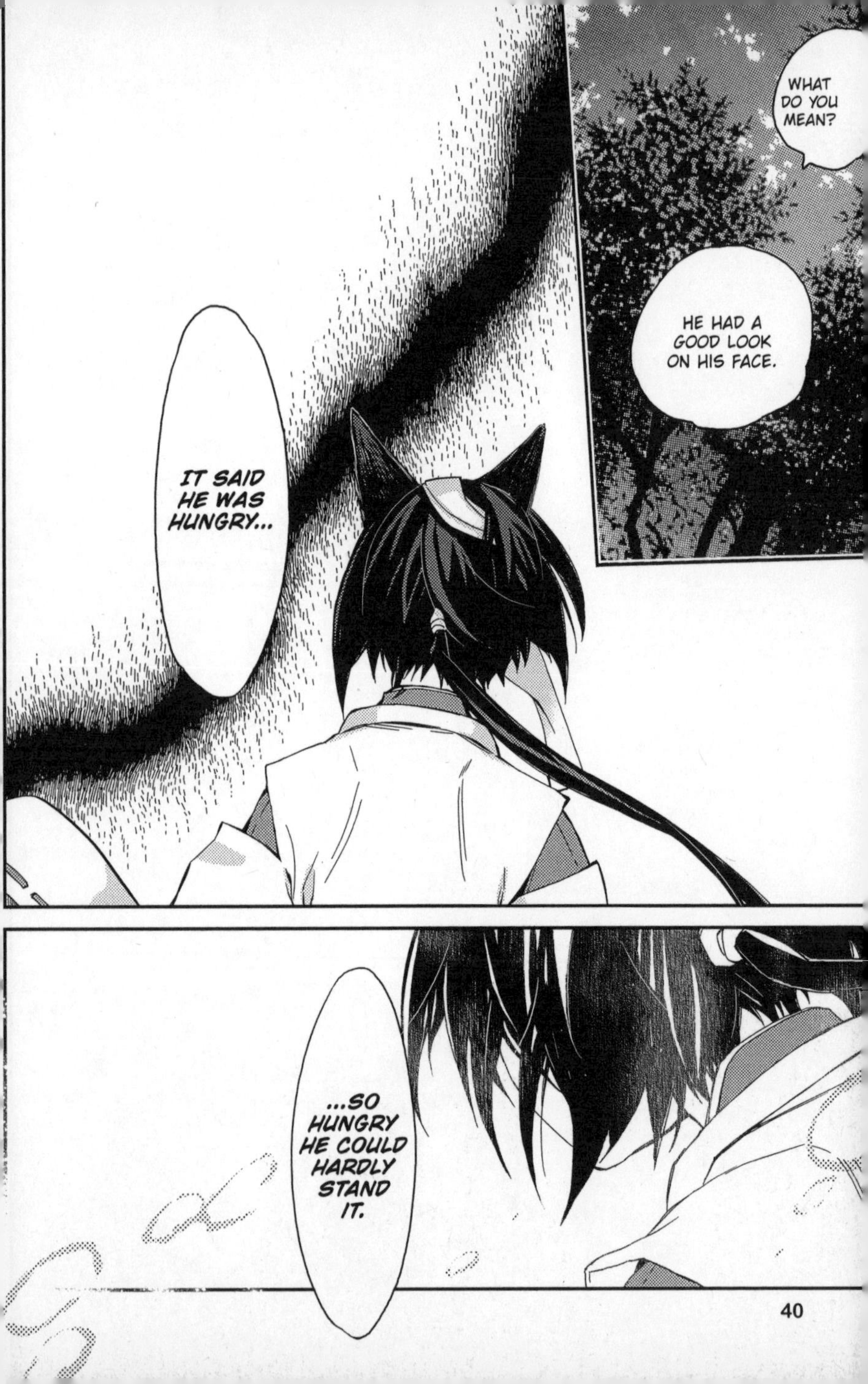
WHAT DO YOU MEAN?
HE HAD A GOOD LOOK ON HIS FACE.
IT SAID HE WAS HUNGRY...
...SO HUNGRY HE COULD HARDLY STAND IT.

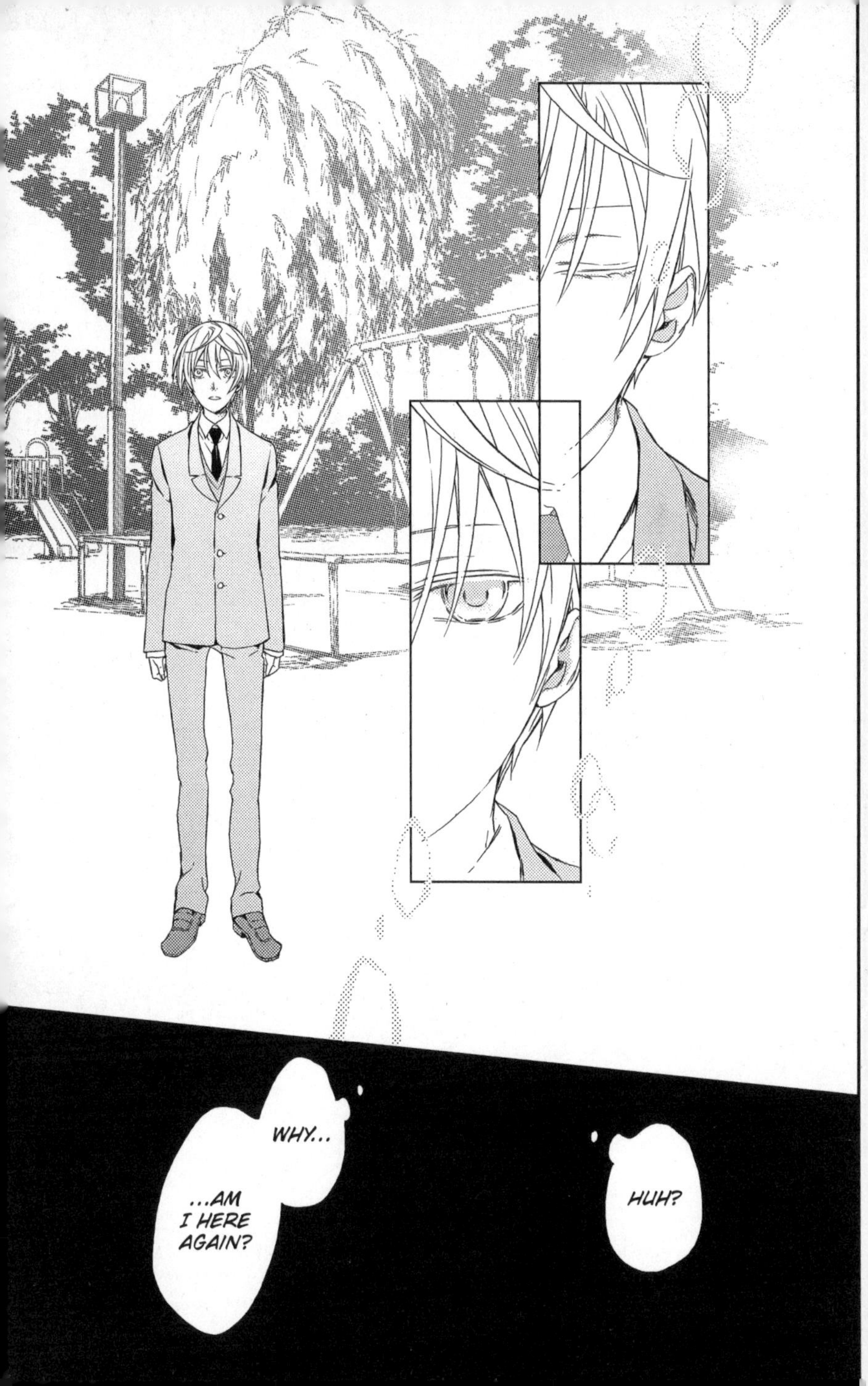
HUH?
WHY...
...AM I HERE AGAIN?

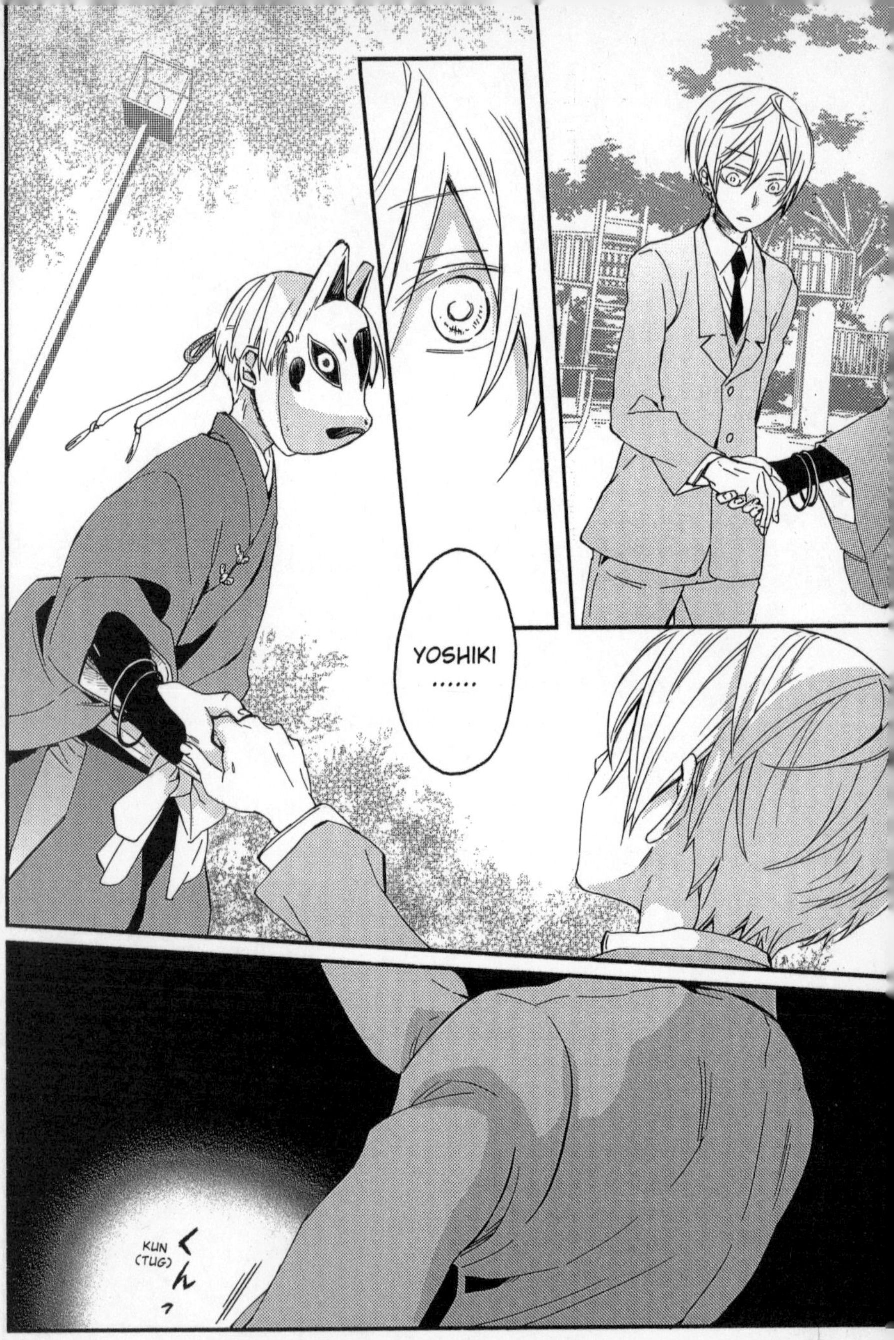
YOSHIKI
......
KUN
(TUG)
くん

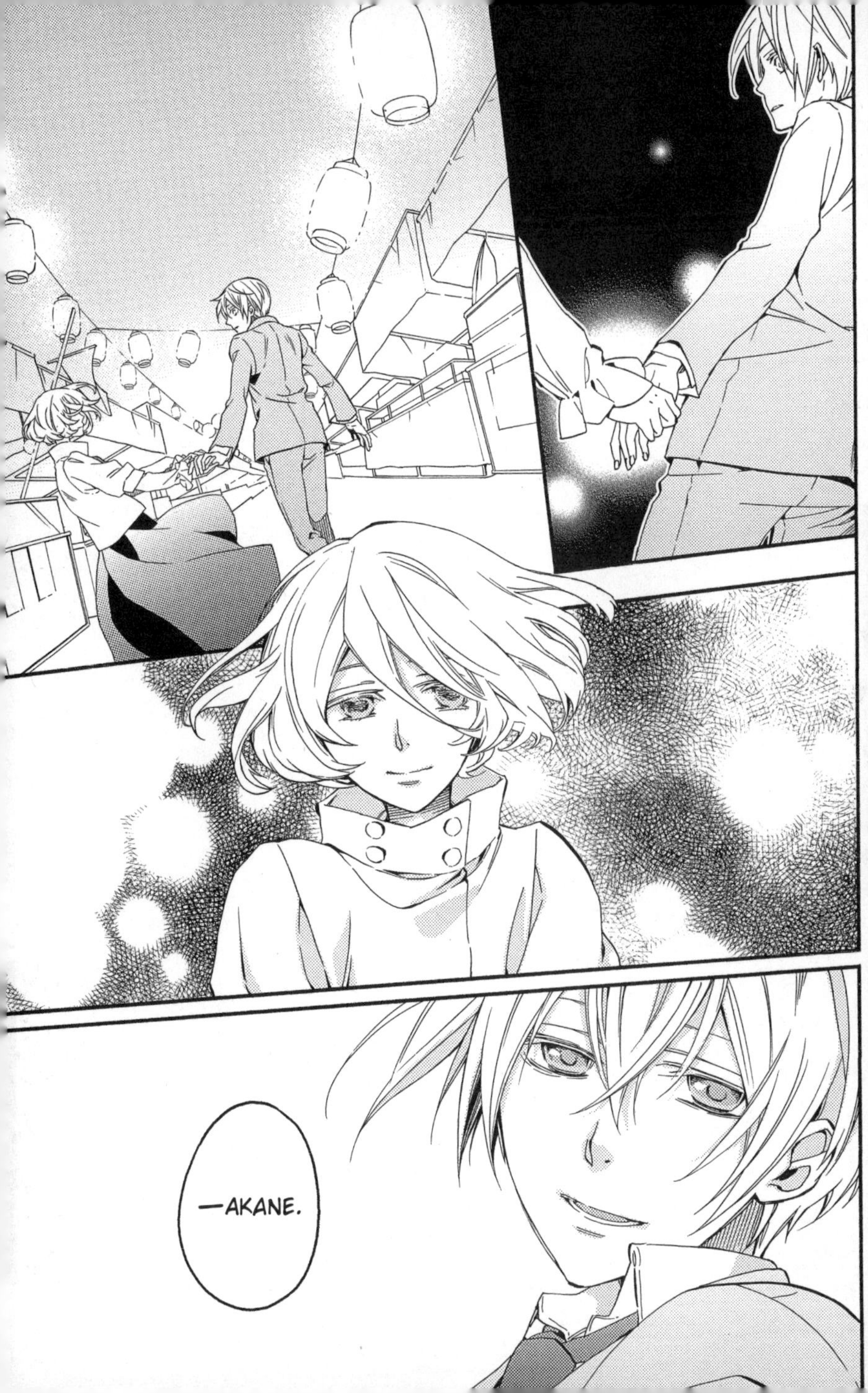
—AKANE.

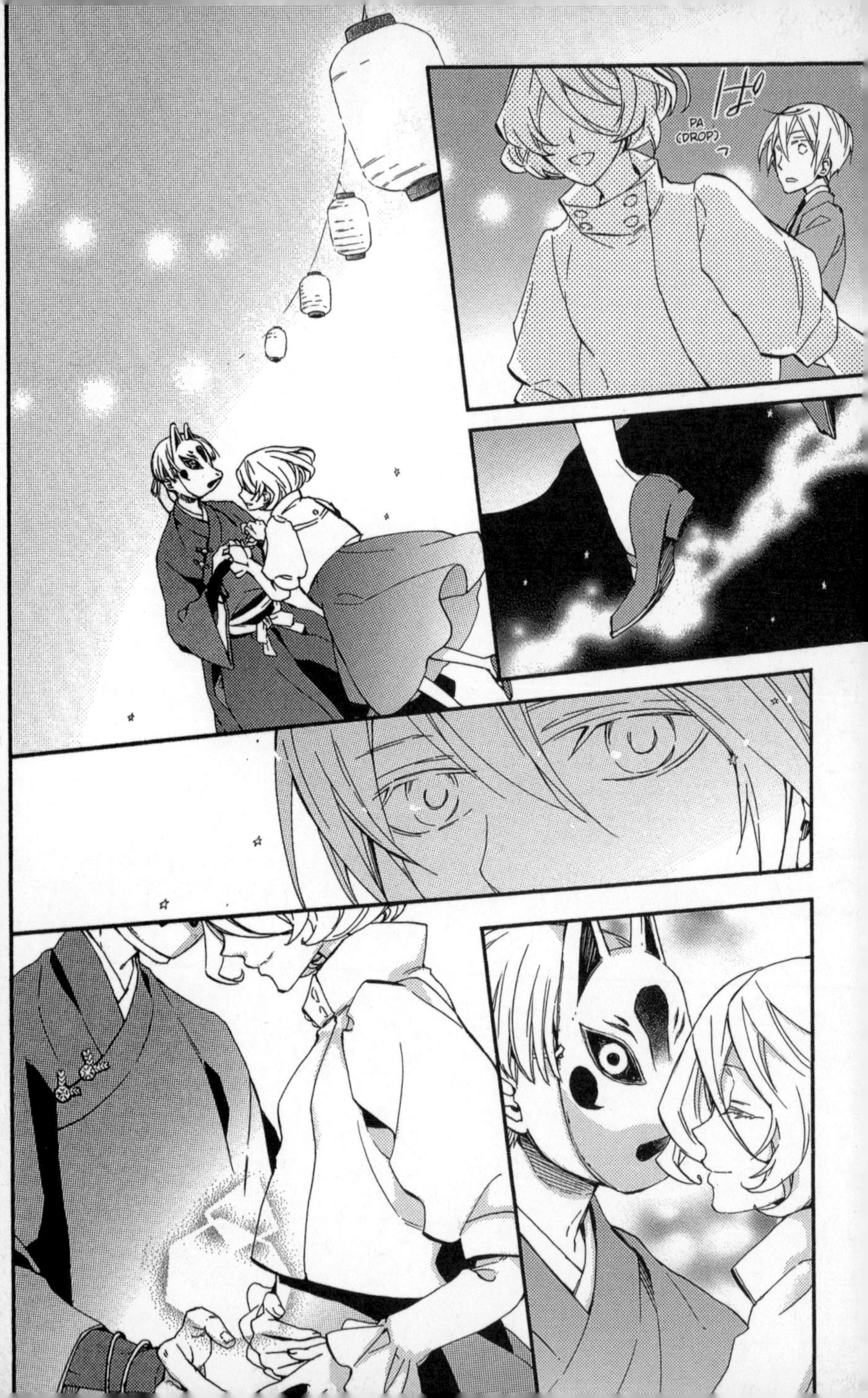
ぱ
PA
(DROP)

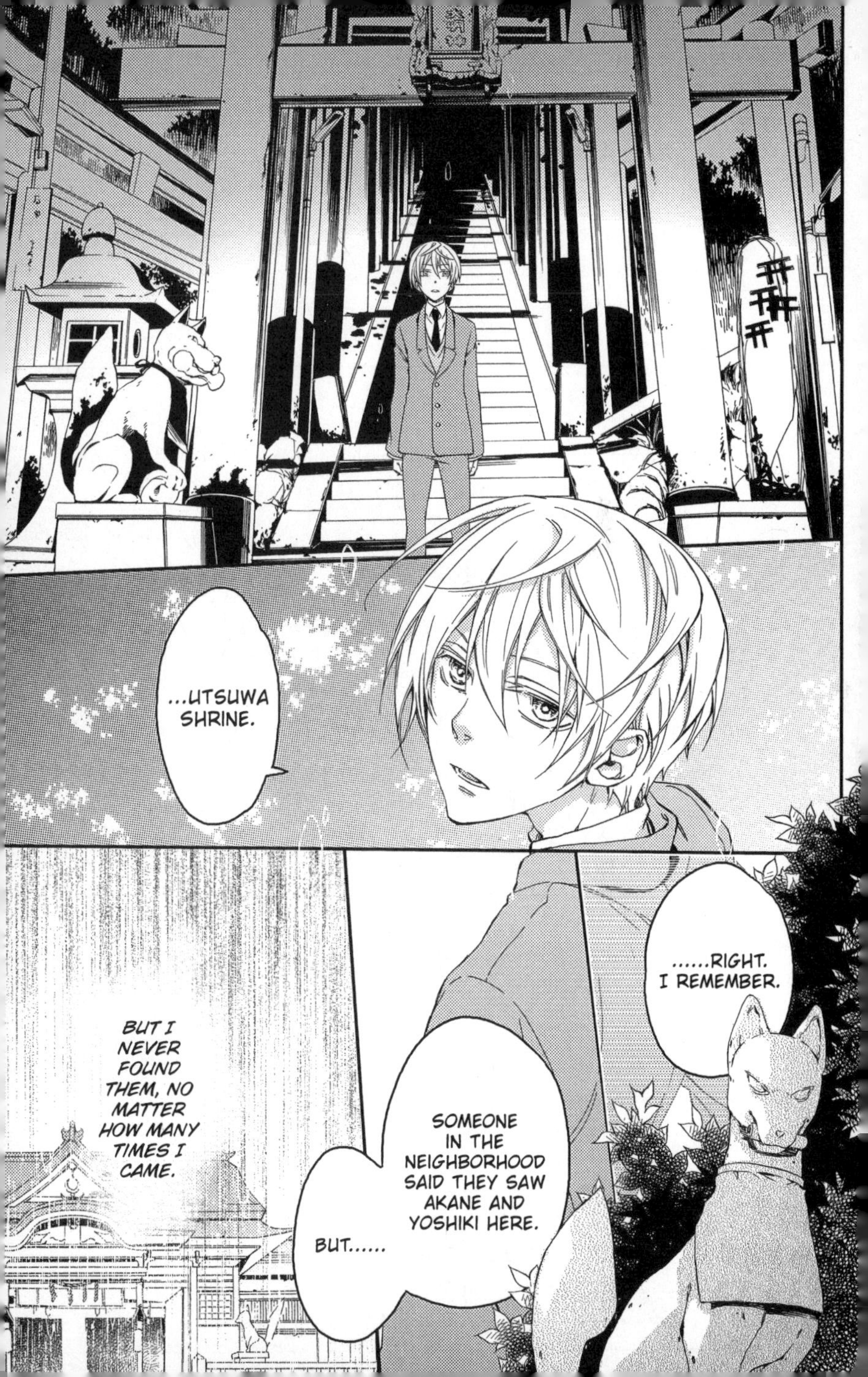
...UTSUWA SHRINE.
......RIGHT. I REMEMBER.
SOMEONE IN THE NEIGHBORHOOD SAID THEY SAW AKANE AND YOSHIKI HERE.
BUT......
BUT I NEVER FOUND THEM, NO MATTER HOW MANY TIMES I CAME.

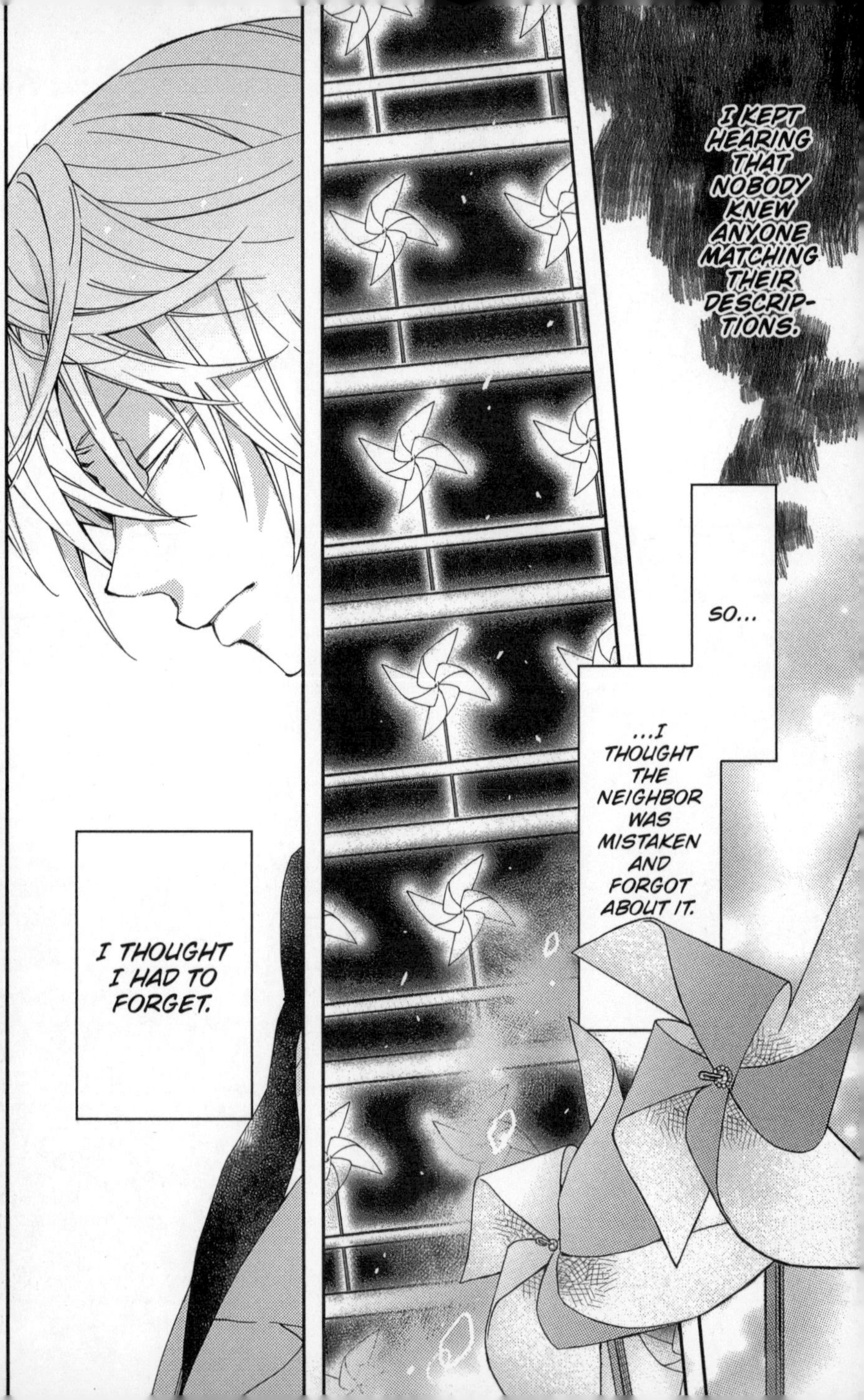
I KEPT HEARING THAT NOBODY KNEW ANYONE MATCHING THEIR DESCRIPTIONS.
SO...
...I THOUGHT THE NEIGHBOR WAS MISTAKEN AND FORGOT ABOUT IT.
I THOUGHT I HAD TO FORGET.

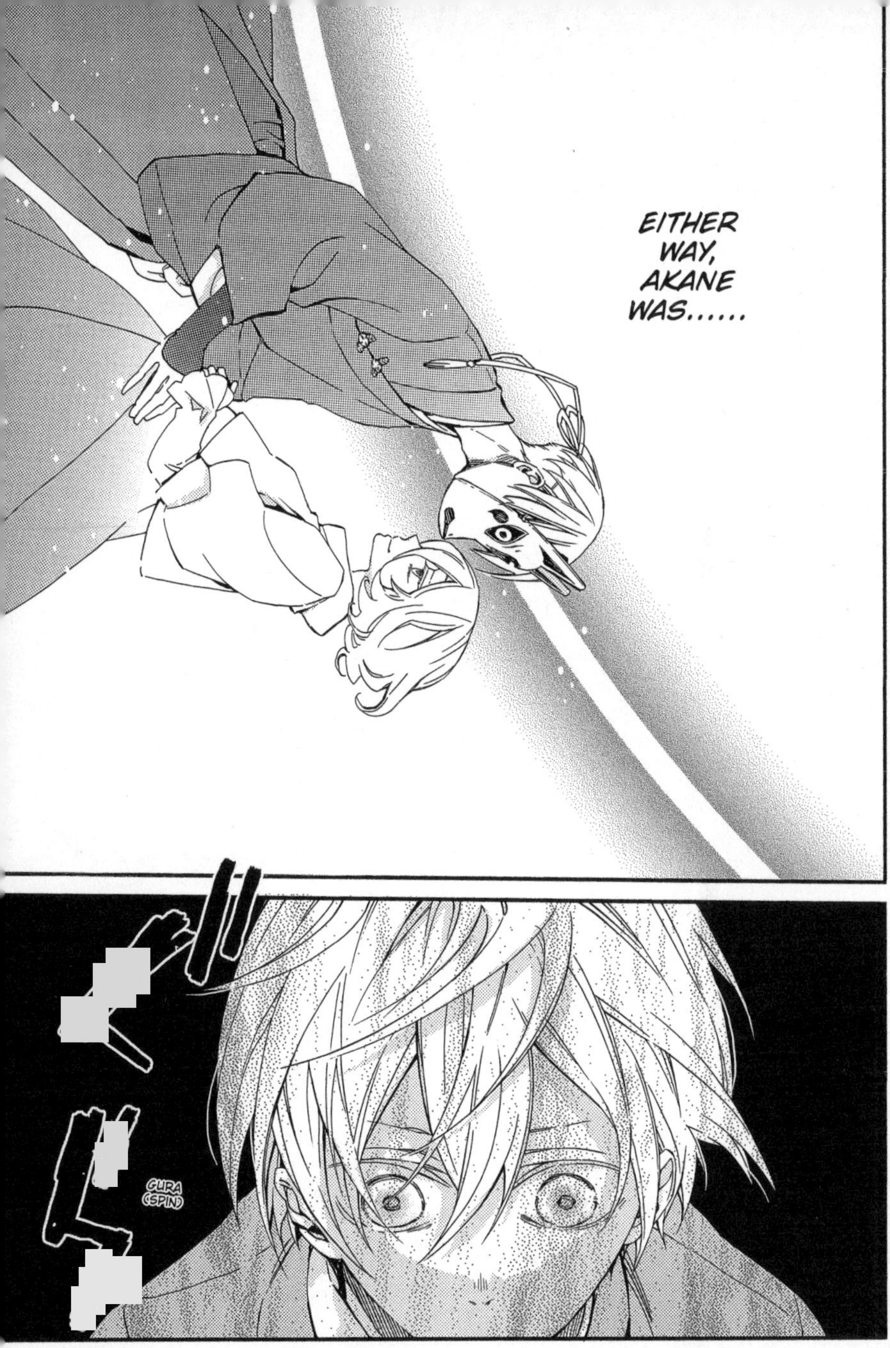
EITHER WAY, AKANE WAS......
GURA (SPIN)

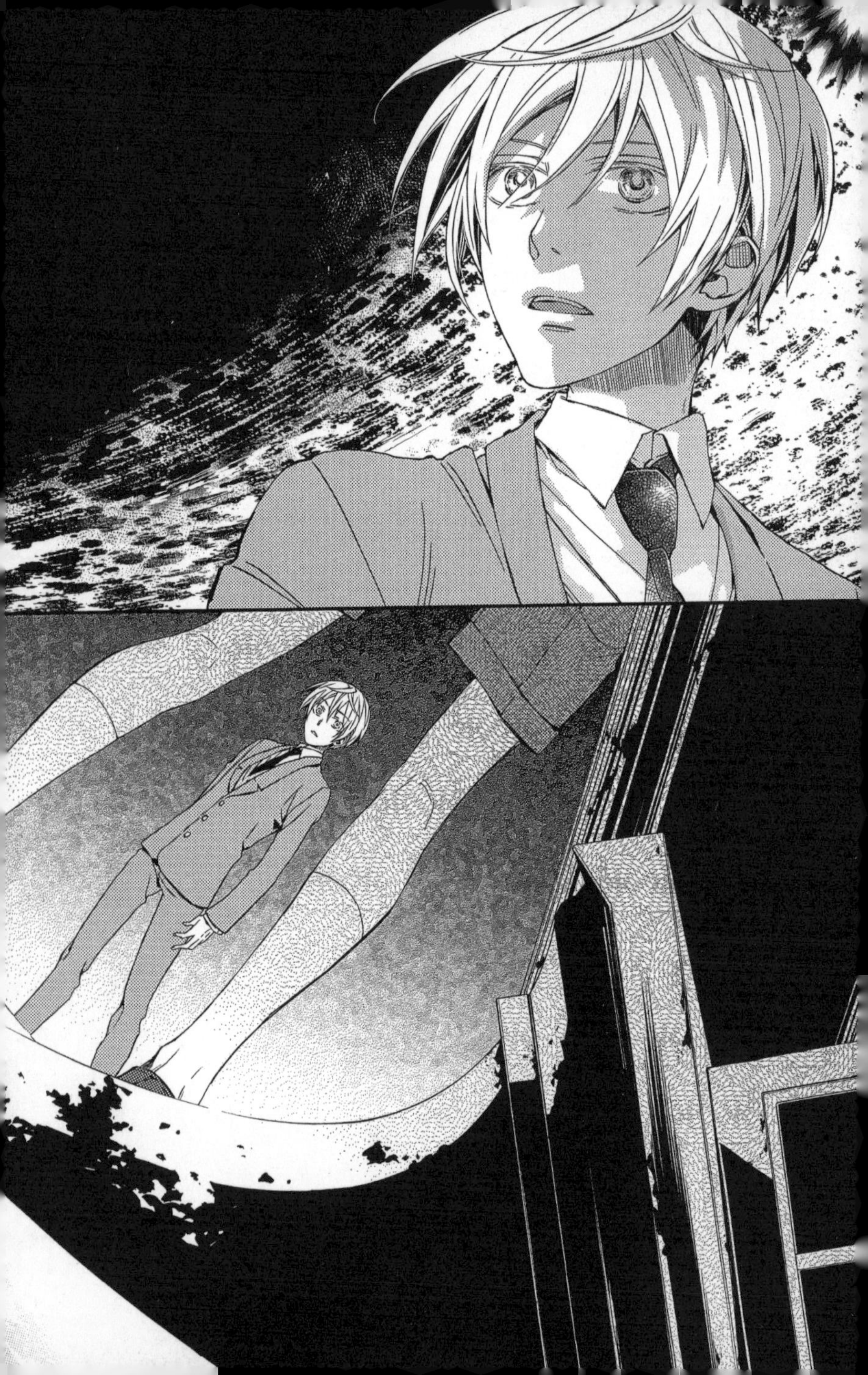

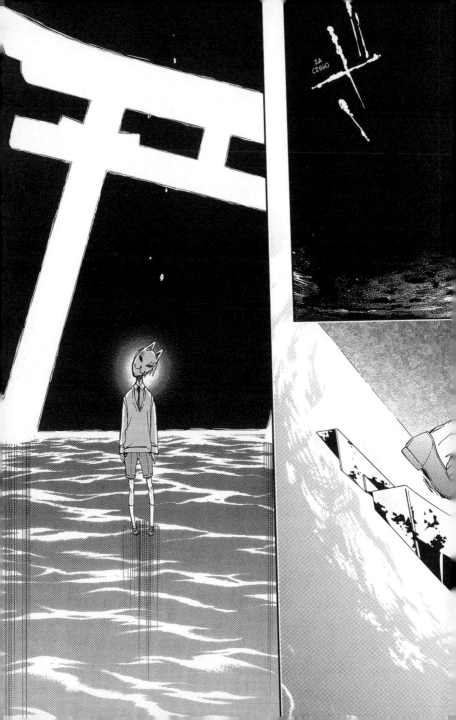

ZA
(ZSH)

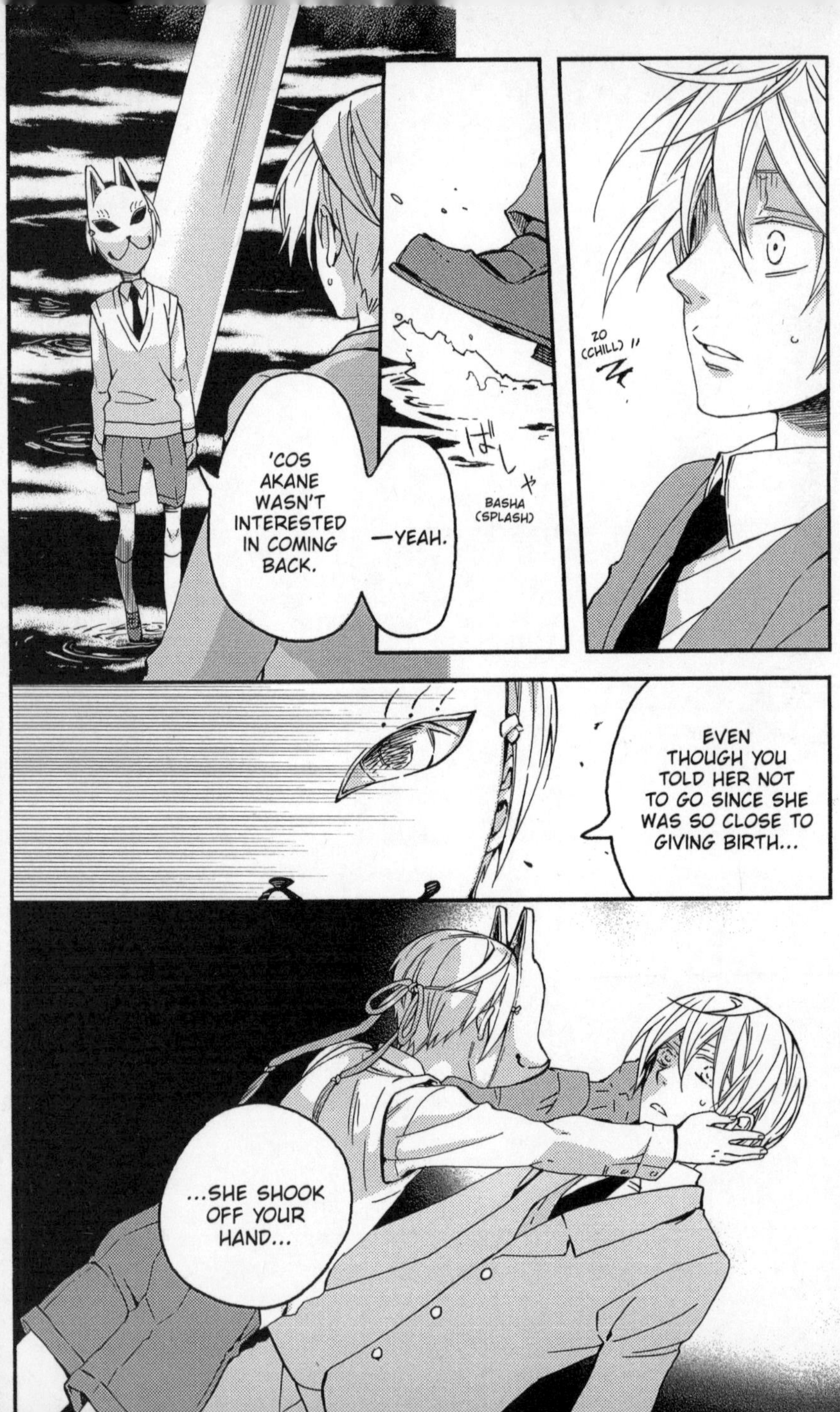
ZO (CHILL)
ばしゃ
BASHA (SPLASH)
—YEAH.
'COS AKANE WASN'T INTERESTED IN COMING BACK.
EVEN THOUGH YOU TOLD HER NOT TO GO SINCE SHE WAS SO CLOSE TO GIVING BIRTH...
...SHE SHOOK OFF YOUR HAND...

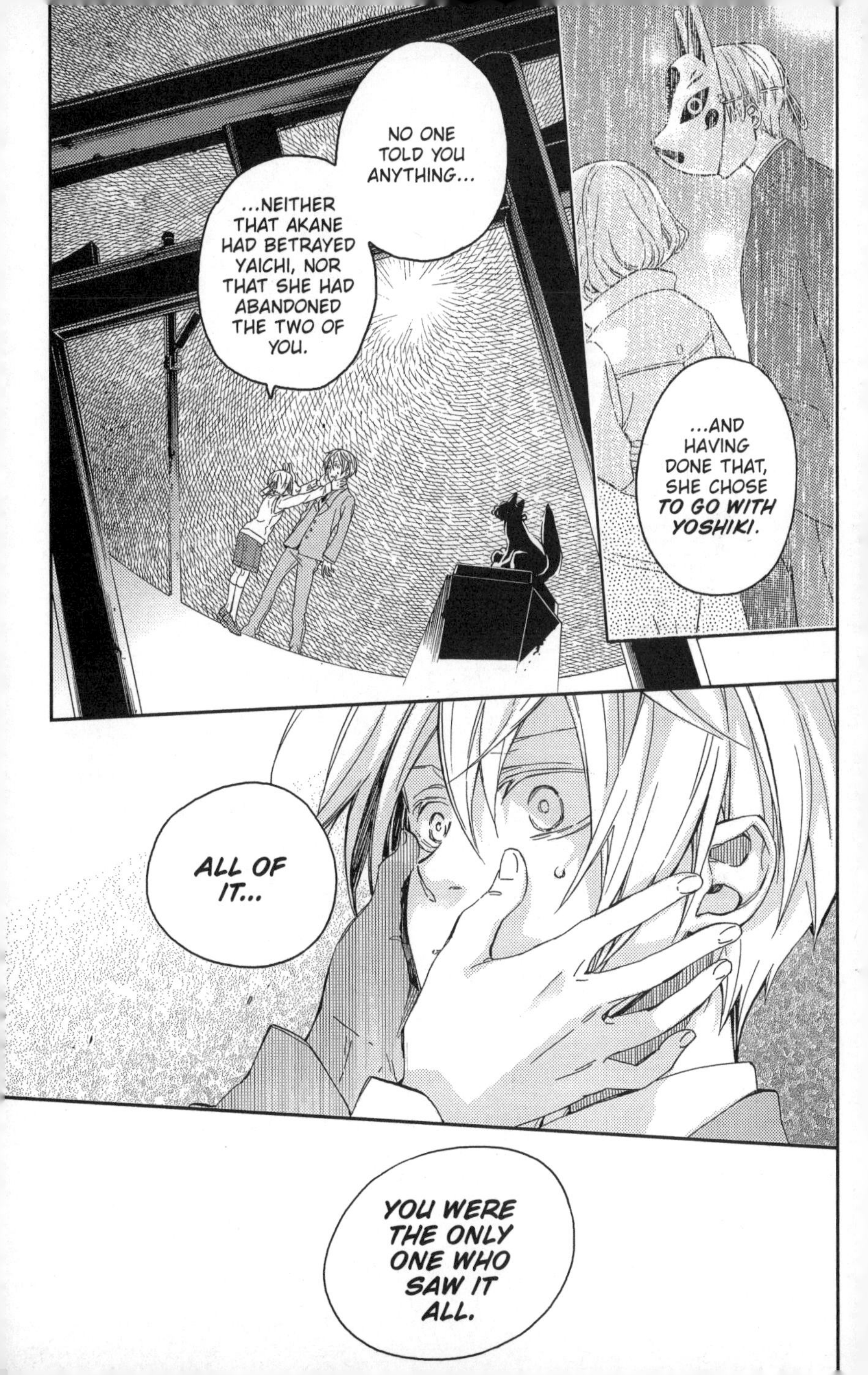
NO ONE TOLD YOU ANYTHING...
...NEITHER THAT AKANE HAD BETRAYED YAICHI, NOR THAT SHE HAD ABANDONED THE TWO OF YOU.
...AND HAVING DONE THAT, SHE CHOSE TO GO WITH YOSHIKI.
ALL OF IT...
YOU WERE THE ONLY ONE WHO SAW IT ALL.

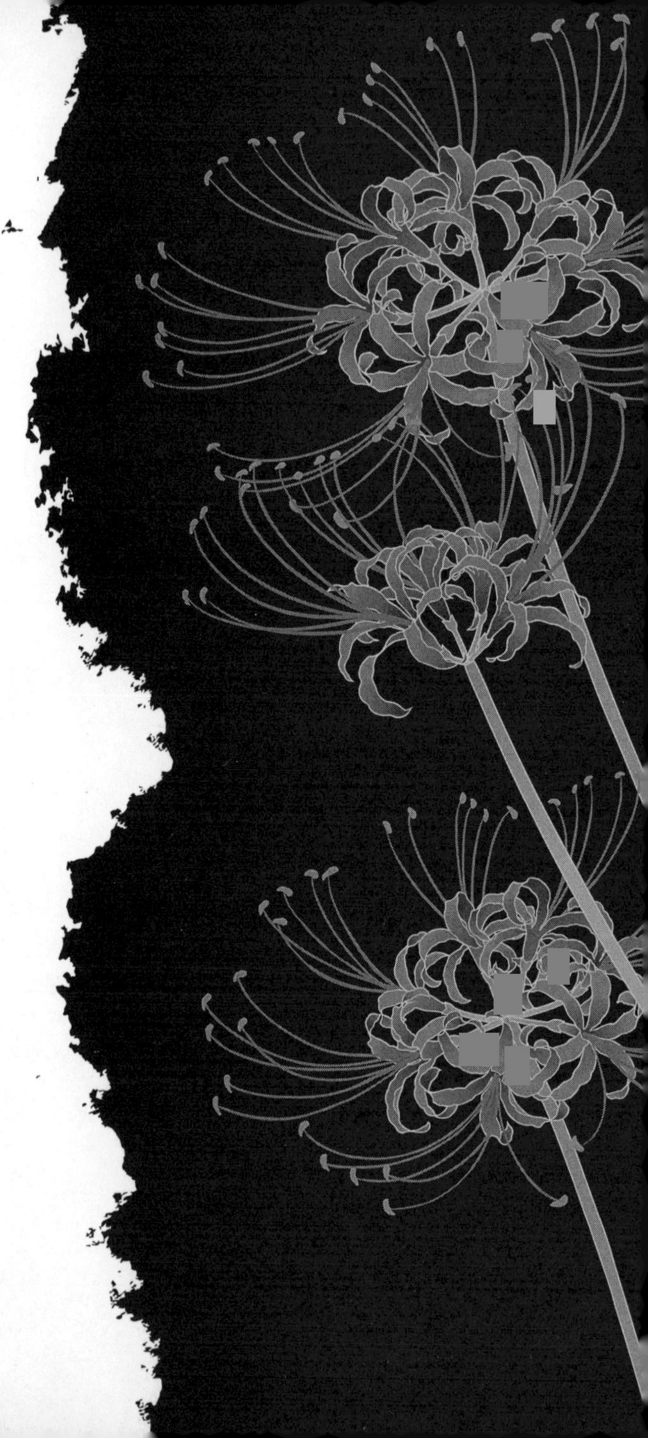

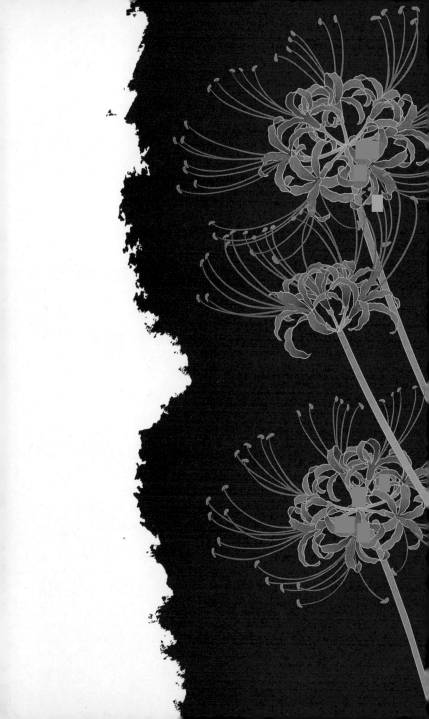

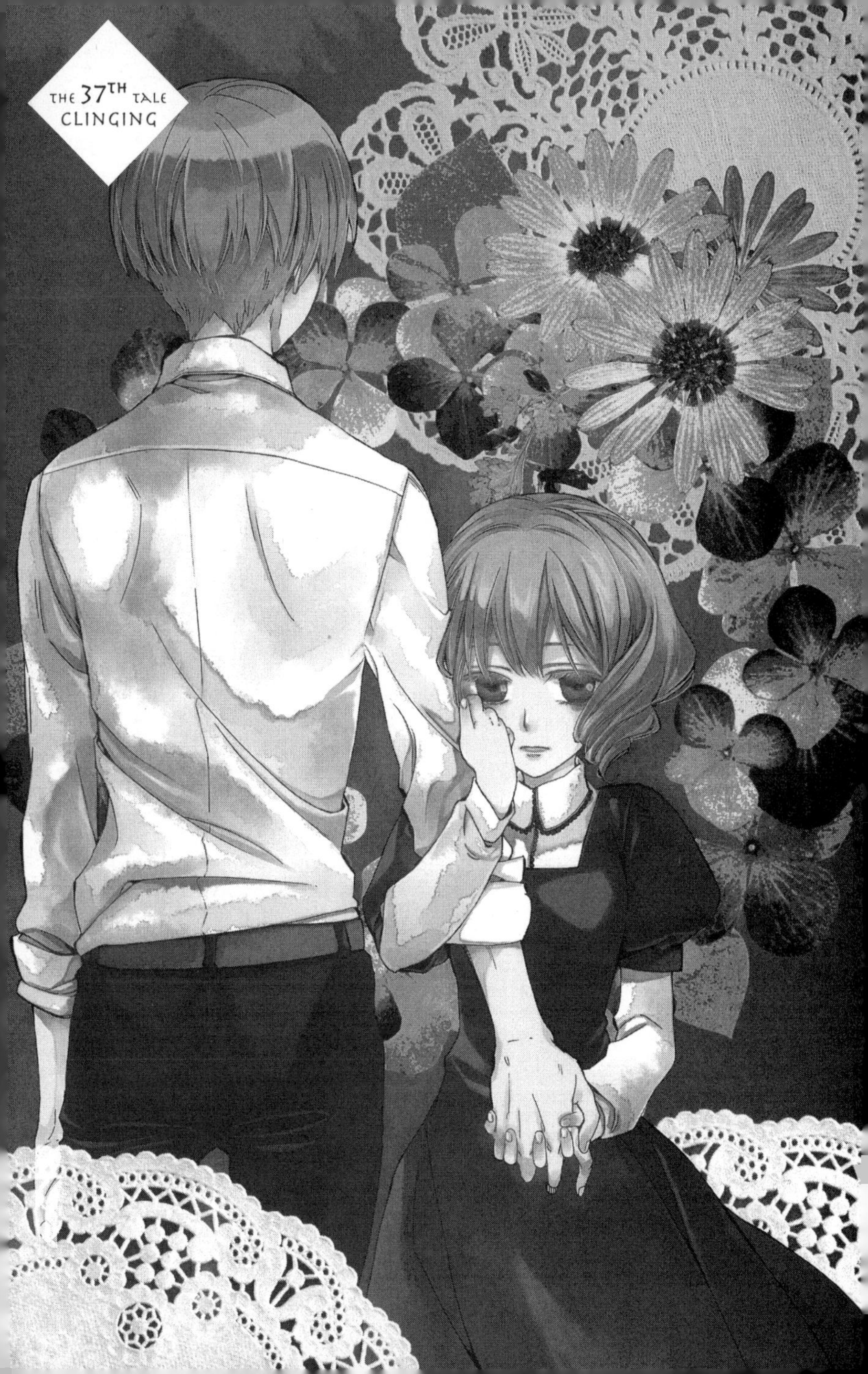
THE 37TH TALE
CLINGING

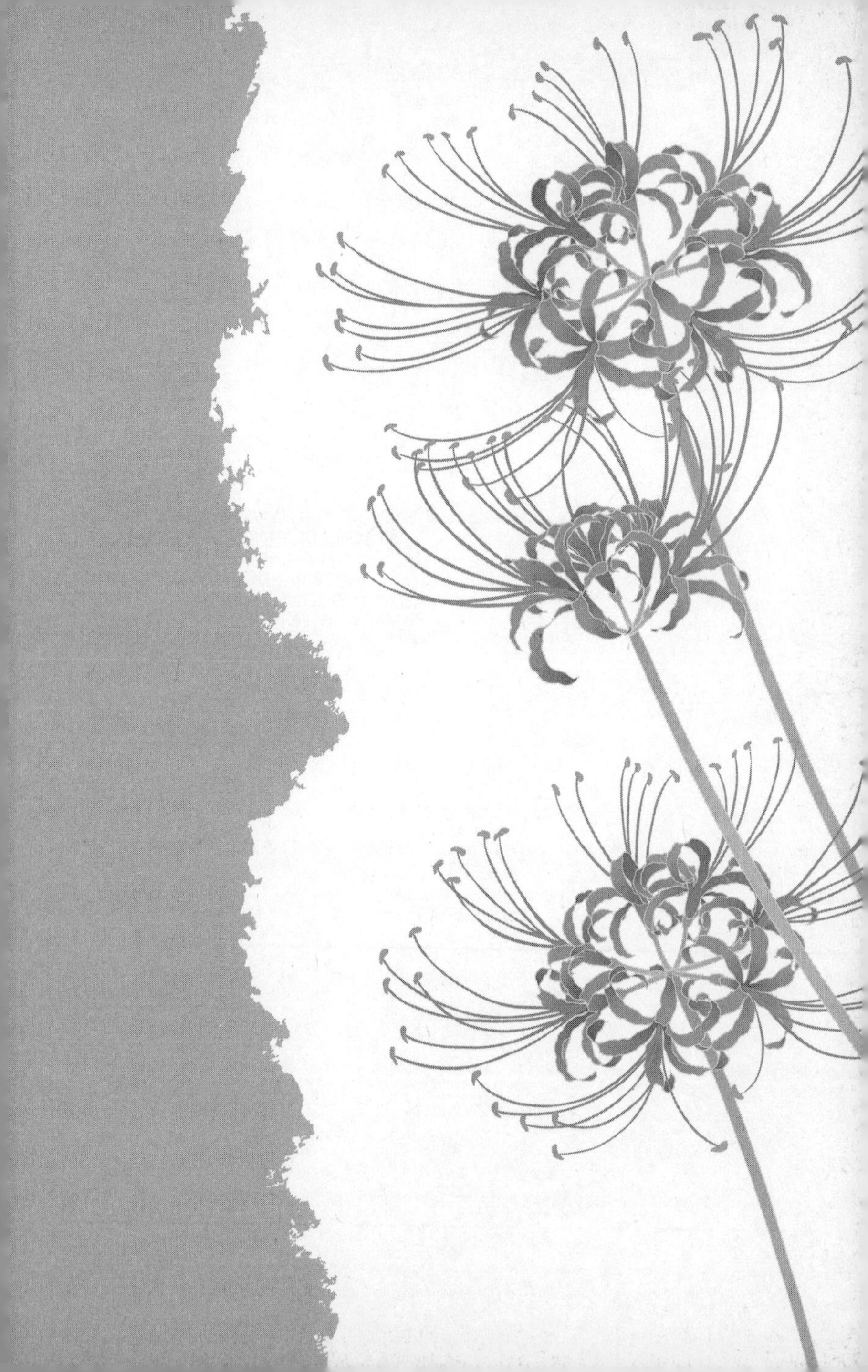

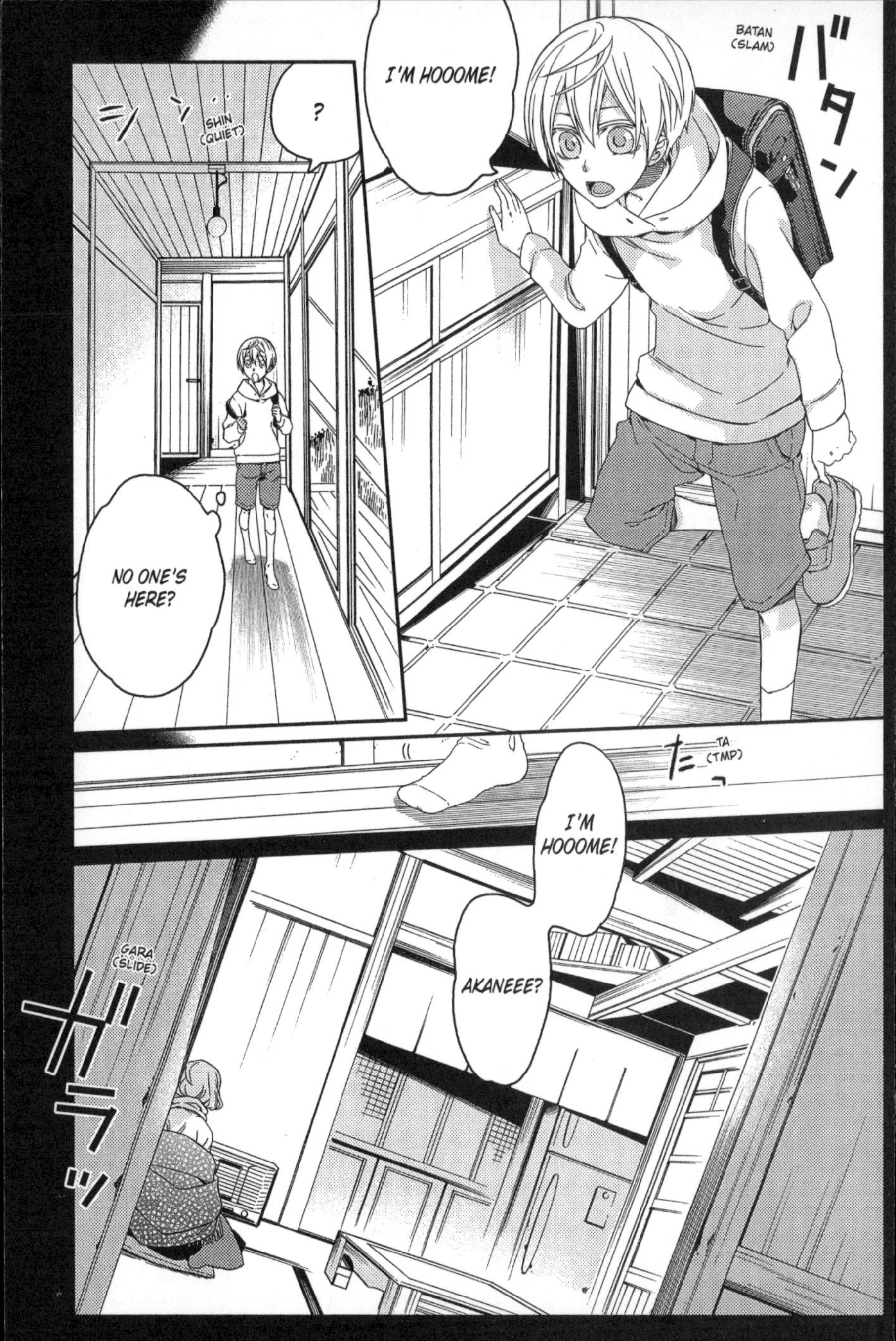
バタン
BATAN (SLAM)
I'M HOOOME!
?
シン
SHIN (QUIET)
NO ONE'S HERE?
たっ
TA (TMP)
I'M HOOOME!
AKANEEE?
GARA (SLIDE)
ガラッ

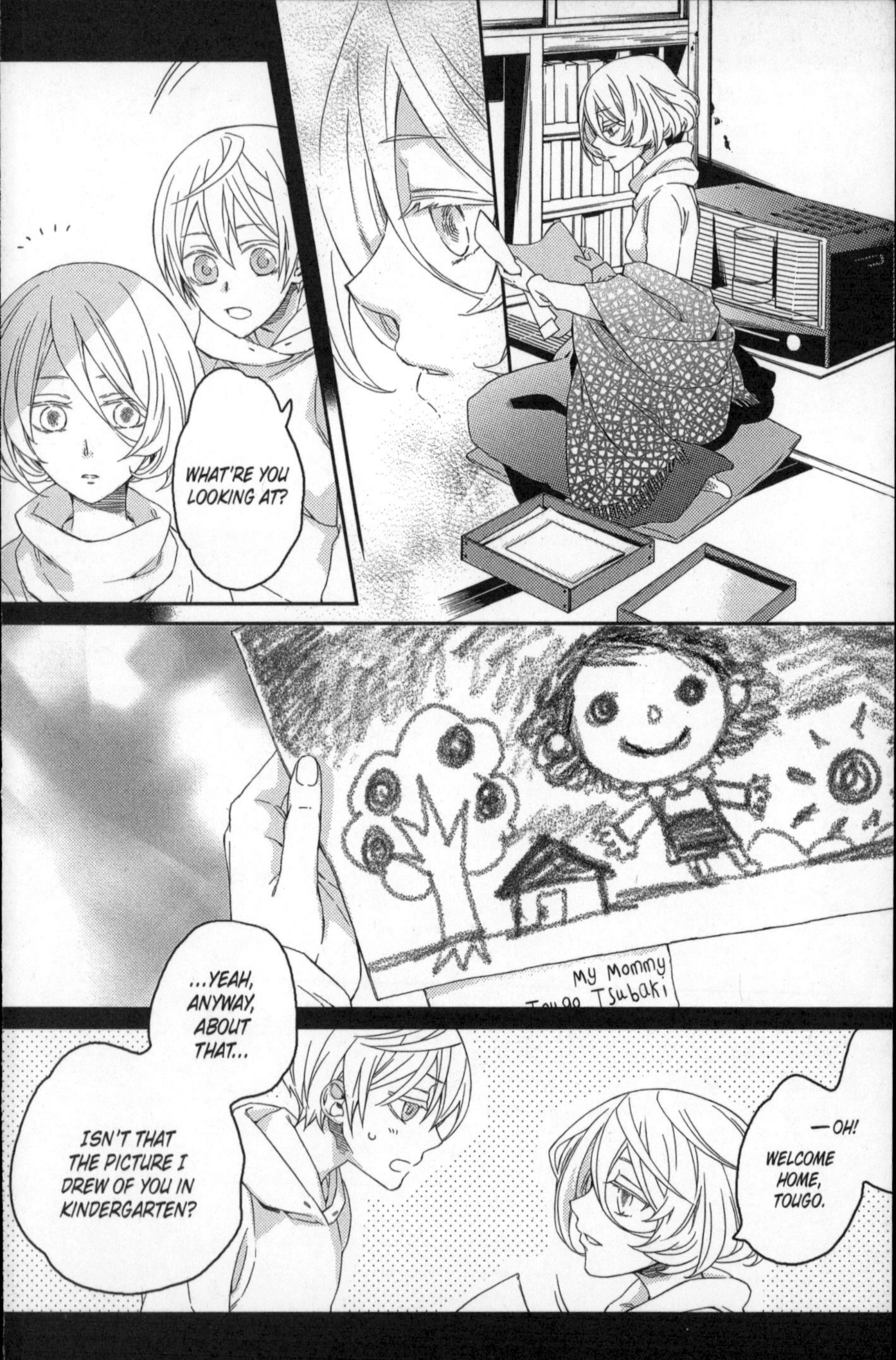
WHAT'RE YOU LOOKING AT?
My Mommy
Tougo Tsubaki
—OH! WELCOME HOME, TOUGO.
...YEAH, ANYWAY, ABOUT THAT...
ISN'T THAT THE PICTURE I DREW OF YOU IN KINDERGARTEN?

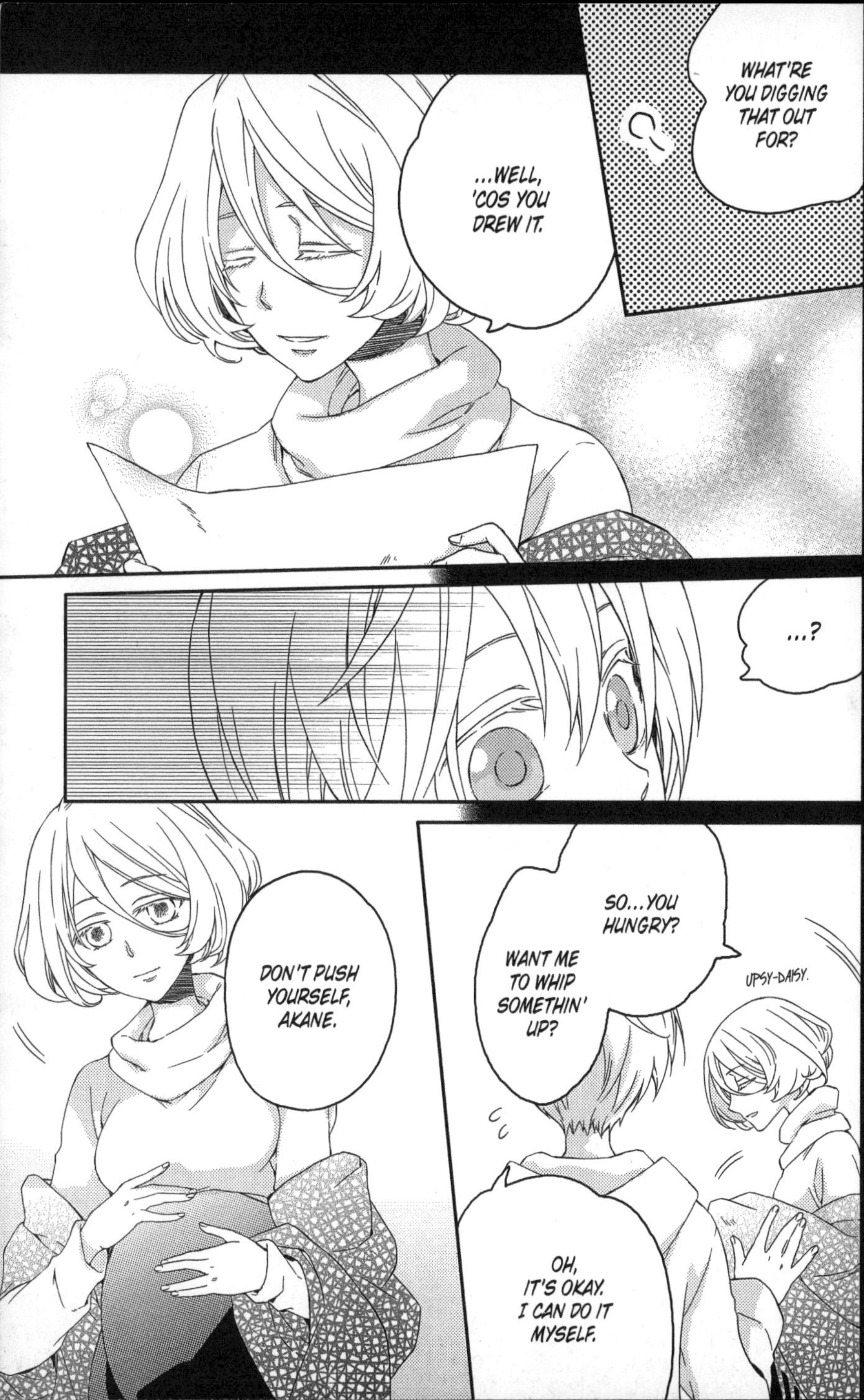
WHAT'RE YOU DIGGING THAT OUT FOR?
...WELL, 'COS YOU DREW IT.
...?
SO...YOU HUNGRY?
WANT ME TO WHIP SOMETHIN' UP?
UPSY-DAISY.
OH, IT'S OKAY. I CAN DO IT MYSELF.
DON'T PUSH YOURSELF, AKANE.

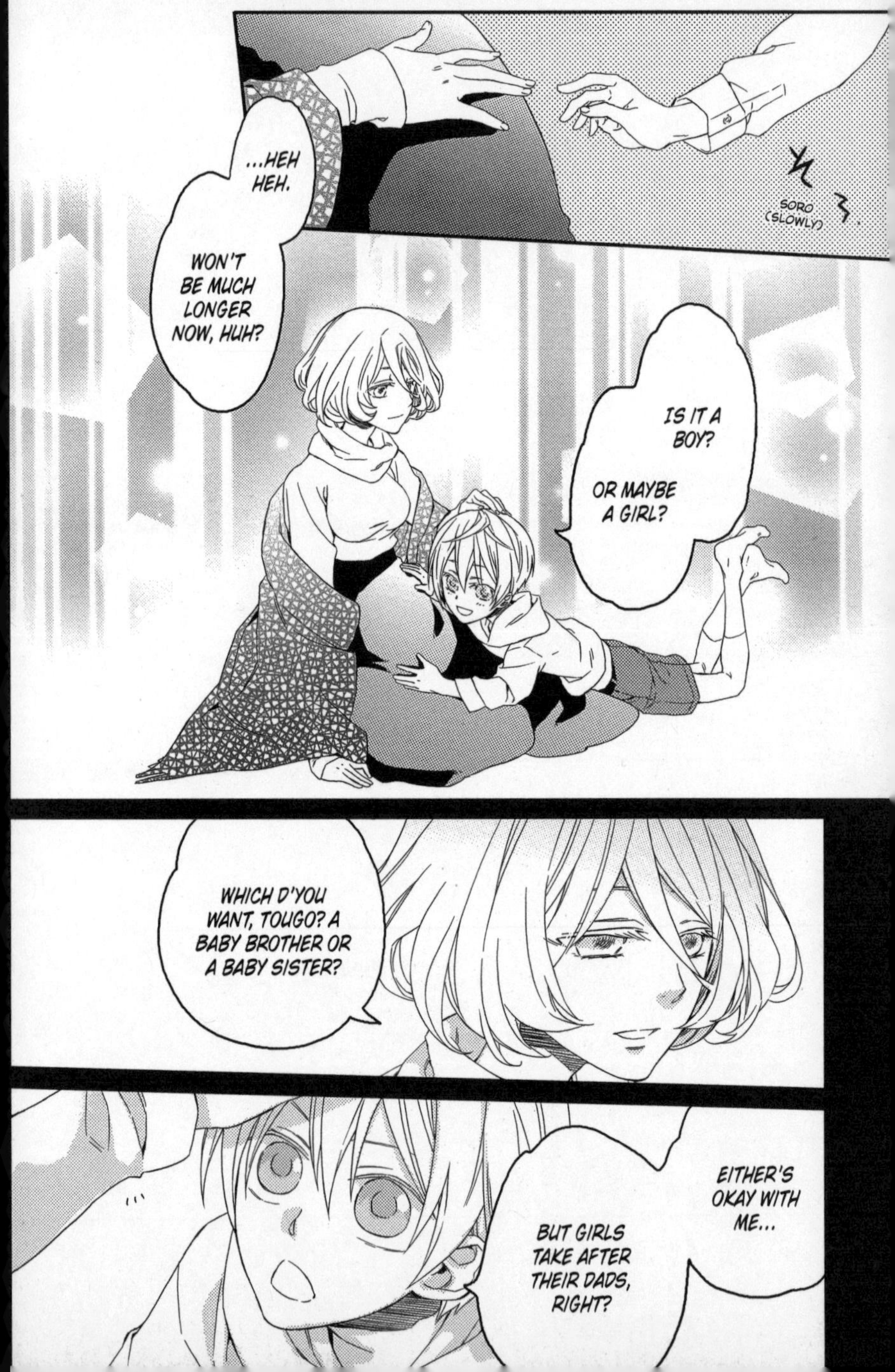
SORO (SLOWLY)
...HEH HEH.
WON'T BE MUCH LONGER NOW, HUH?
IS IT A BOY?
OR MAYBE A GIRL?
WHICH D'YOU WANT, TOUGO? A BABY BROTHER OR A BABY SISTER?
EITHER'S OKAY WITH ME...
BUT GIRLS TAKE AFTER THEIR DADS, RIGHT?
...

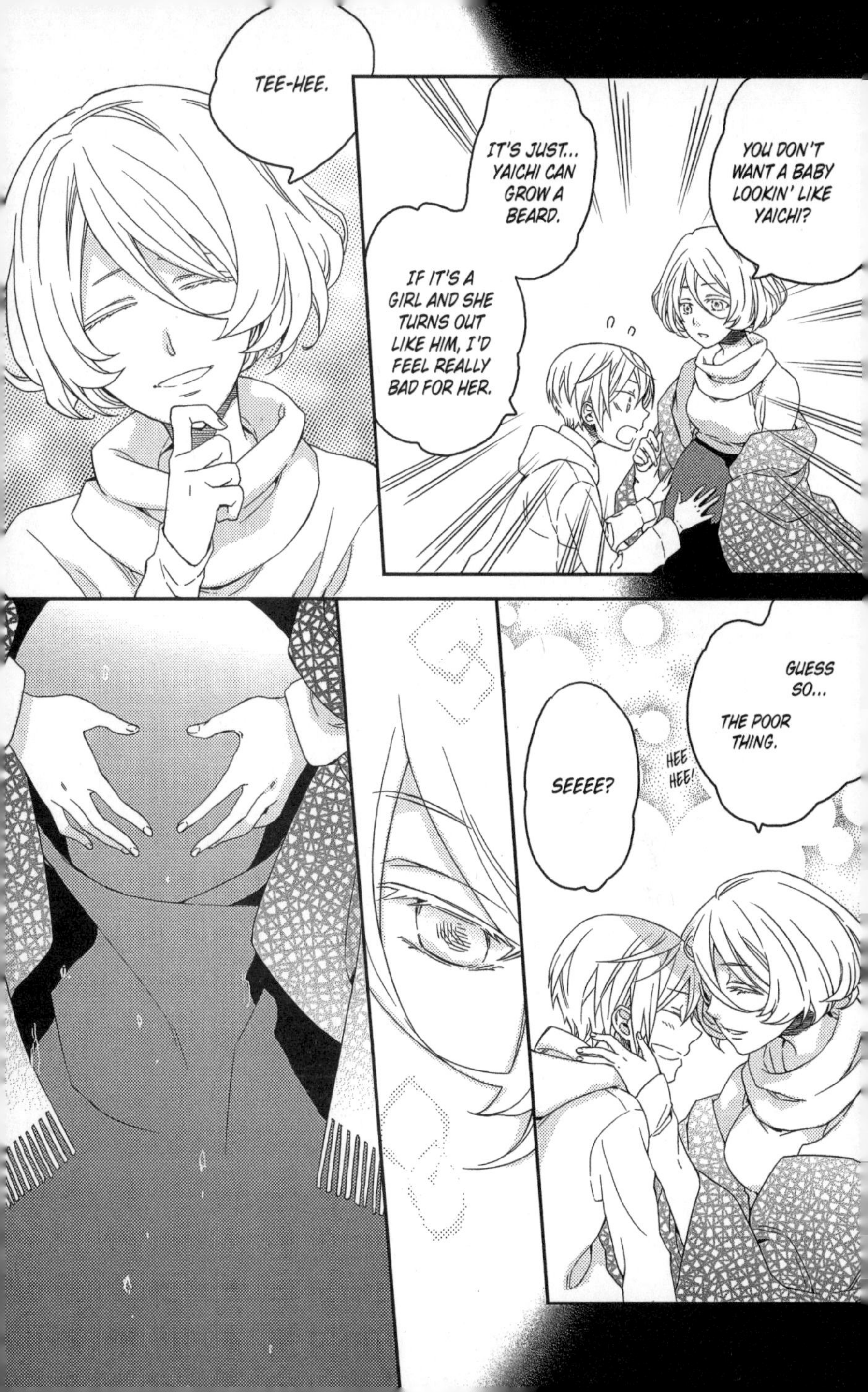
YOU DON'T WANT A BABY LOOKIN' LIKE YAICHI?
IT'S JUST... YAICHI CAN GROW A BEARD.
IF IT'S A GIRL AND SHE TURNS OUT LIKE HIM, I'D FEEL REALLY BAD FOR HER.
TEE-HEE.
GUESS SO...
THE POOR THING.
HEE HEE!
SEEEE?

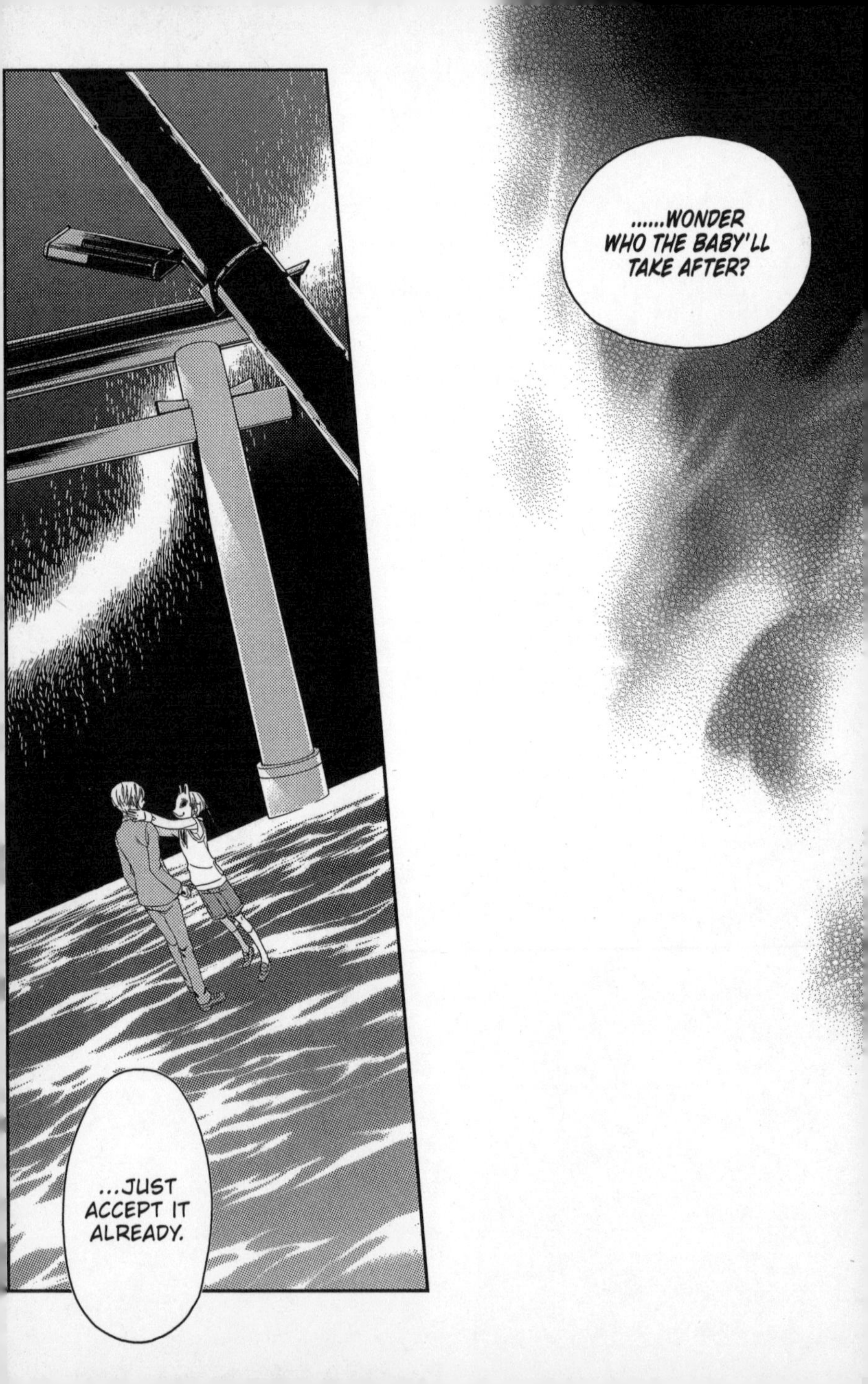
......WONDER WHO THE BABY'LL TAKE AFTER?
...JUST ACCEPT IT ALREADY.

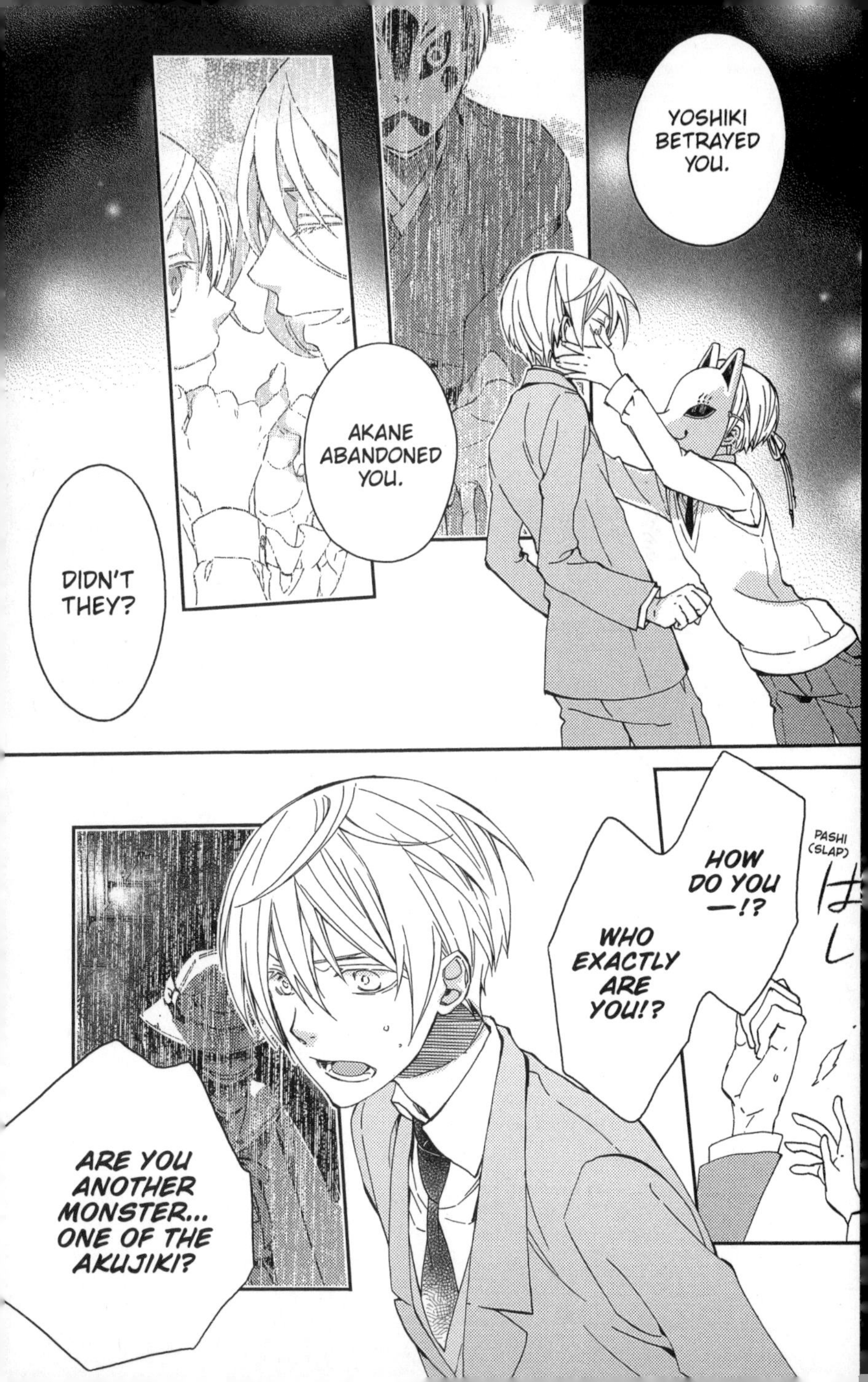
YOSHIKI BETRAYED YOU.
AKANE ABANDONED YOU.
DIDN'T THEY?
PASHI (SLAP)
はし
HOW DO YOU—!?
WHO EXACTLY ARE YOU!?
ARE YOU ANOTHER MONSTER... ONE OF THE AKUJIKI?

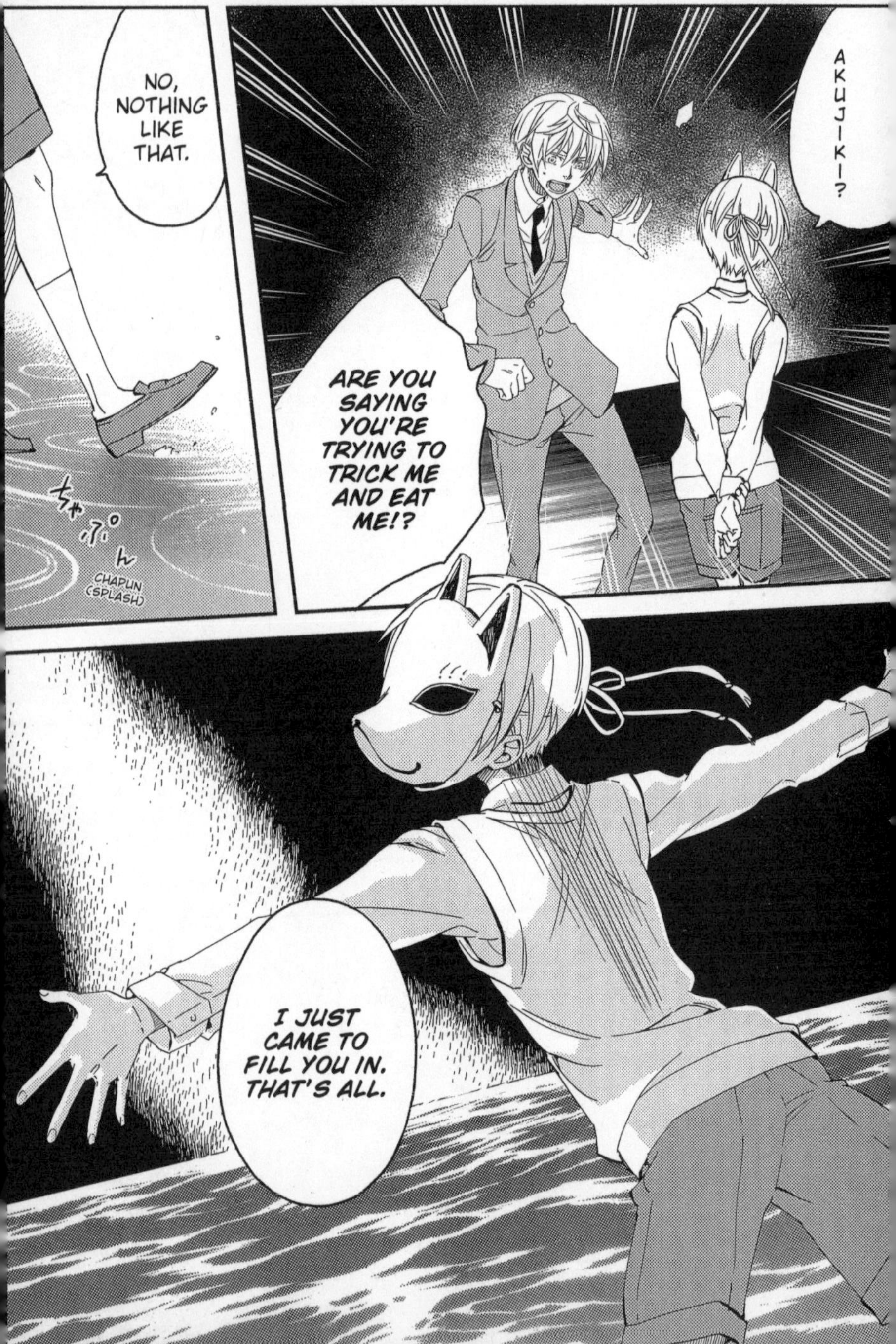
AKUJIKI?
ARE YOU SAYING YOU'RE TRYING TO TRICK ME AND EAT ME!?
NO, NOTHING LIKE THAT.
ちゃぷん
CHAPUN (SPLASH)
I JUST CAME TO FILL YOU IN. THAT'S ALL.

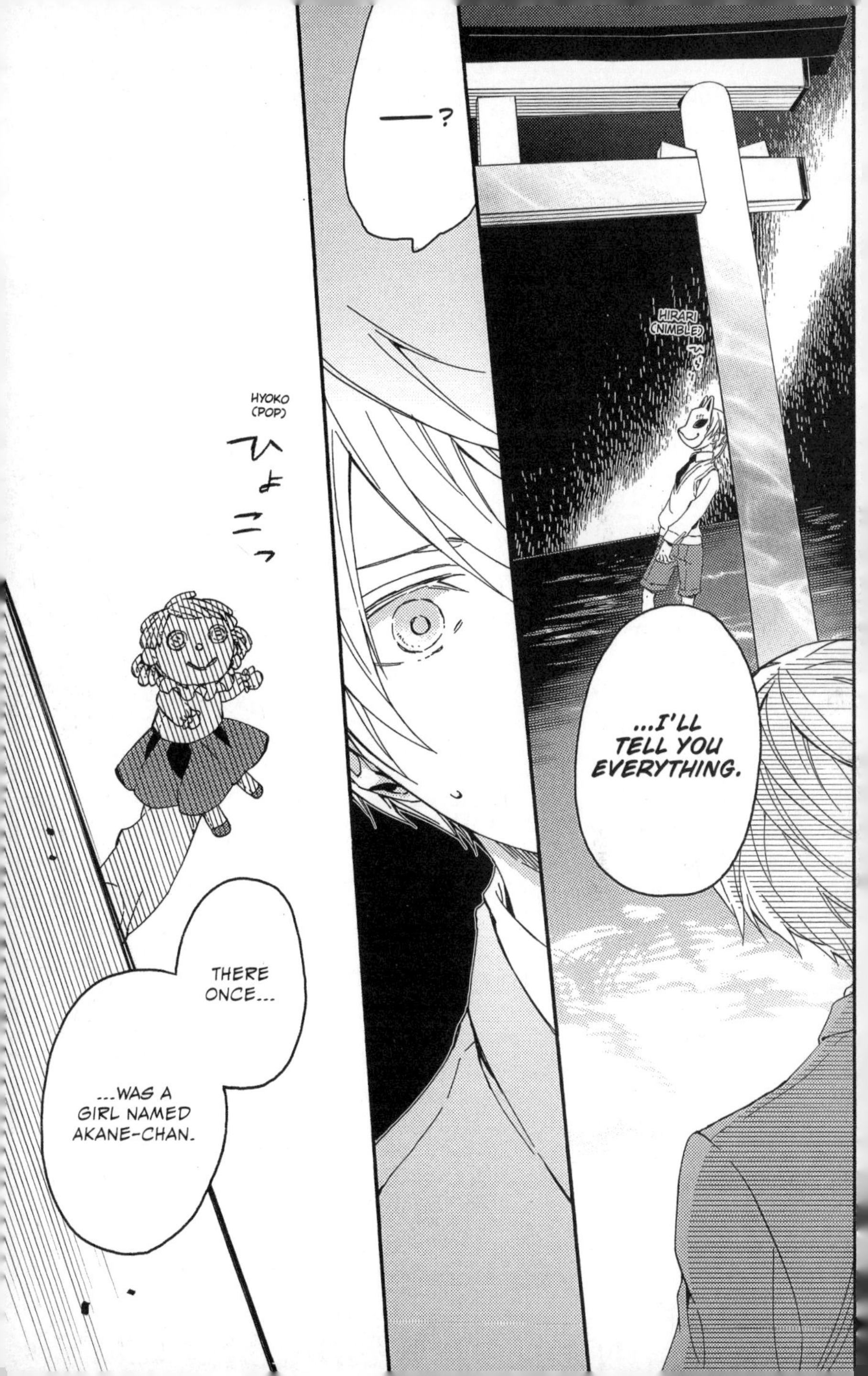
HIRARI (NIMBLE)
...I'LL TELL YOU EVERYTHING.
—?
HYOKO (POP)
ひょこっ
THERE ONCE...
...WAS A GIRL NAMED AKANE-CHAN.

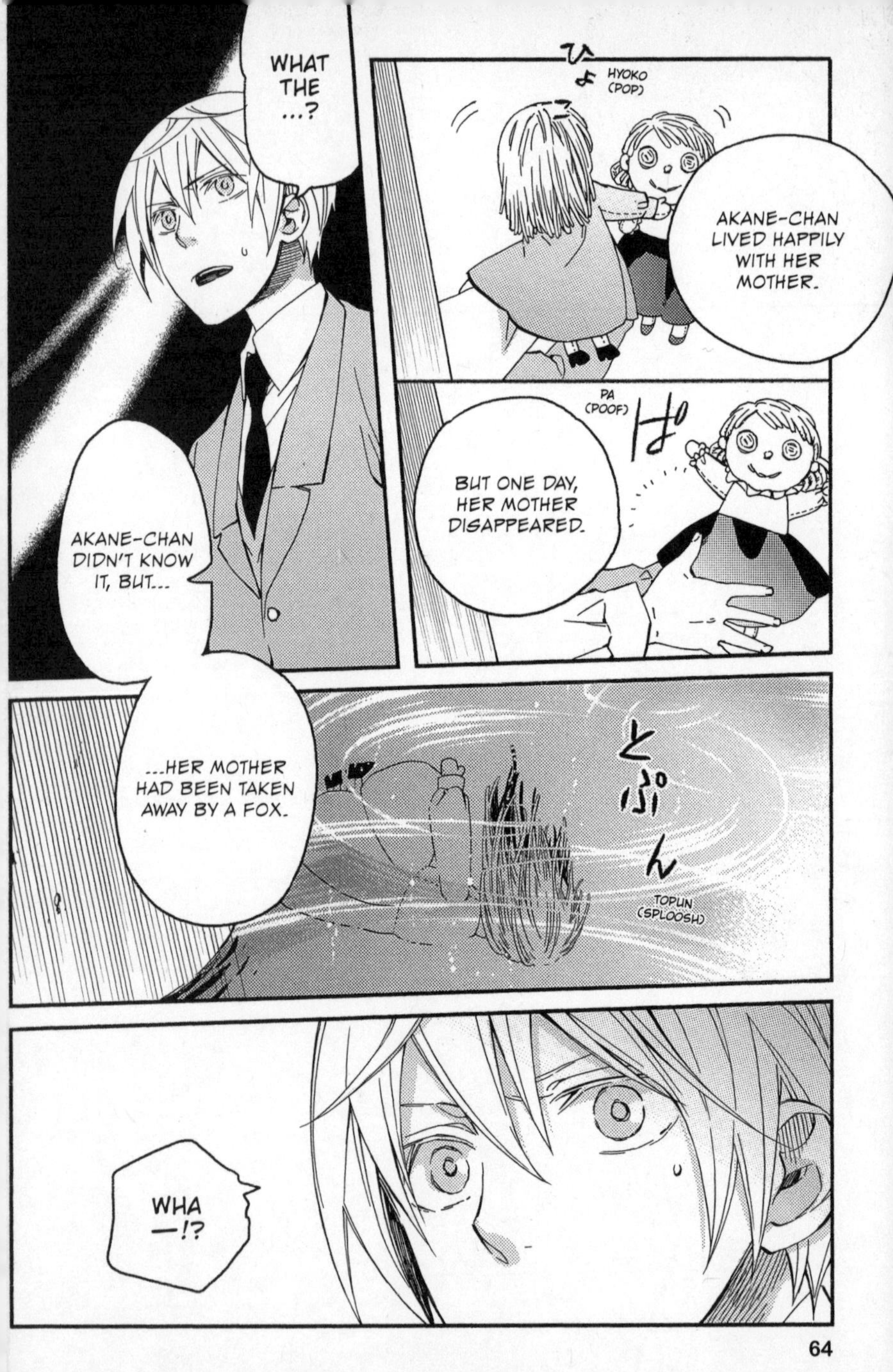

ひょ
HYOKO (POP)
AKANE-CHAN LIVED HAPPILY WITH HER MOTHER.
ぱ
PA (POOF)
BUT ONE DAY, HER MOTHER DISAPPEARED.
WHAT THE ...?
AKANE-CHAN DIDN'T KNOW IT, BUT...
...HER MOTHER HAD BEEN TAKEN AWAY BY A FOX.
とぷん
TOPUN (SPLOOSH)
WHA—!?

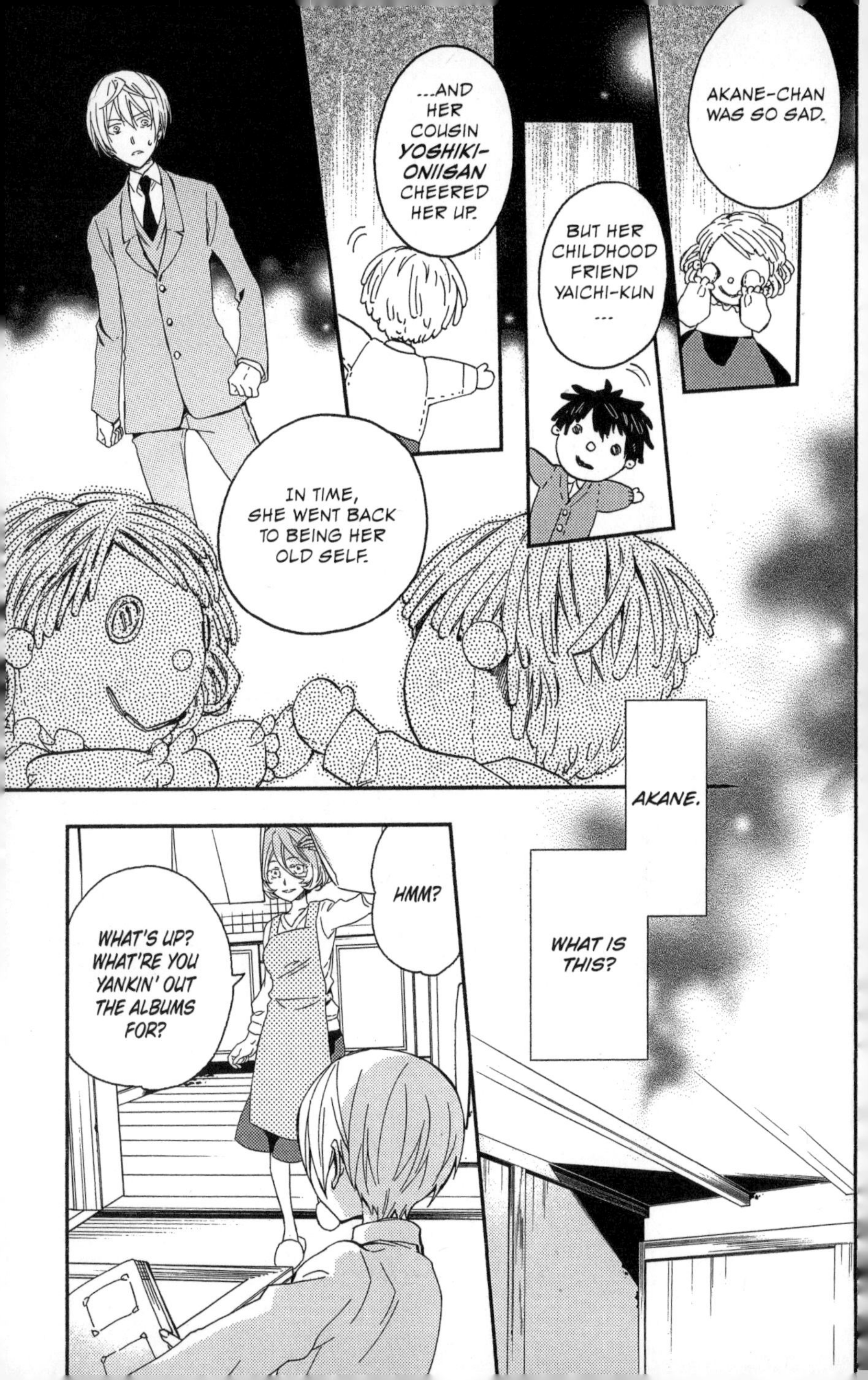
AKANE-CHAN WAS SO SAD.
BUT HER CHILDHOOD FRIEND YAICHI-KUN ...
...AND HER COUSIN YOSHIKI-ONIISAN CHEERED HER UP.
IN TIME, SHE WENT BACK TO BEING HER OLD SELF.
AKANE.
WHAT IS THIS?
HMM?
WHAT'S UP? WHAT'RE YOU YANKIN' OUT THE ALBUMS FOR?

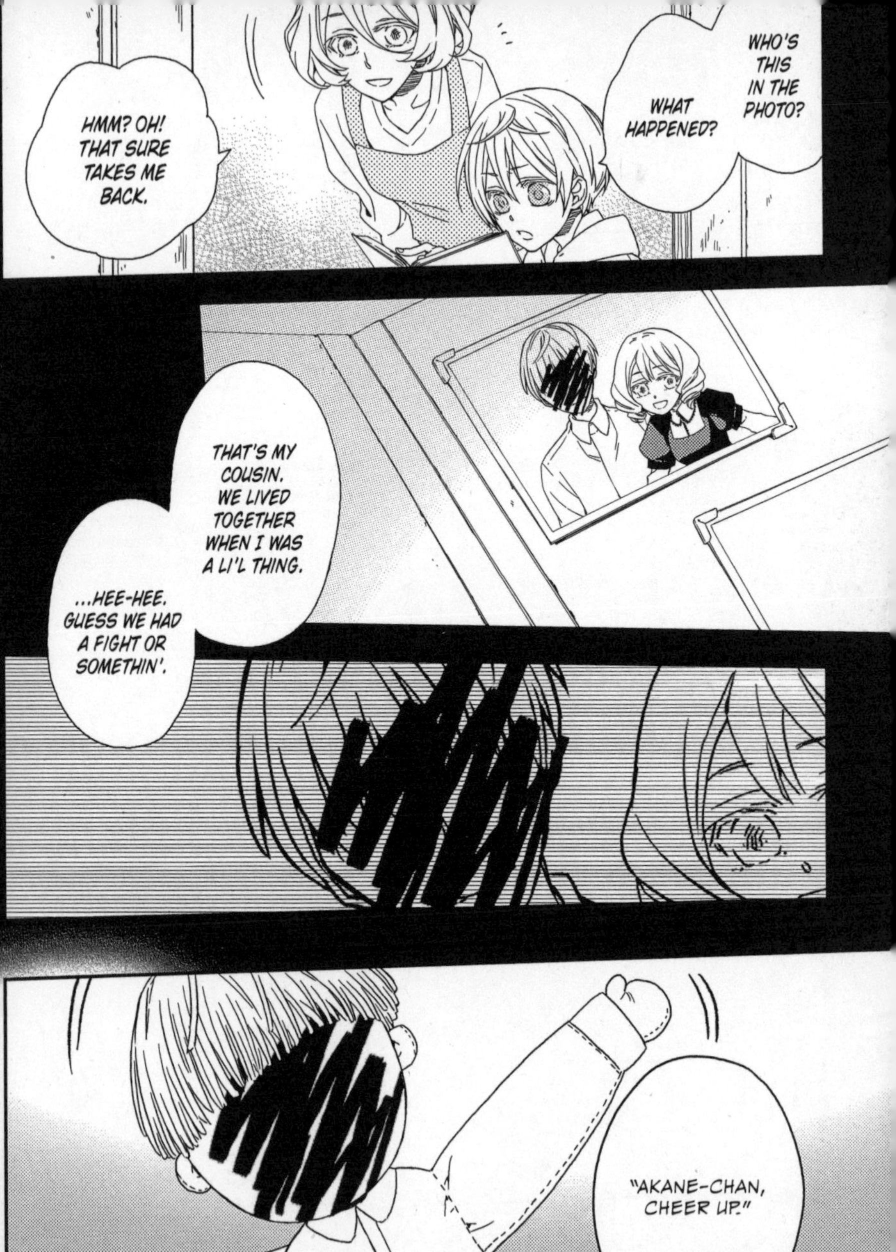
WHO'S THIS IN THE PHOTO?
WHAT HAPPENED?
HMM? OH! THAT SURE TAKES ME BACK.
THAT'S MY COUSIN. WE LIVED TOGETHER WHEN I WAS A LI'L THING.
...HEE-HEE. GUESS WE HAD A FIGHT OR SOMETHIN'.
"AKANE-CHAN, CHEER UP."

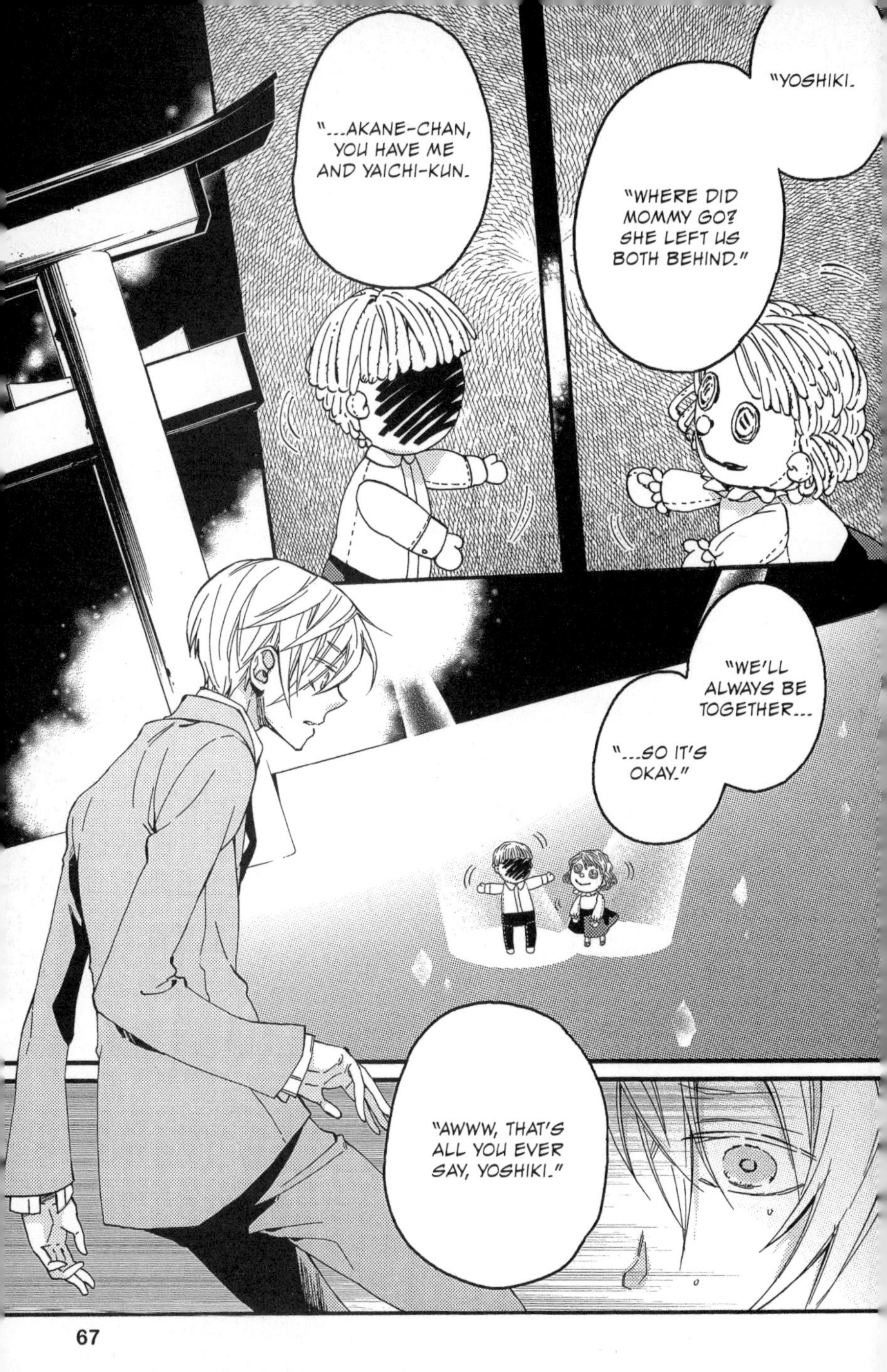
"YOSHIKI.
"WHERE DID MOMMY GO? SHE LEFT US BOTH BEHIND."
"...AKANE-CHAN, YOU HAVE ME AND YAICHI-KUN.
"WE'LL ALWAYS BE TOGETHER...
"...SO IT'S OKAY."
"AWWW, THAT'S ALL YOU EVER SAY, YOSHIKI."

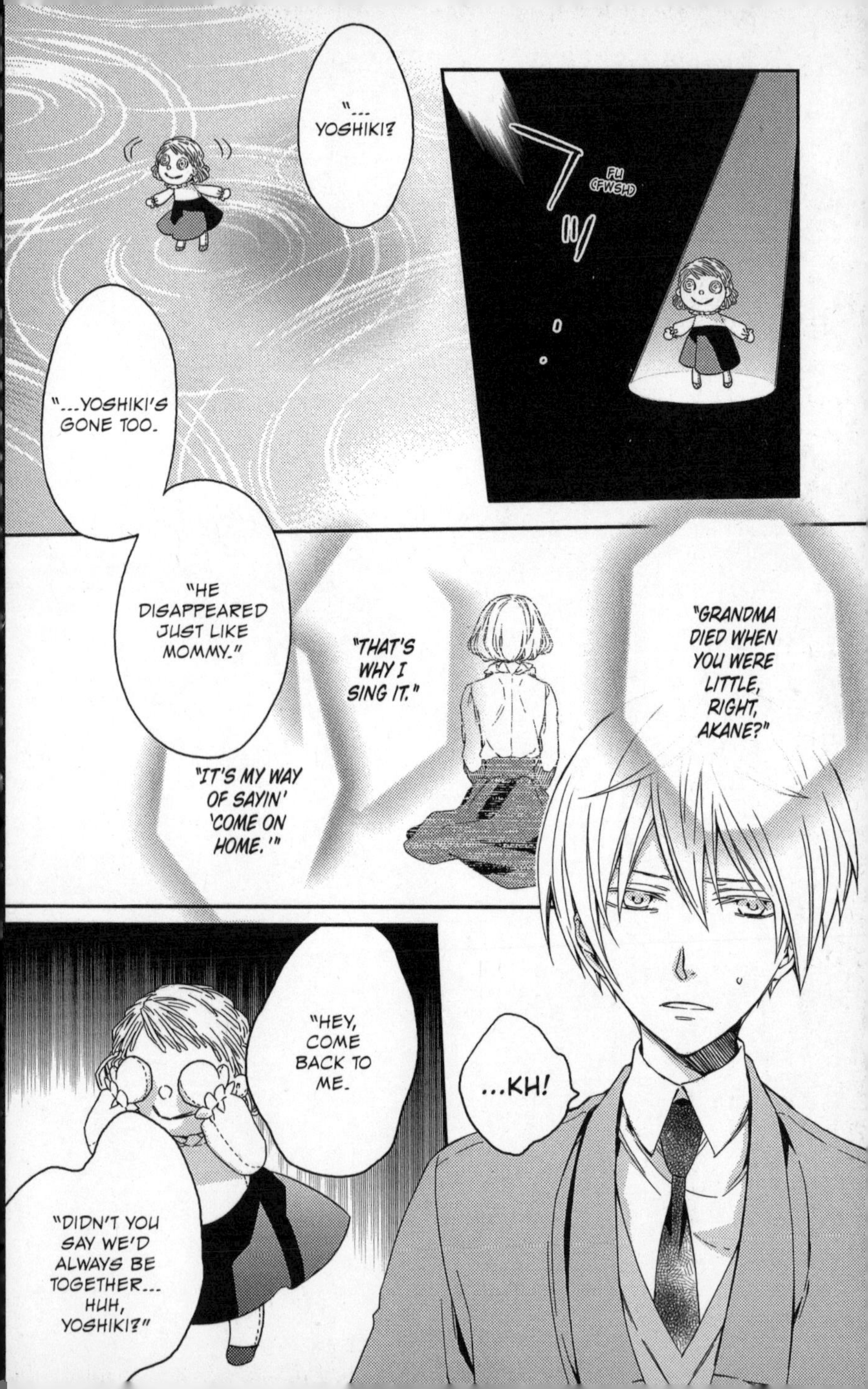
FU (FWSH)
"...YOSHIKI?
"...YOSHIKI'S GONE TOO.
"HE DISAPPEARED JUST LIKE MOMMY."
"GRANDMA DIED WHEN YOU WERE LITTLE, RIGHT, AKANE?"
"THAT'S WHY I SING IT."
"IT'S MY WAY OF SAYIN' 'COME ON HOME.'"
...KH!
"HEY, COME BACK TO ME.
"DIDN'T YOU SAY WE'D ALWAYS BE TOGETHER... HUH, YOSHIKI?"

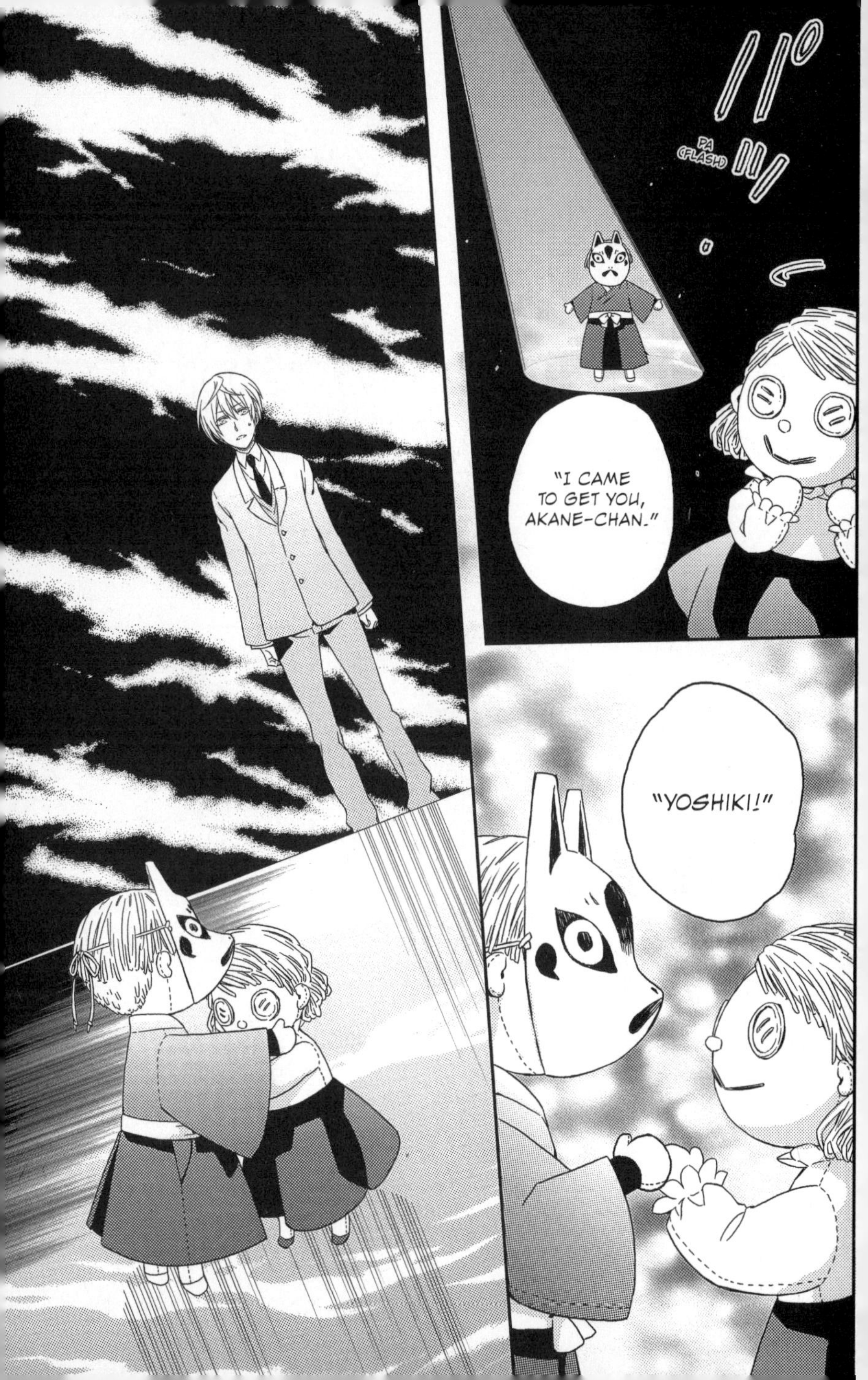
PA (FLASH)
"I CAME TO GET YOU, AKANE-CHAN."
"YOSHIKI!"

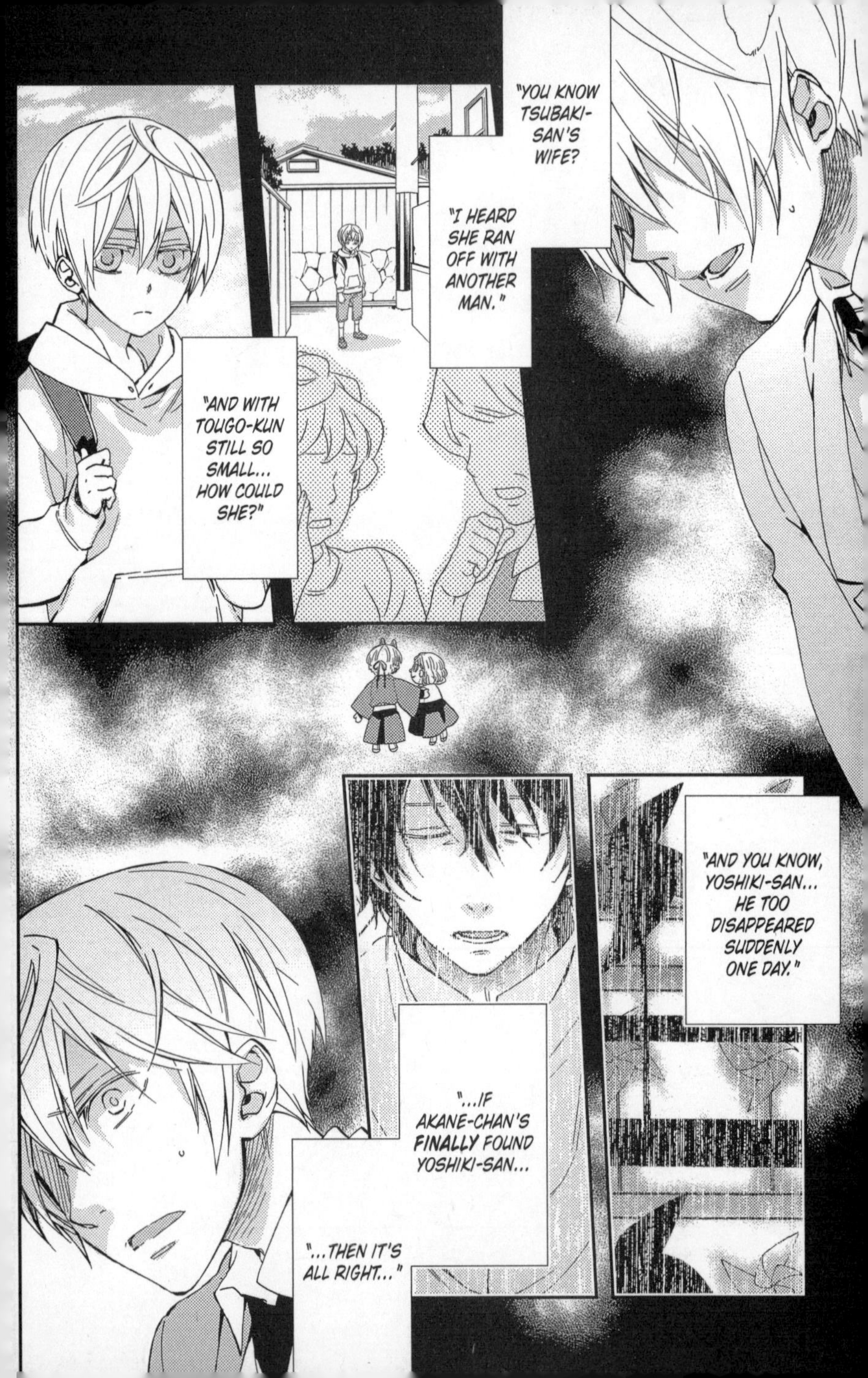
"YOU KNOW TSUBAKI-SAN'S WIFE?
"I HEARD SHE RAN OFF WITH ANOTHER MAN."
"AND WITH TOUGO-KUN STILL SO SMALL... HOW COULD SHE?"
"AND YOU KNOW, YOSHIKI-SAN... HE TOO DISAPPEARED SUDDENLY ONE DAY."
"...IF AKANE-CHAN'S FINALLY FOUND YOSHIKI-SAN...
"...THEN IT'S ALL RIGHT..."

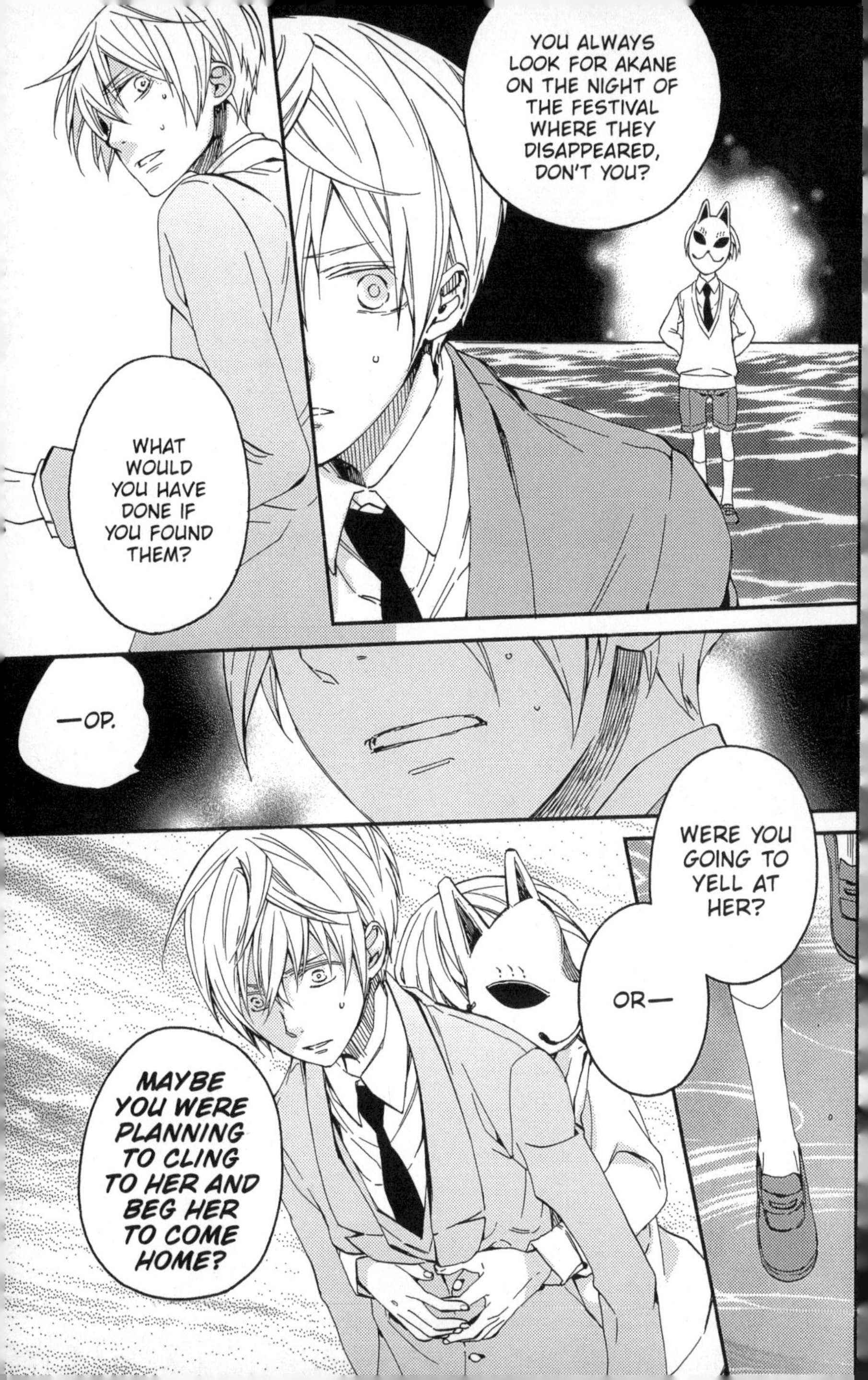
YOU ALWAYS LOOK FOR AKANE ON THE NIGHT OF THE FESTIVAL WHERE THEY DISAPPEARED, DON'T YOU?
WHAT WOULD YOU HAVE DONE IF YOU FOUND THEM?
—OP.
WERE YOU GOING TO YELL AT HER?
OR—
MAYBE YOU WERE PLANNING TO CLING TO HER AND BEG HER TO COME HOME?

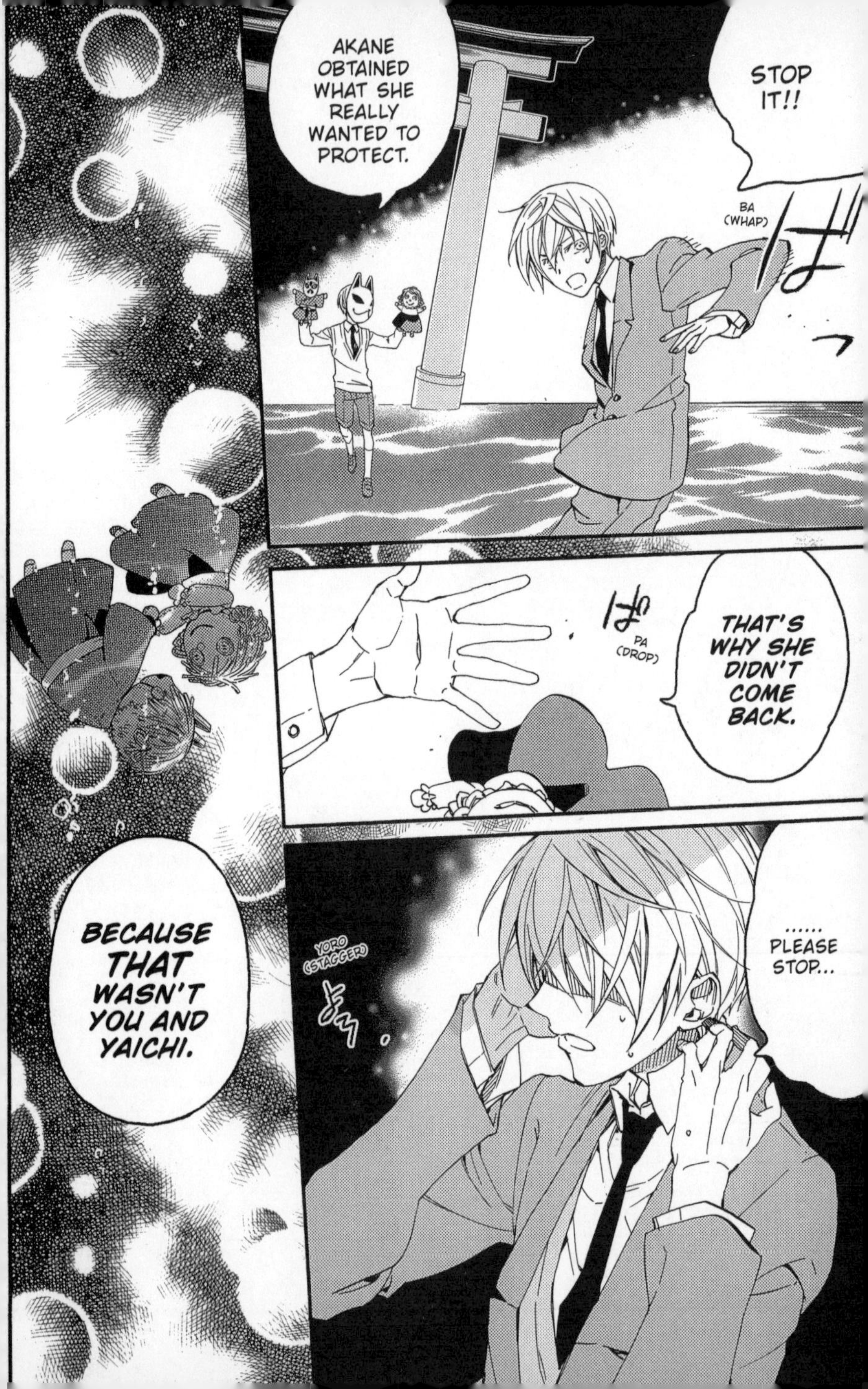
STOP IT!!
BA (WHAP)
ばっ
AKANE OBTAINED WHAT SHE REALLY WANTED TO PROTECT.
THAT'S WHY SHE DIDN'T COME BACK.
ぱ
PA (DROP)
...... PLEASE STOP...
YORO (STAGGER)
よろ
BECAUSE THAT WASN'T YOU AND YAICHI.

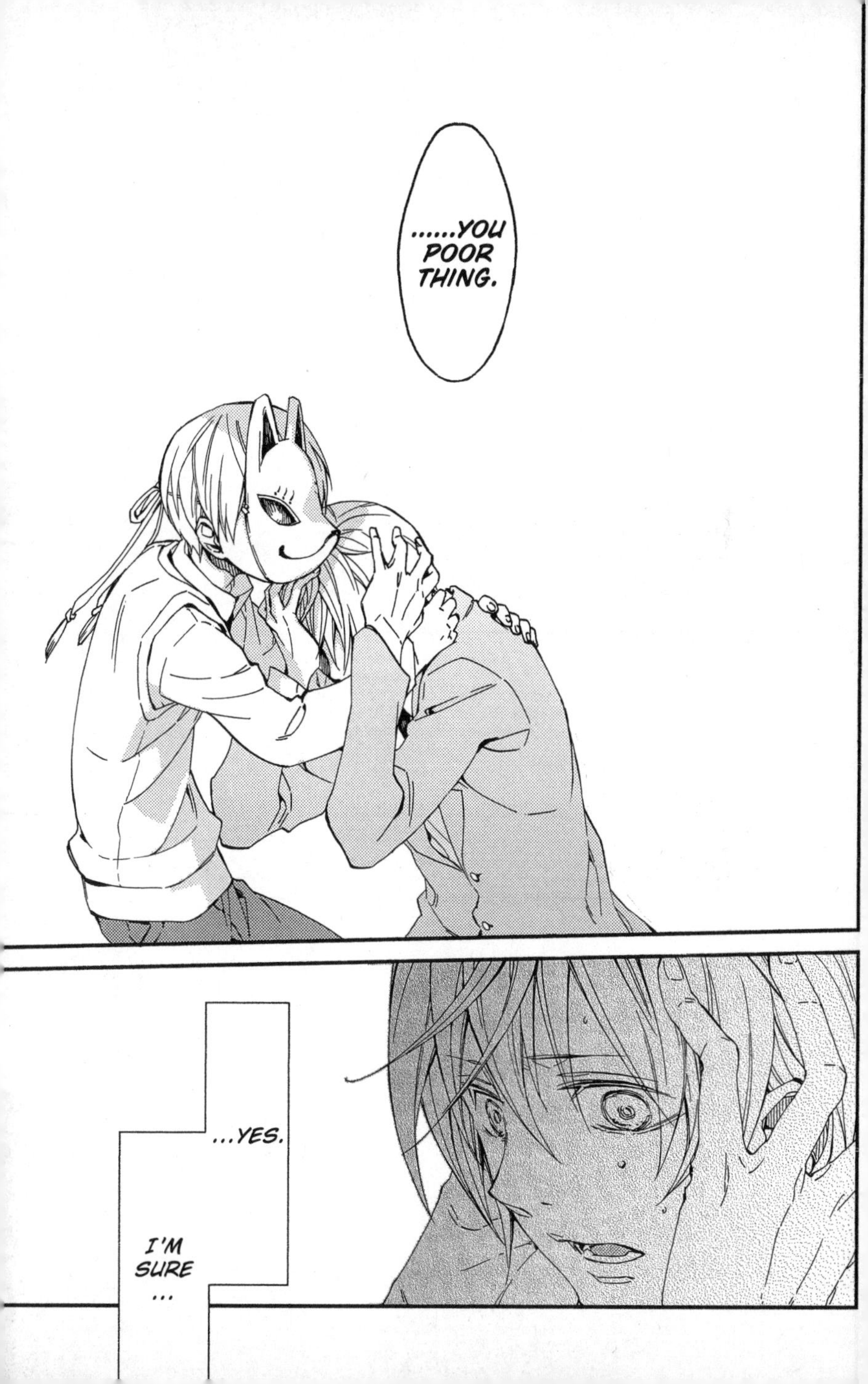
......YOU POOR THING.
...YES.
I'M SURE ...

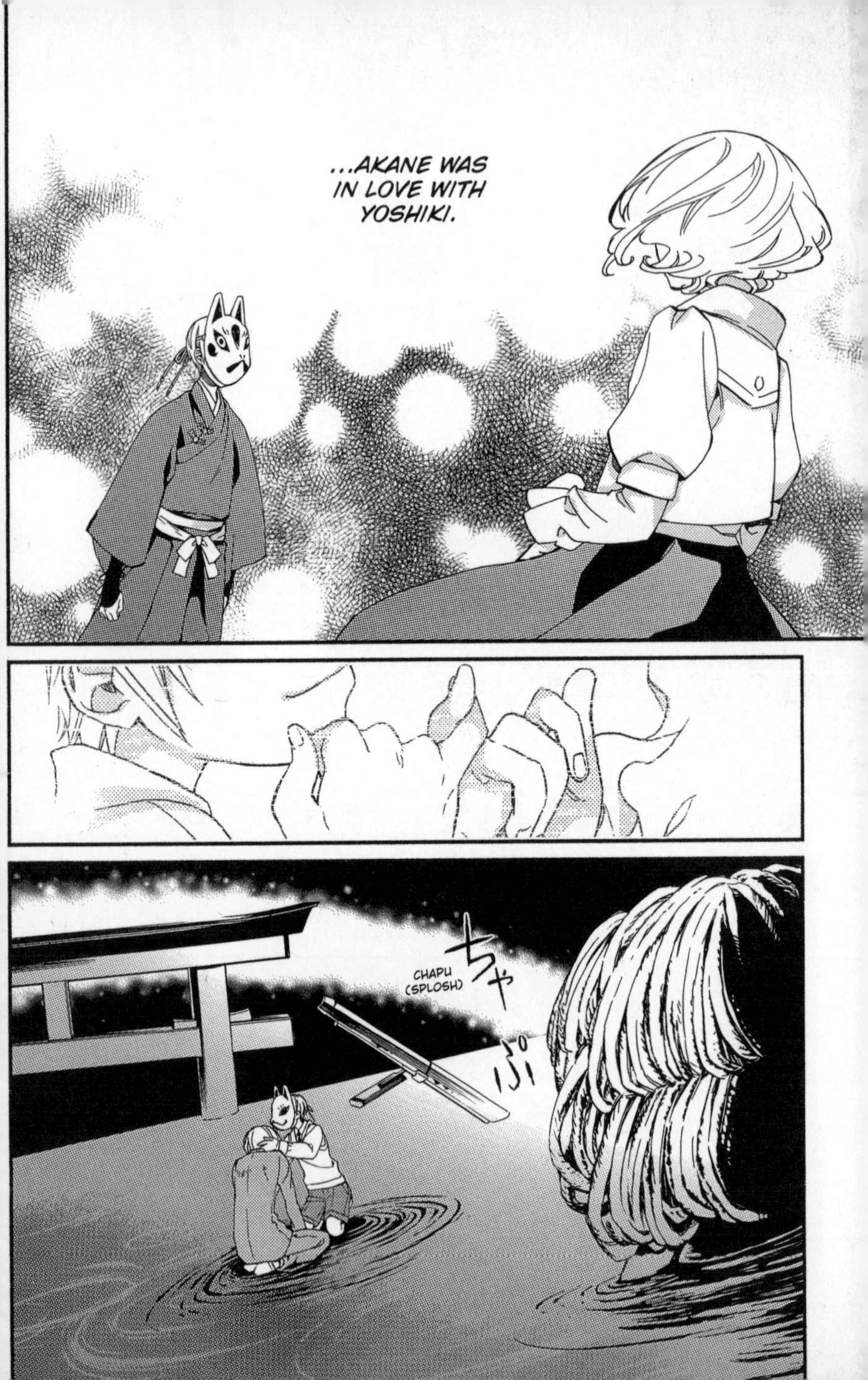
...AKANE WAS IN LOVE WITH YOSHIKI.
ちゃぷ
CHAPU (SPLOSH)

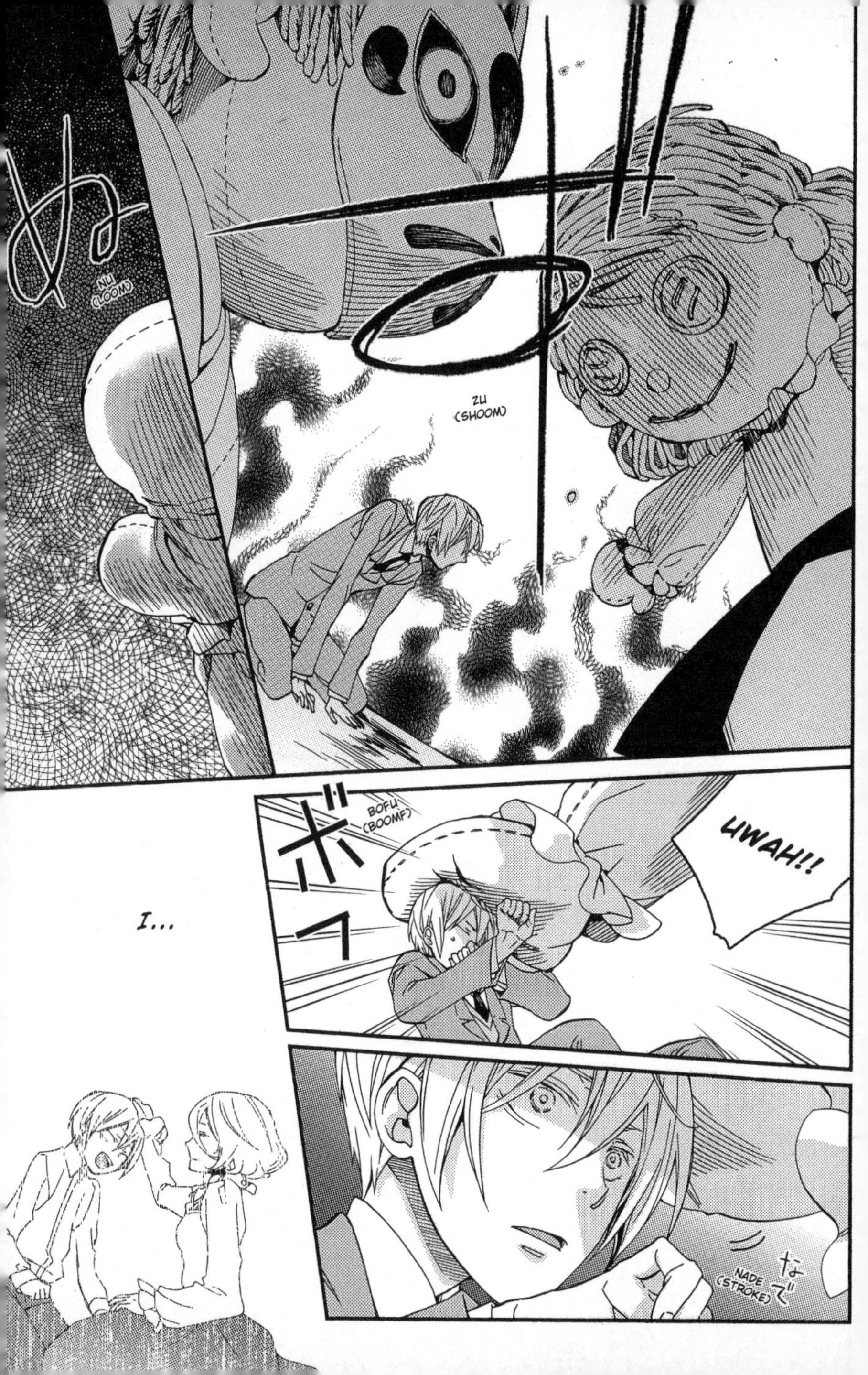
ZU
(SHOOM)
ぬ
NU
(LOOM)
UWAH!!
ボフ
BOFU
(BOOMF)
なで
NADE
(STROKE)
I...

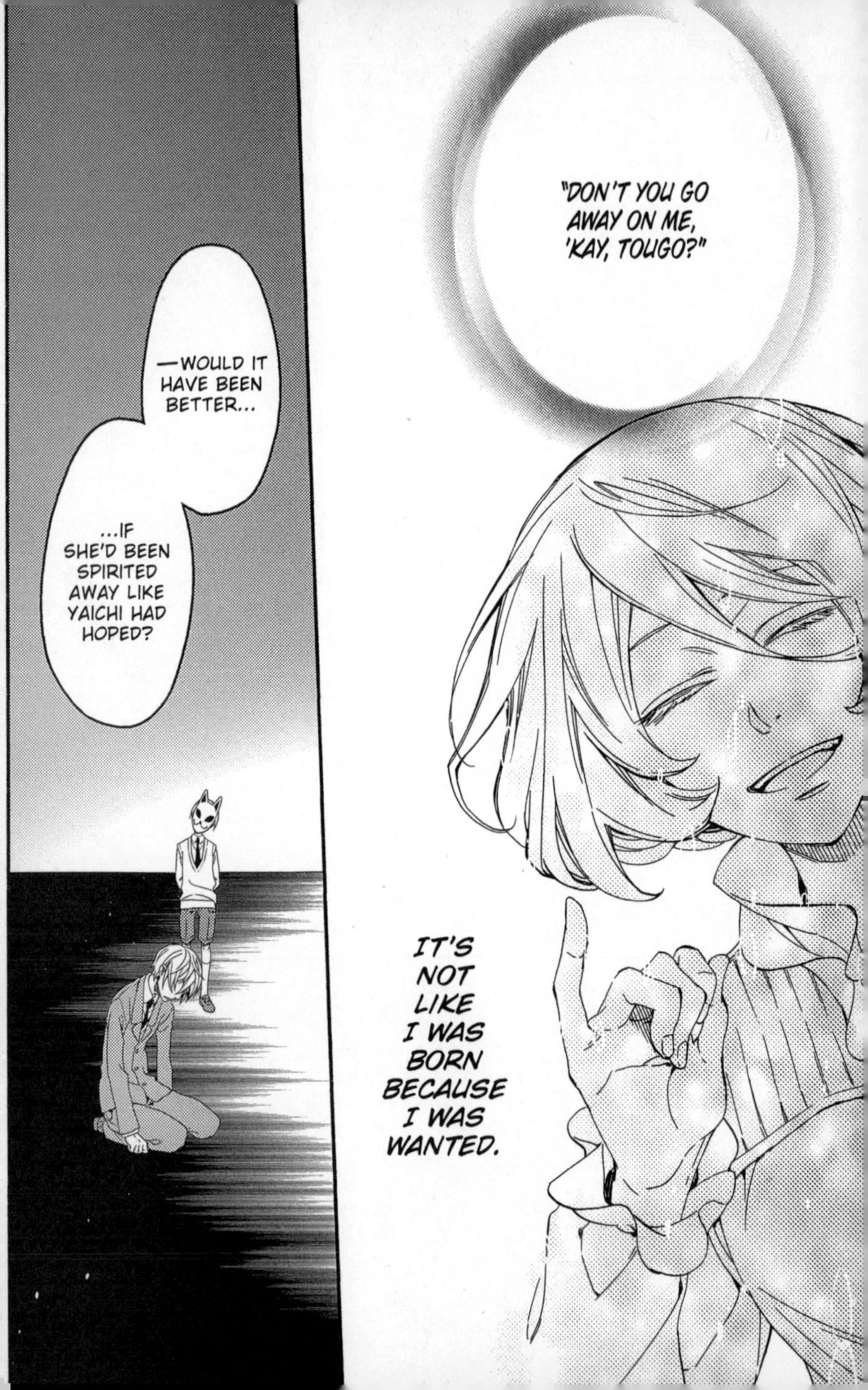
"DON'T YOU GO AWAY ON ME, 'KAY, TOUGO?"
IT'S NOT LIKE I WAS BORN BECAUSE I WAS WANTED.
—WOULD IT HAVE BEEN BETTER...
...IF SHE'D BEEN SPIRITED AWAY LIKE YAICHI HAD HOPED?

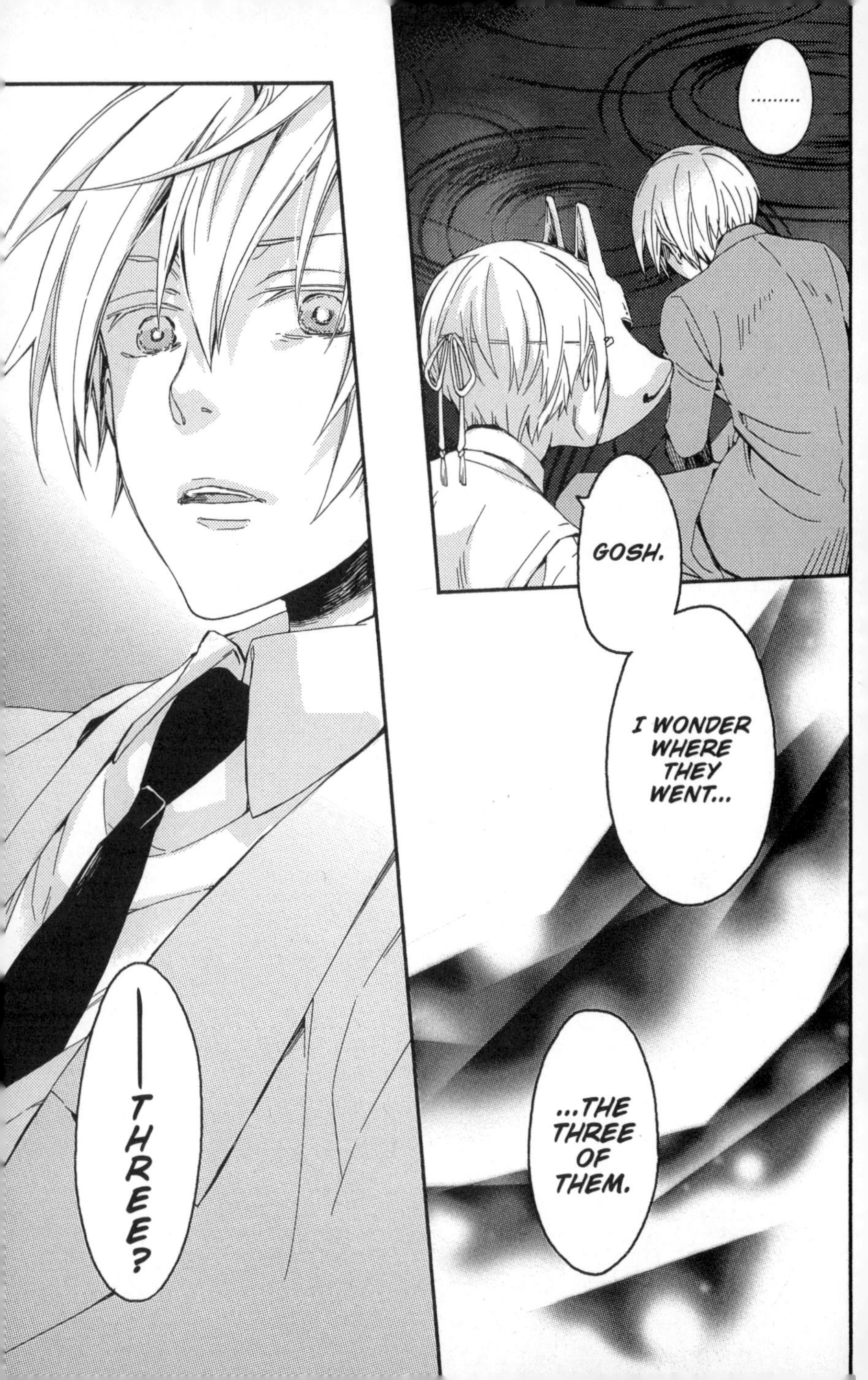
....
GOSH.
I WONDER WHERE THEY WENT...
...THE THREE OF THEM.
—THREE?

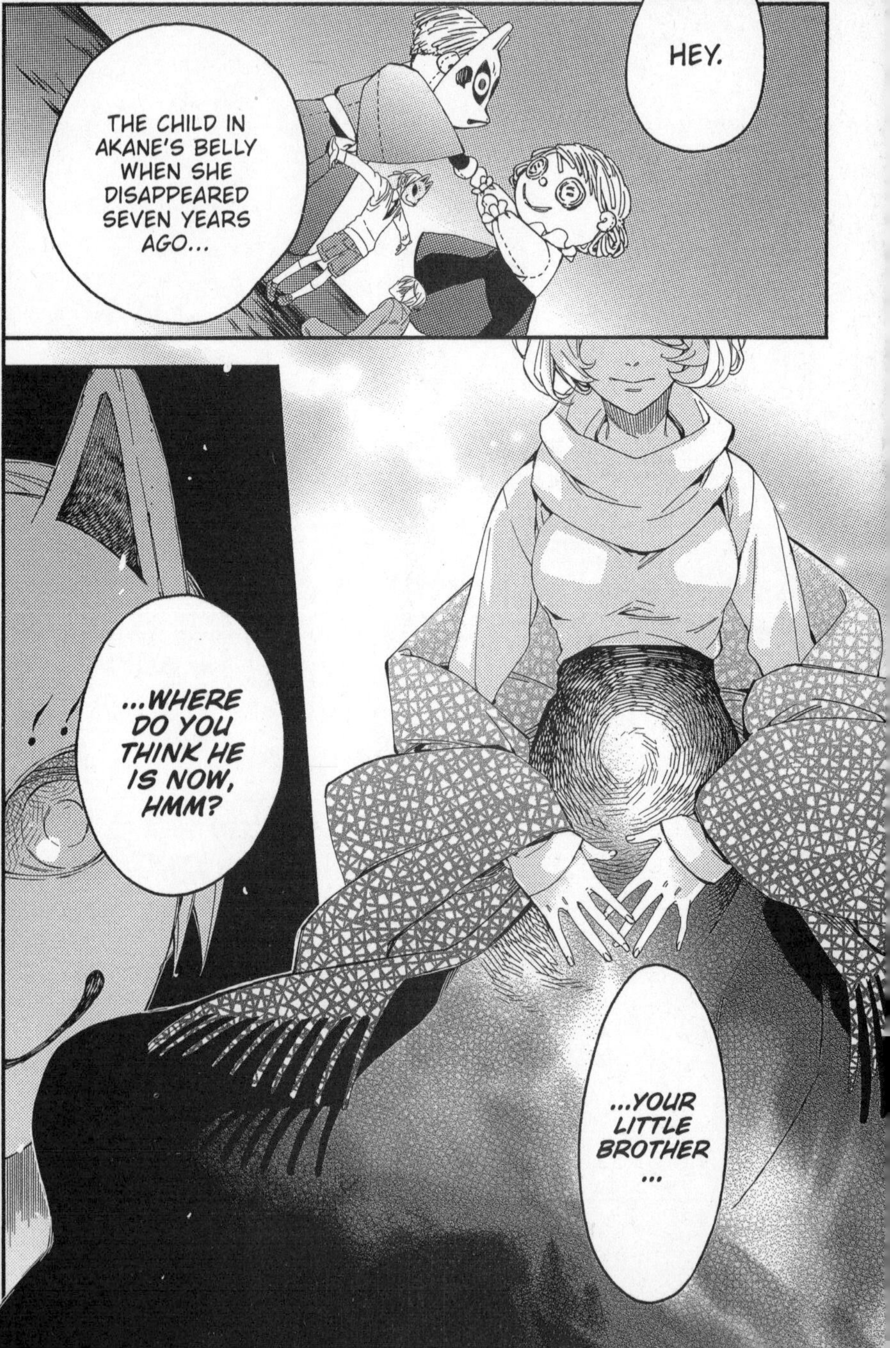
HEY.
THE CHILD IN AKANE'S BELLY WHEN SHE DISAPPEARED SEVEN YEARS AGO...
...WHERE DO YOU THINK HE IS NOW, HMM?
...YOUR LITTLE BROTHER ...

Of the Red,
the Light,
and the
Ayakashi

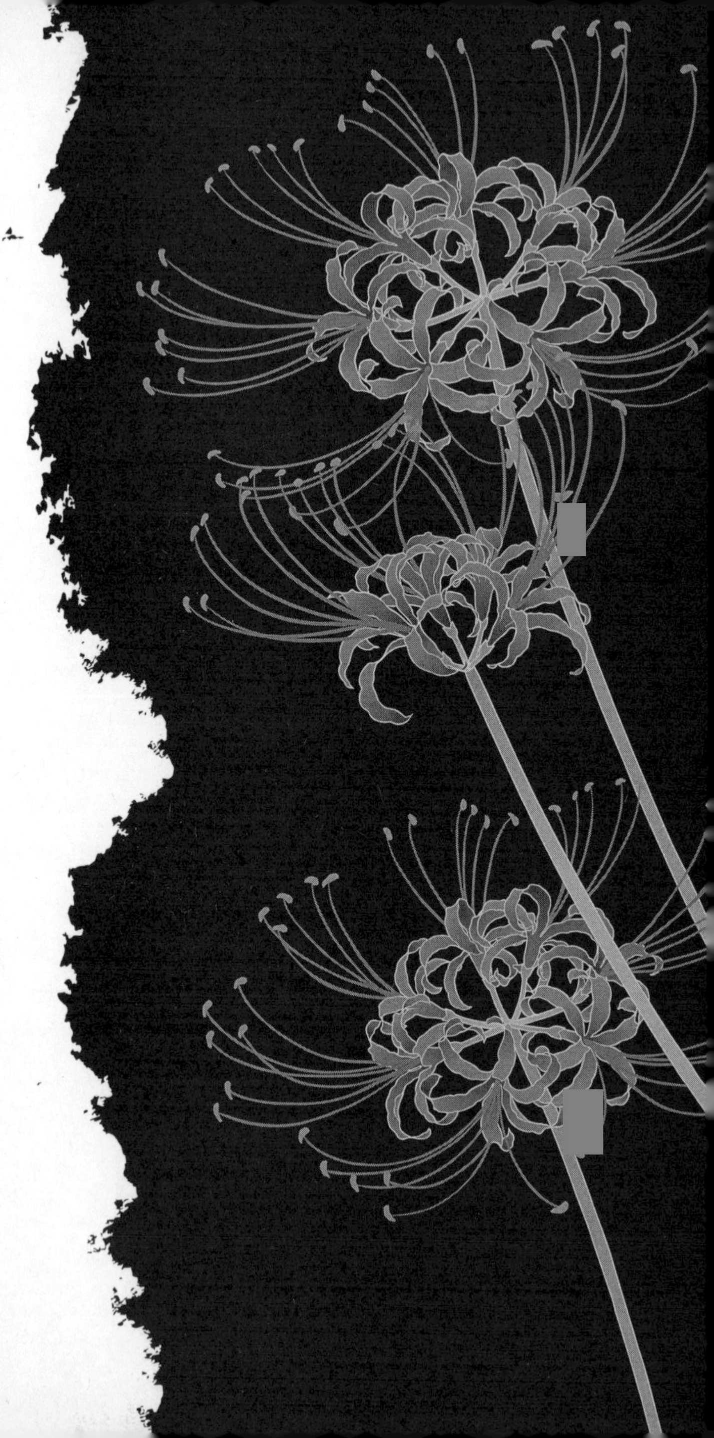

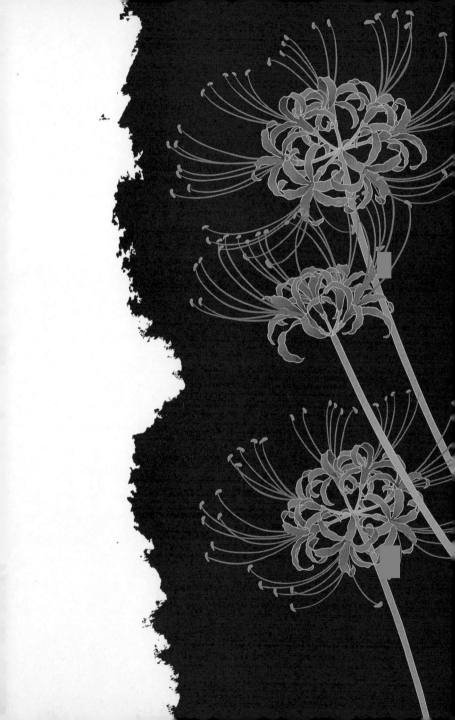

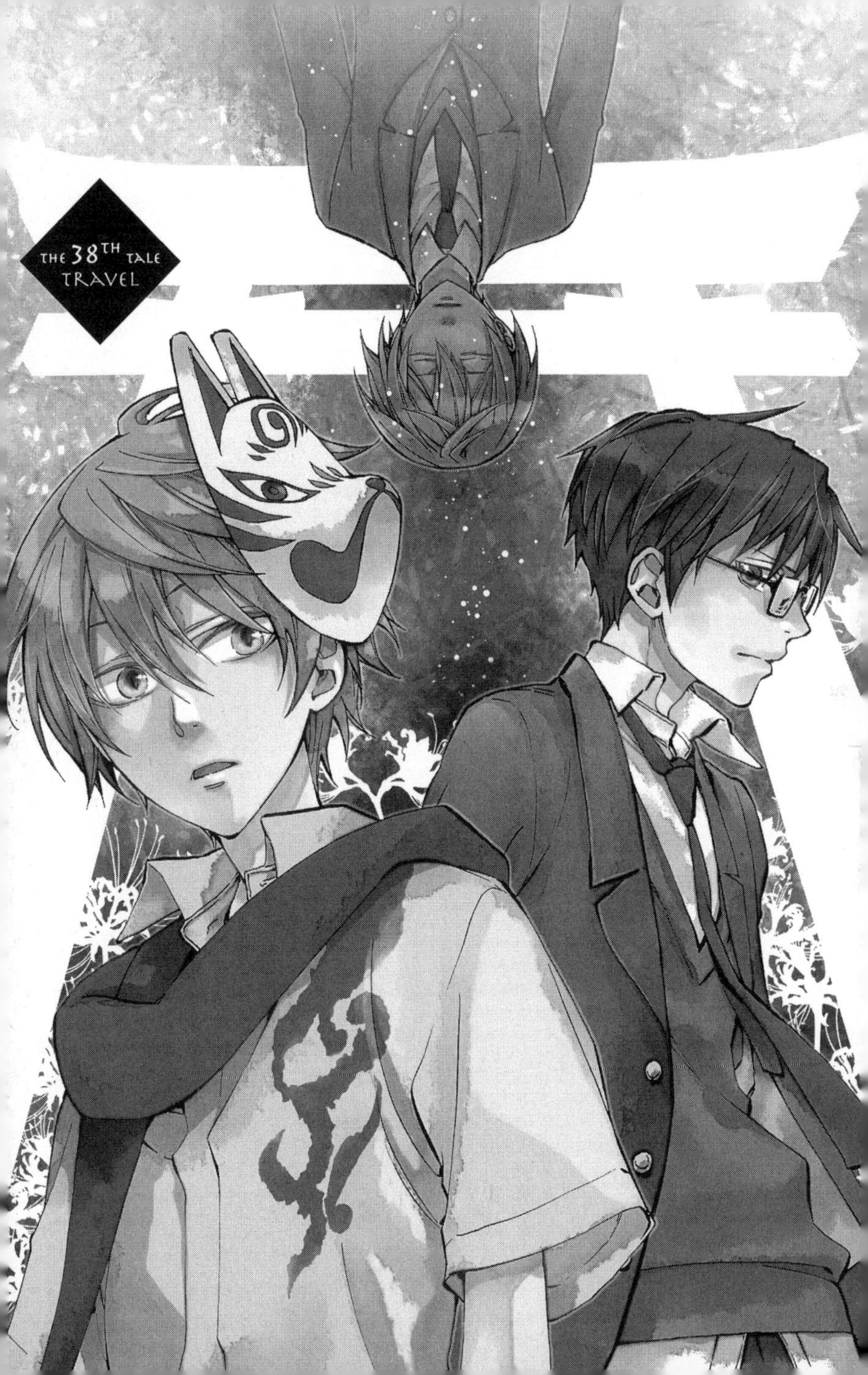
THE 38TH TALE
TRAVEL

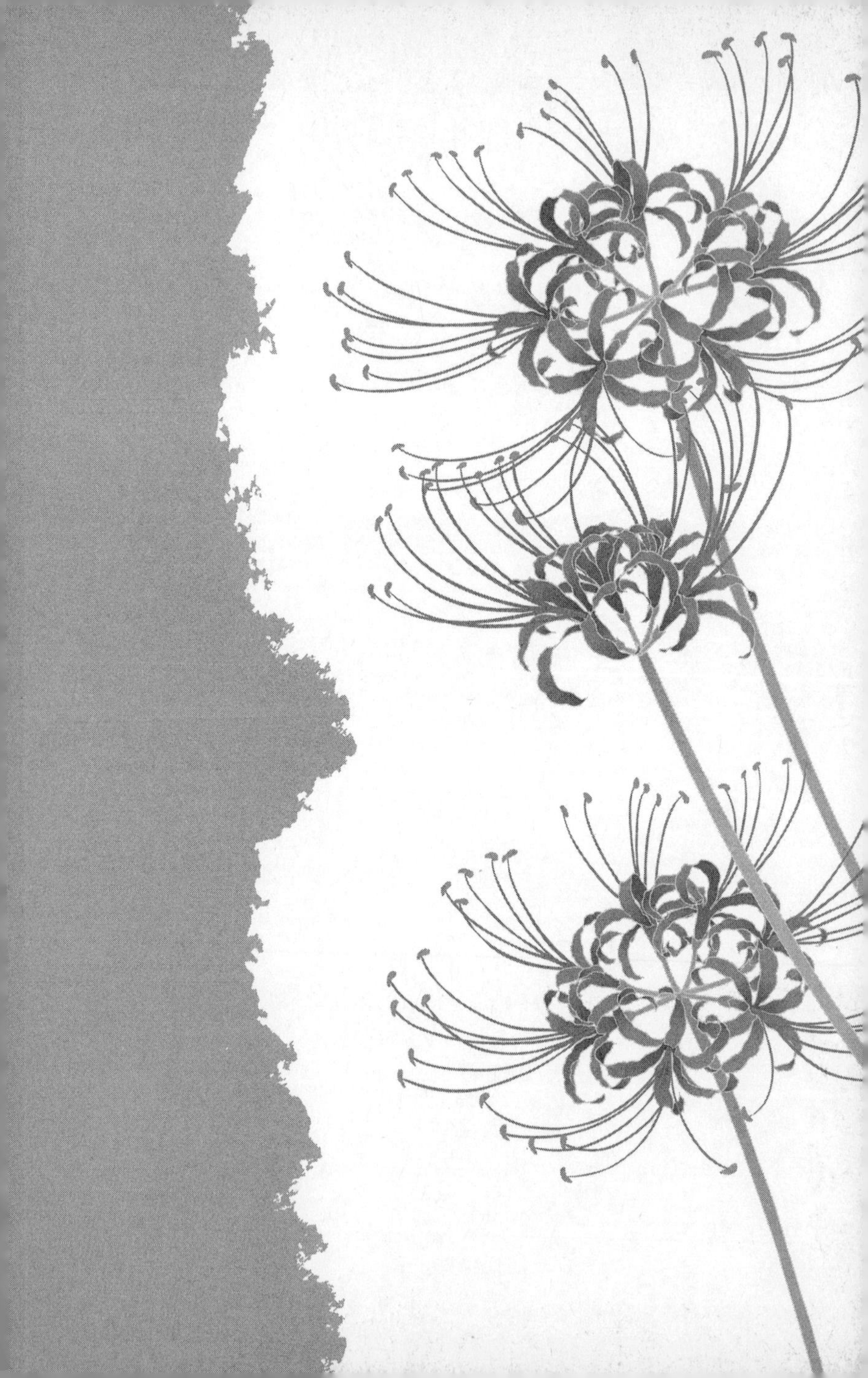

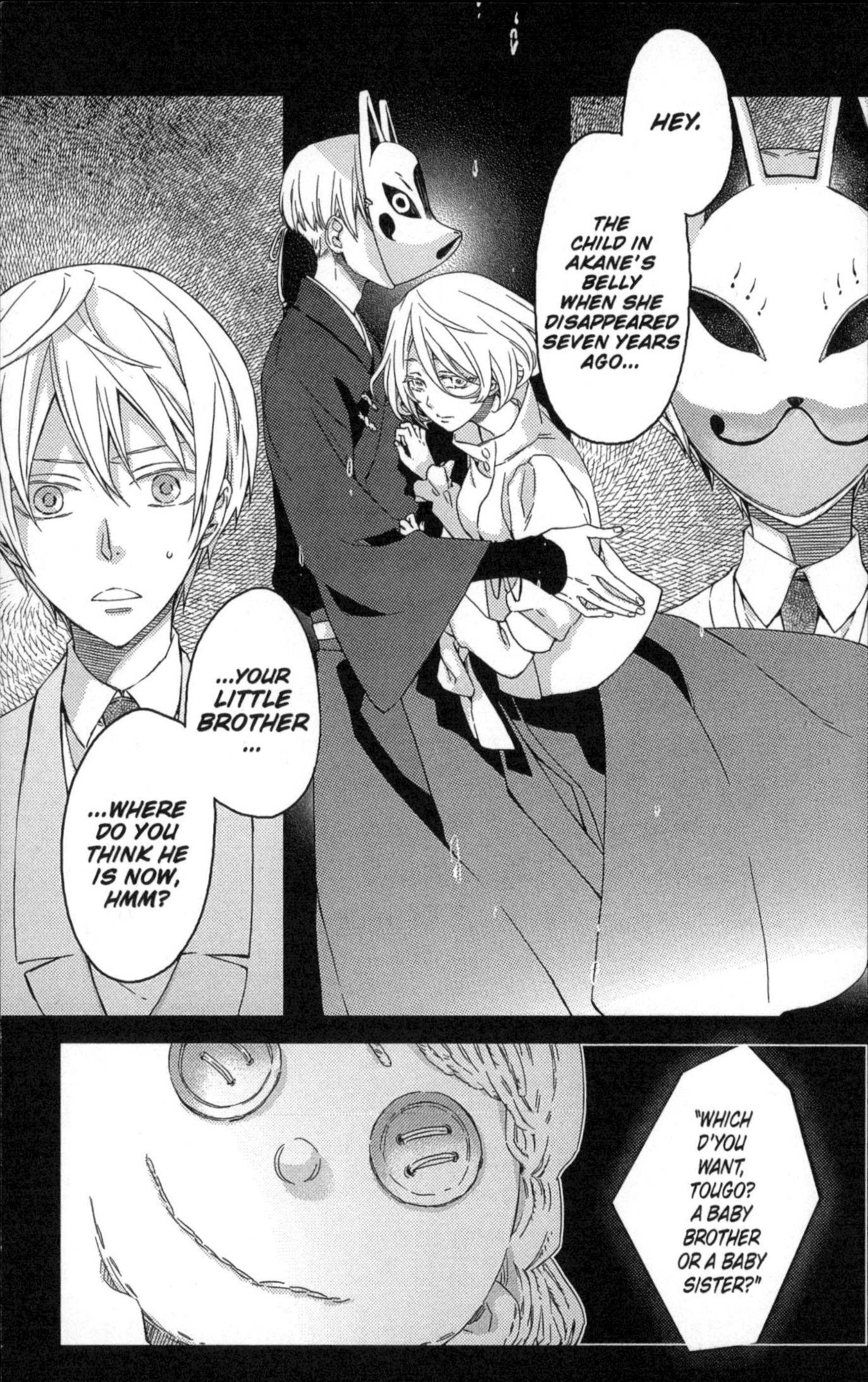
HEY.
THE CHILD IN AKANE'S BELLY WHEN SHE DISAPPEARED SEVEN YEARS AGO...
...YOUR LITTLE BROTHER ...
...WHERE DO YOU THINK HE IS NOW, HMM?
"WHICH D'YOU WANT, TOUGO? A BABY BROTHER OR A BABY SISTER?"

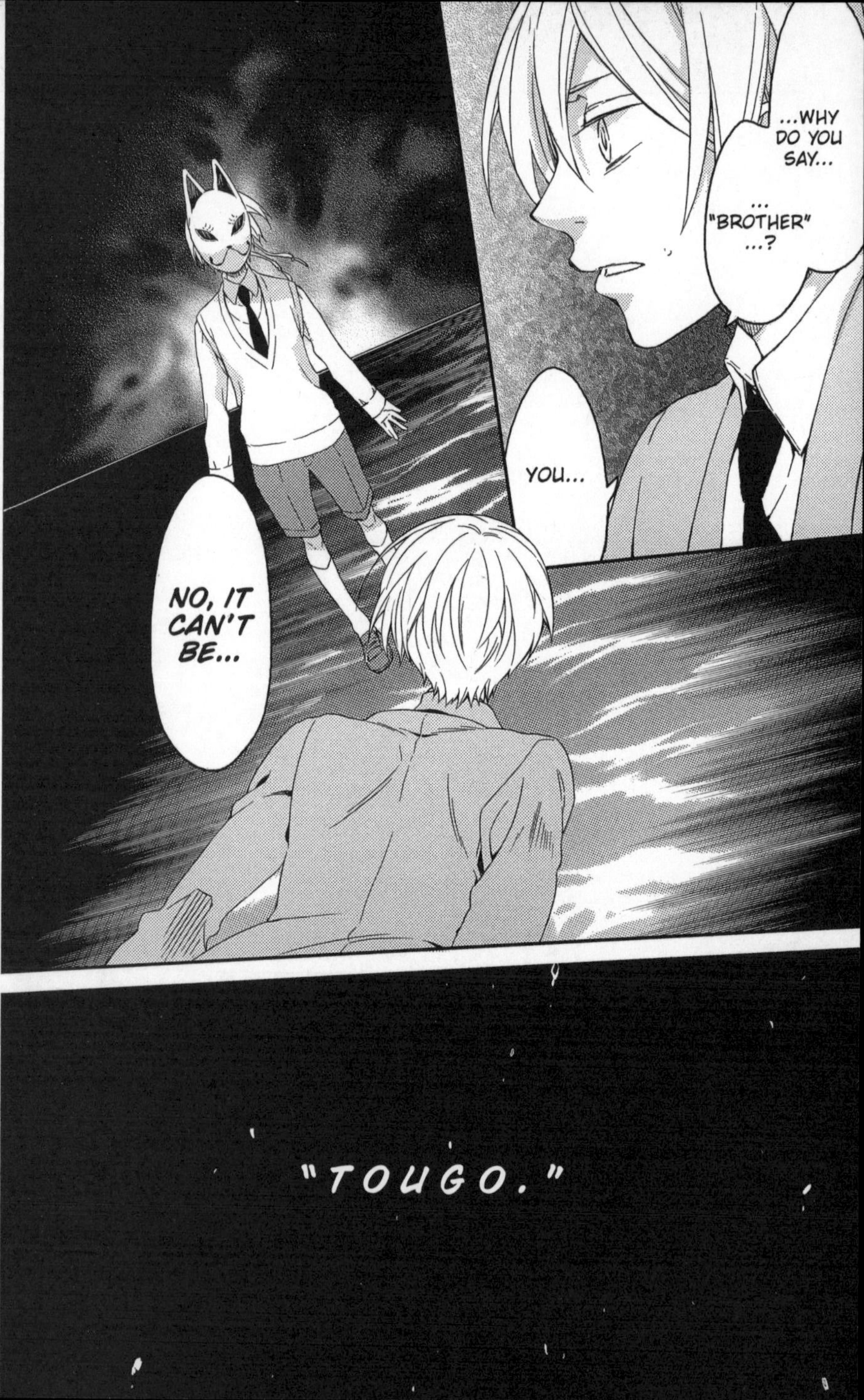
...WHY DO YOU SAY... ... "BROTHER" ...?
YOU...
NO, IT CAN'T BE...
"TOUGO."

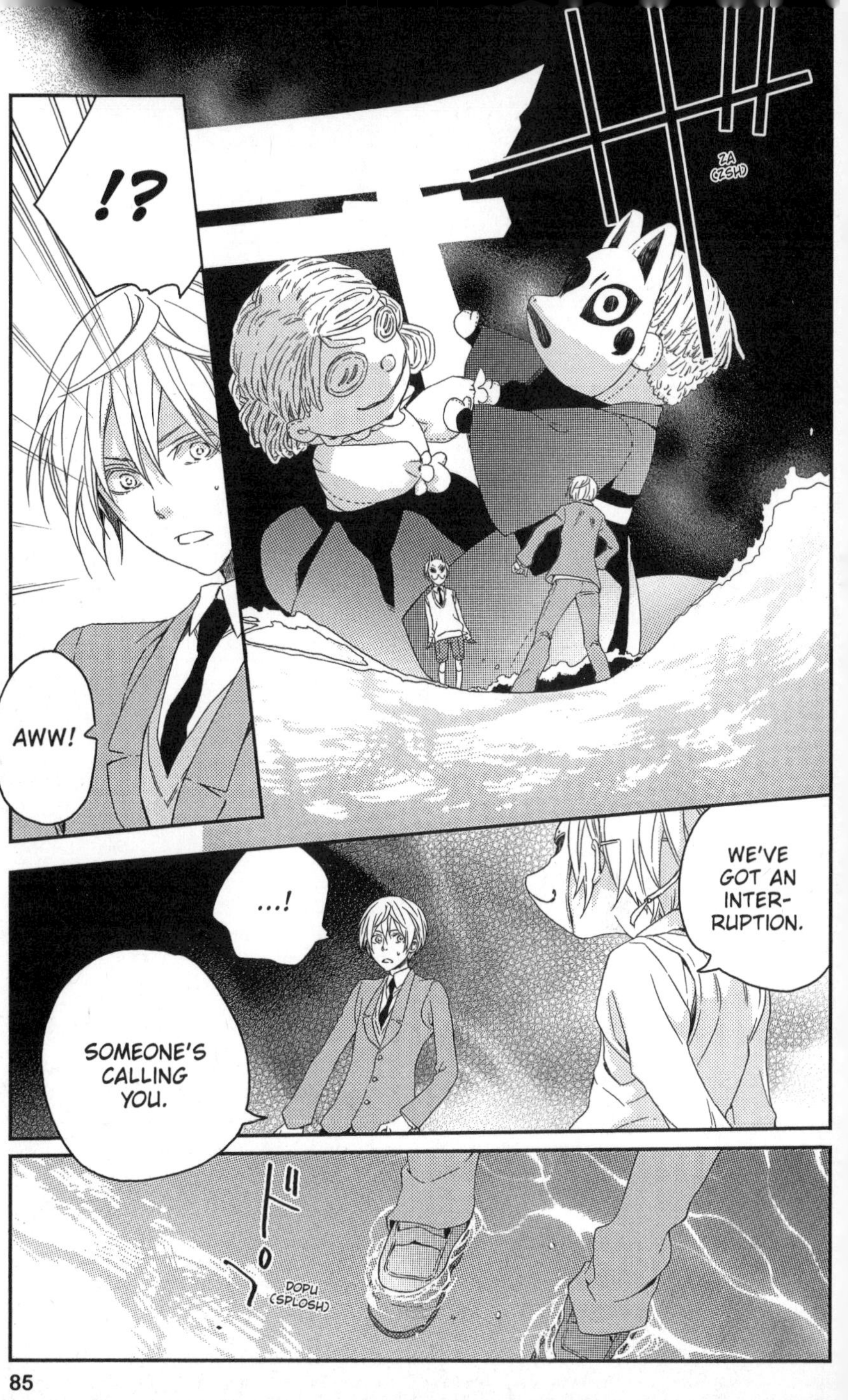
ZA (ZSH)
!?
AWW!
WE'VE GOT AN INTER-RUPTION.
...!
SOMEONE'S CALLING YOU.
DOPU (SPLOSH)

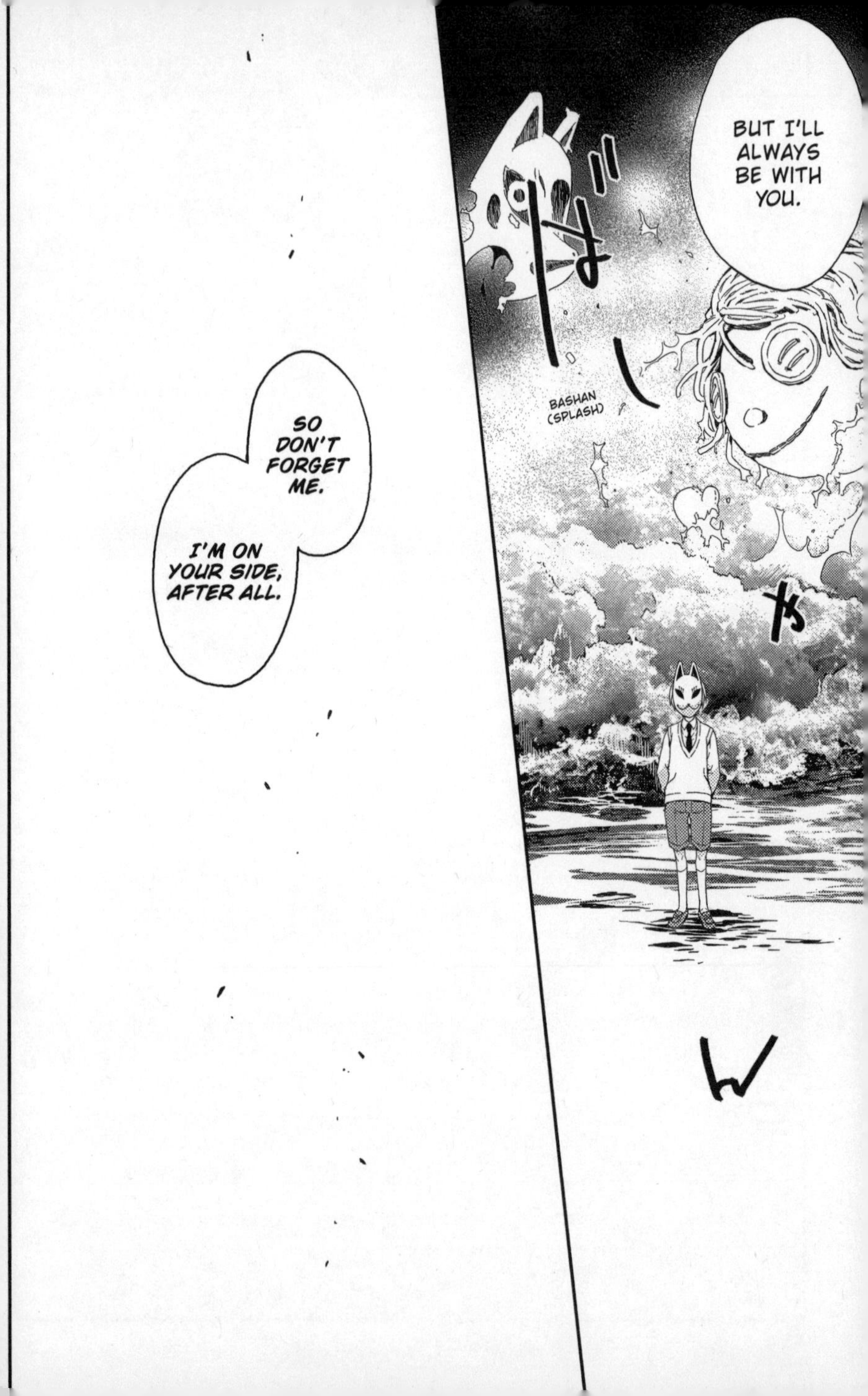
BUT I'LL ALWAYS BE WITH YOU.
BASHAN (SPLASH)
SO DON'T FORGET ME.
I'M ON YOUR SIDE, AFTER ALL.

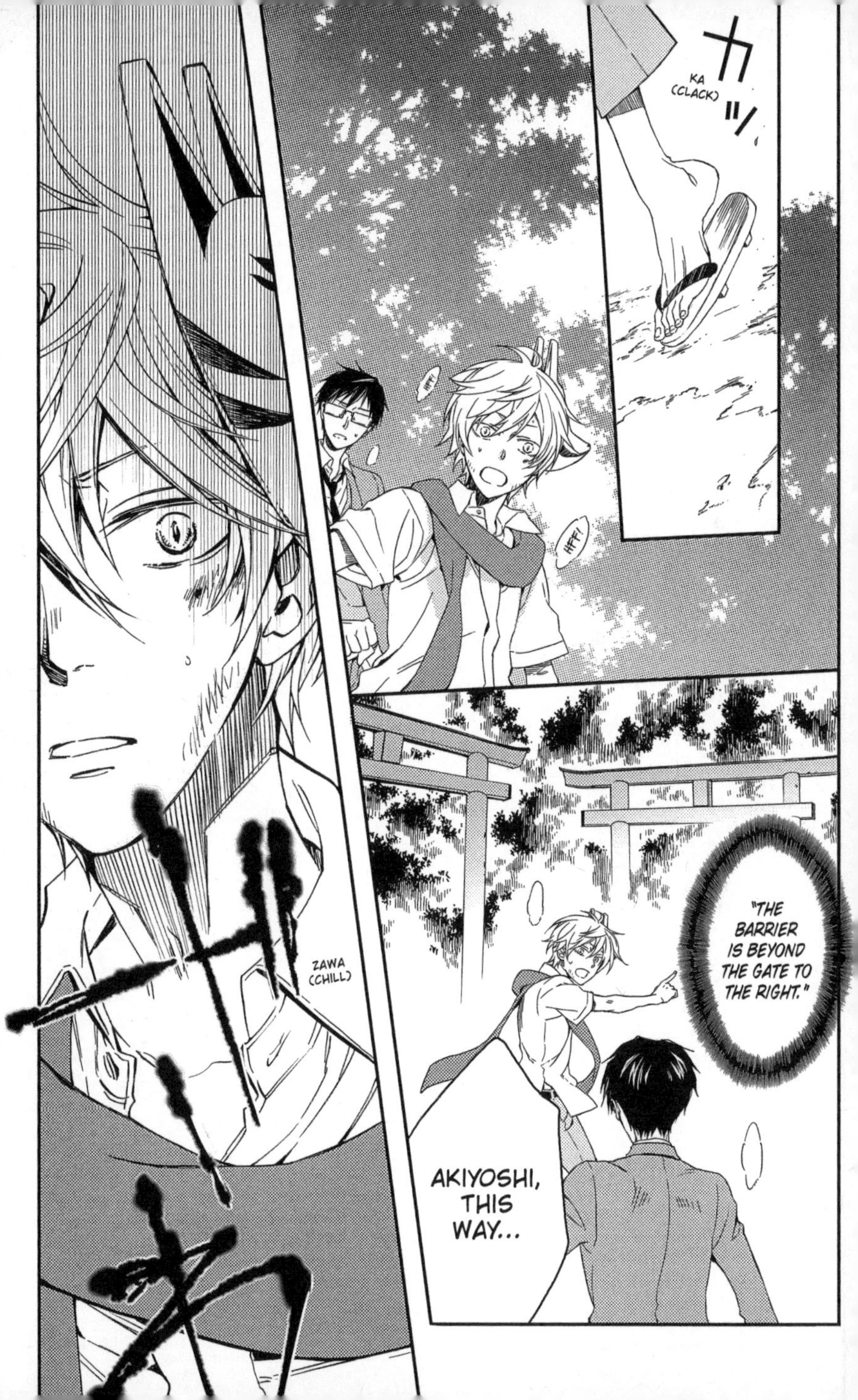
KA (CLACK)
HFF!
"THE BARRIER IS BEYOND THE GATE TO THE RIGHT."
AKIYOSHI, THIS WAY...
ZAWA (CHILL)

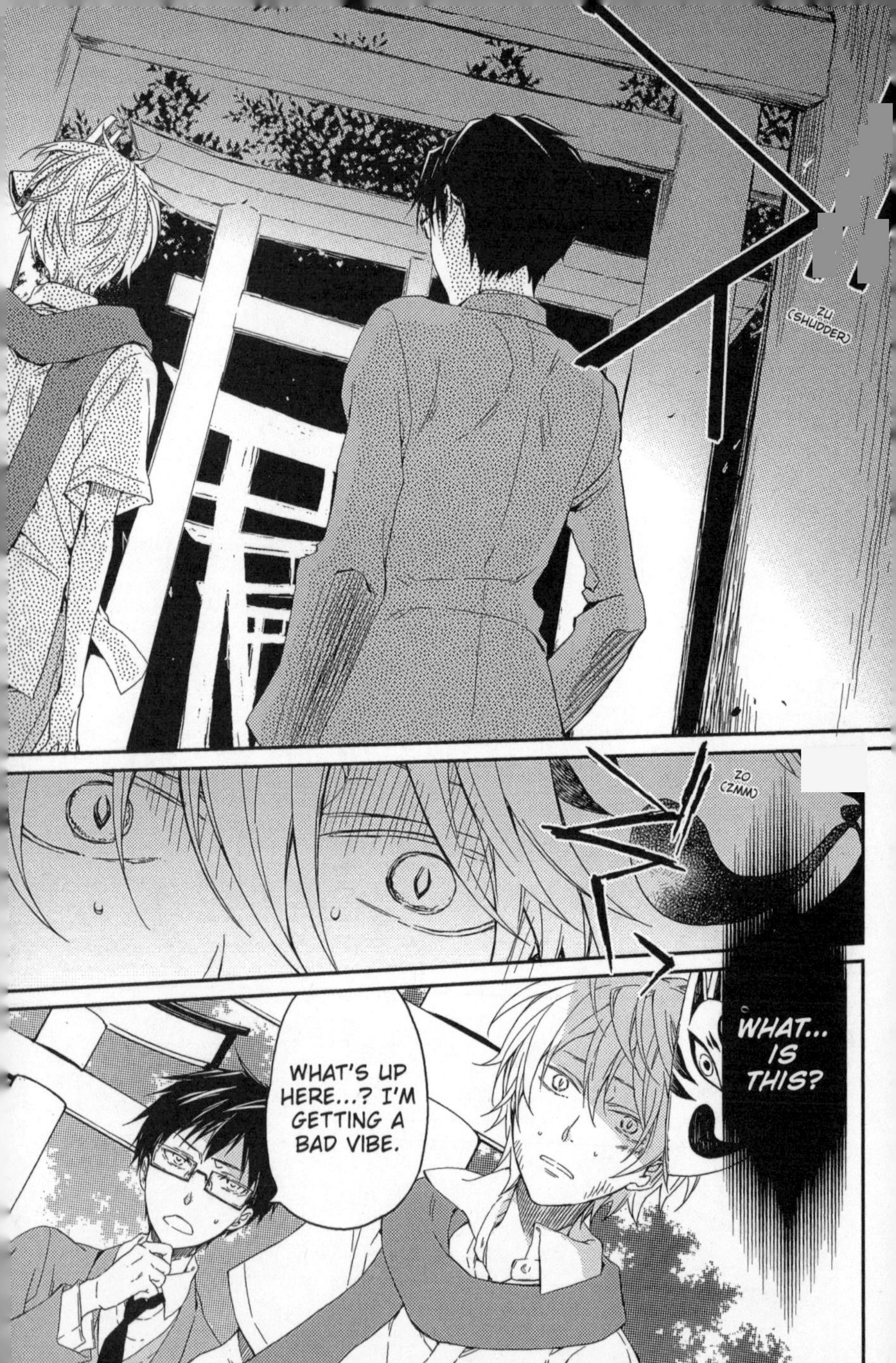
ZU (SHUDDER)
ZO (ZMM)
WHAT... IS THIS?
WHAT'S UP HERE...? I'M GETTING A BAD VIBE.

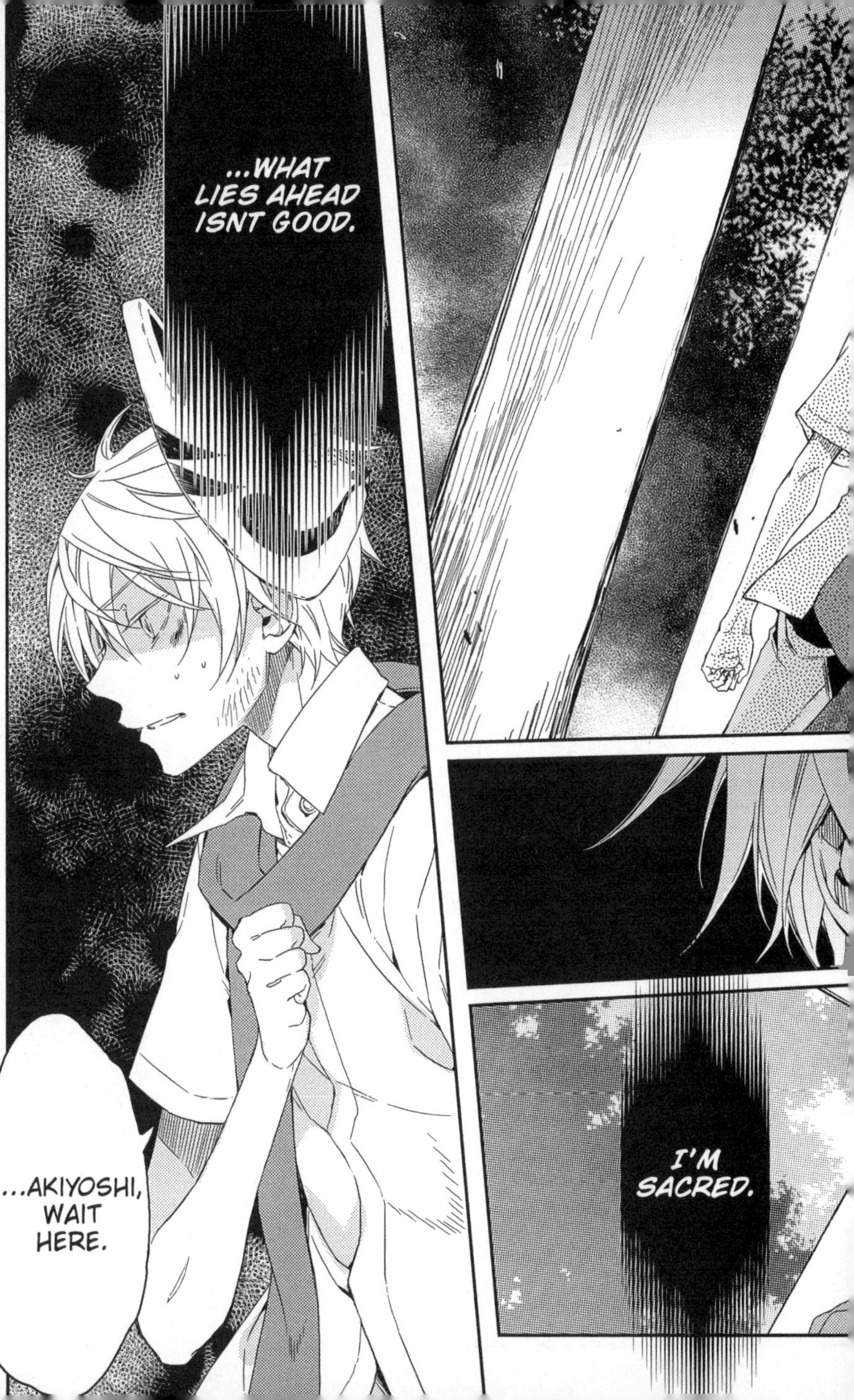
I'M SACRED.
...WHAT LIES AHEAD ISNT GOOD.
...AKIYOSHI, WAIT HERE.

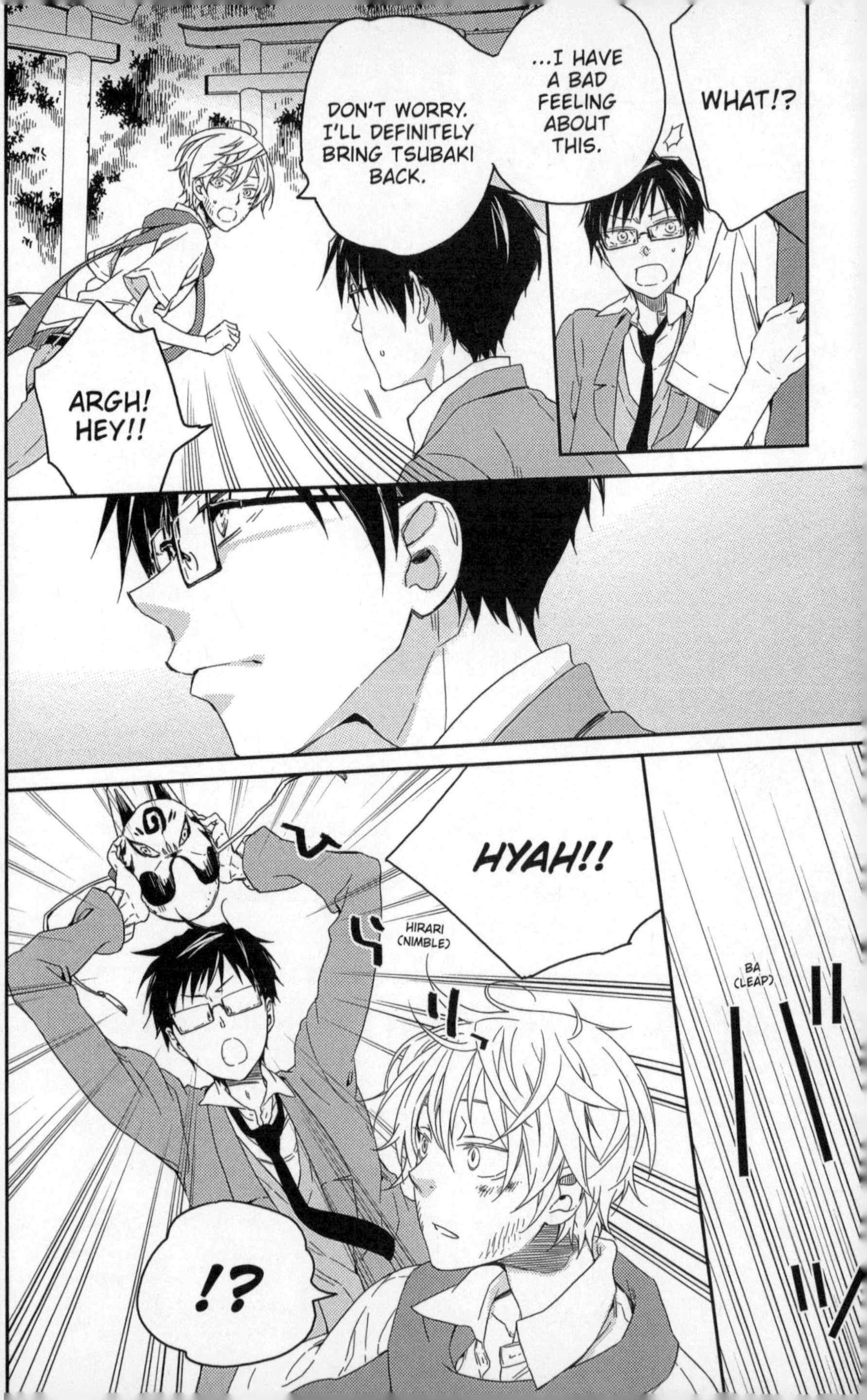
WHAT!?
...I HAVE A BAD FEELING ABOUT THIS.
DON'T WORRY. I'LL DEFINITELY BRING TSUBAKI BACK.
ARGH! HEY!!
BA (LEAP)
HYAH!!
HIRARI (NIMBLE)
!?

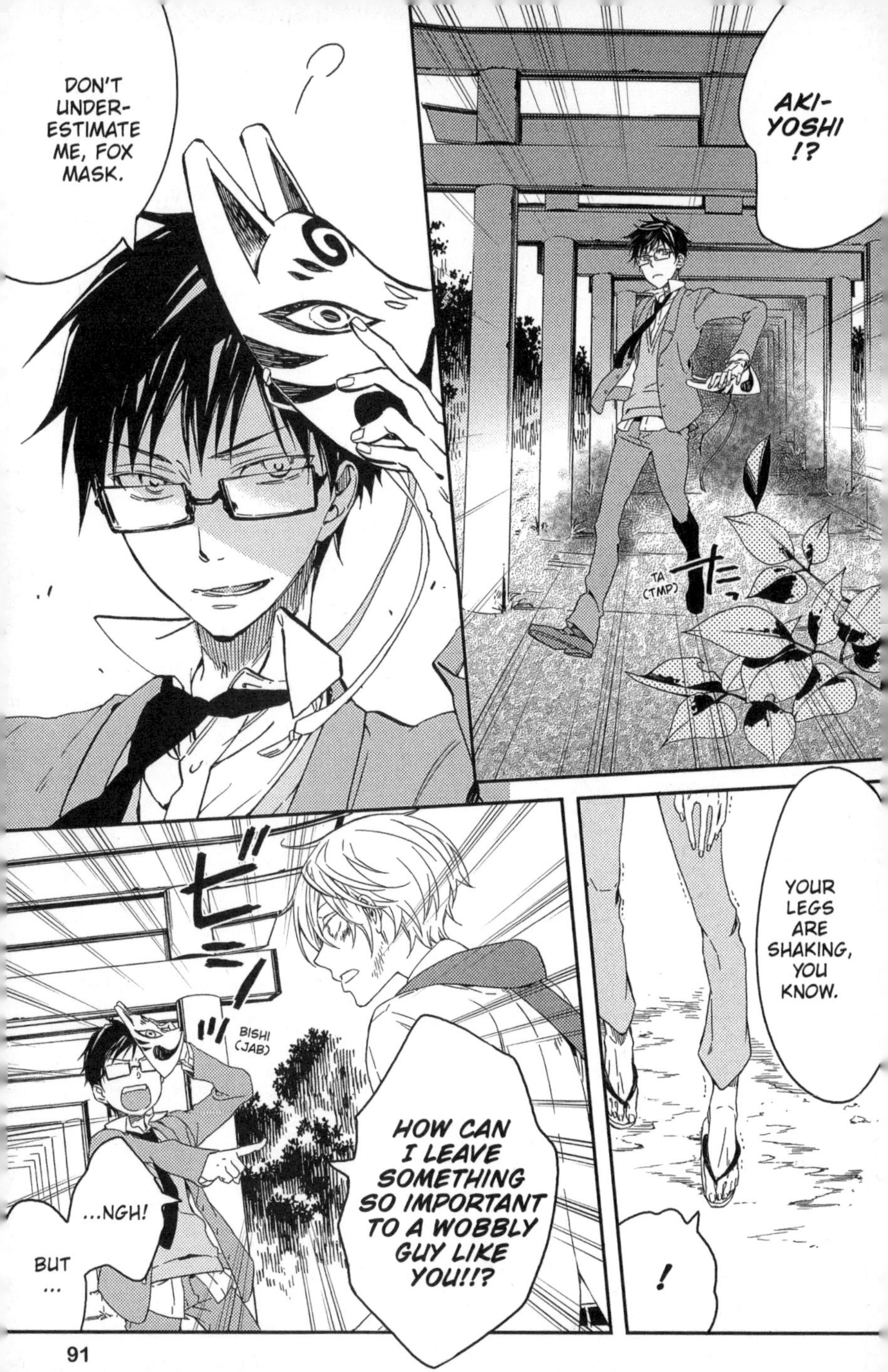
AKI-YOSHI!?
TA (TMP)
DON'T UNDER-ESTIMATE ME, FOX MASK.
?
YOUR LEGS ARE SHAKING, YOU KNOW.
!
HOW CAN I LEAVE SOMETHING SO IMPORTANT TO A WOBBLY GUY LIKE YOU!!?
BISHI (JAB)
...NGH!
BUT ...

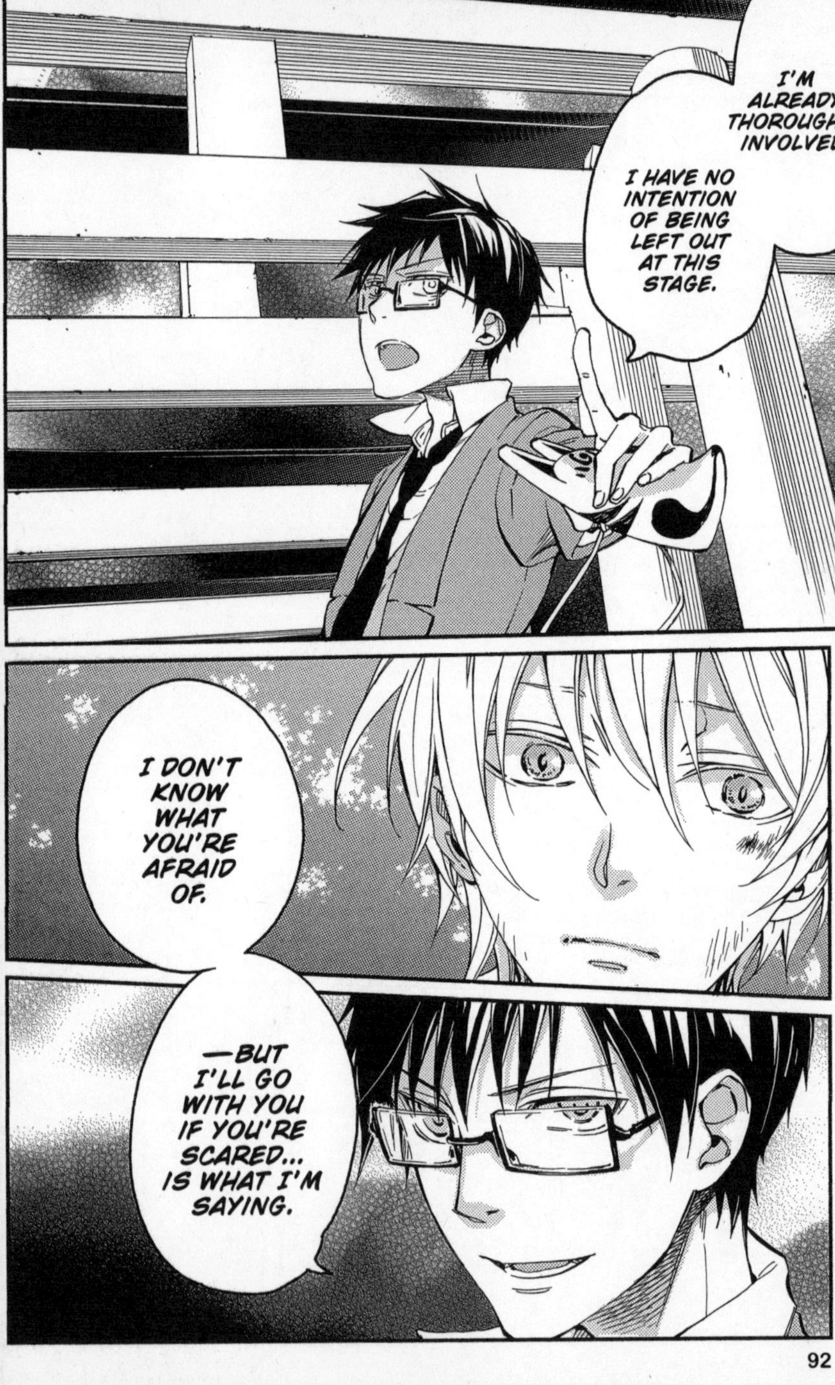
I'M ALREADY THOROUGHLY INVOLVED.
I HAVE NO INTENTION OF BEING LEFT OUT AT THIS STAGE.
I DON'T KNOW WHAT YOU'RE AFRAID OF.
—BUT I'LL GO WITH YOU IF YOU'RE SCARED... IS WHAT I'M SAYING.

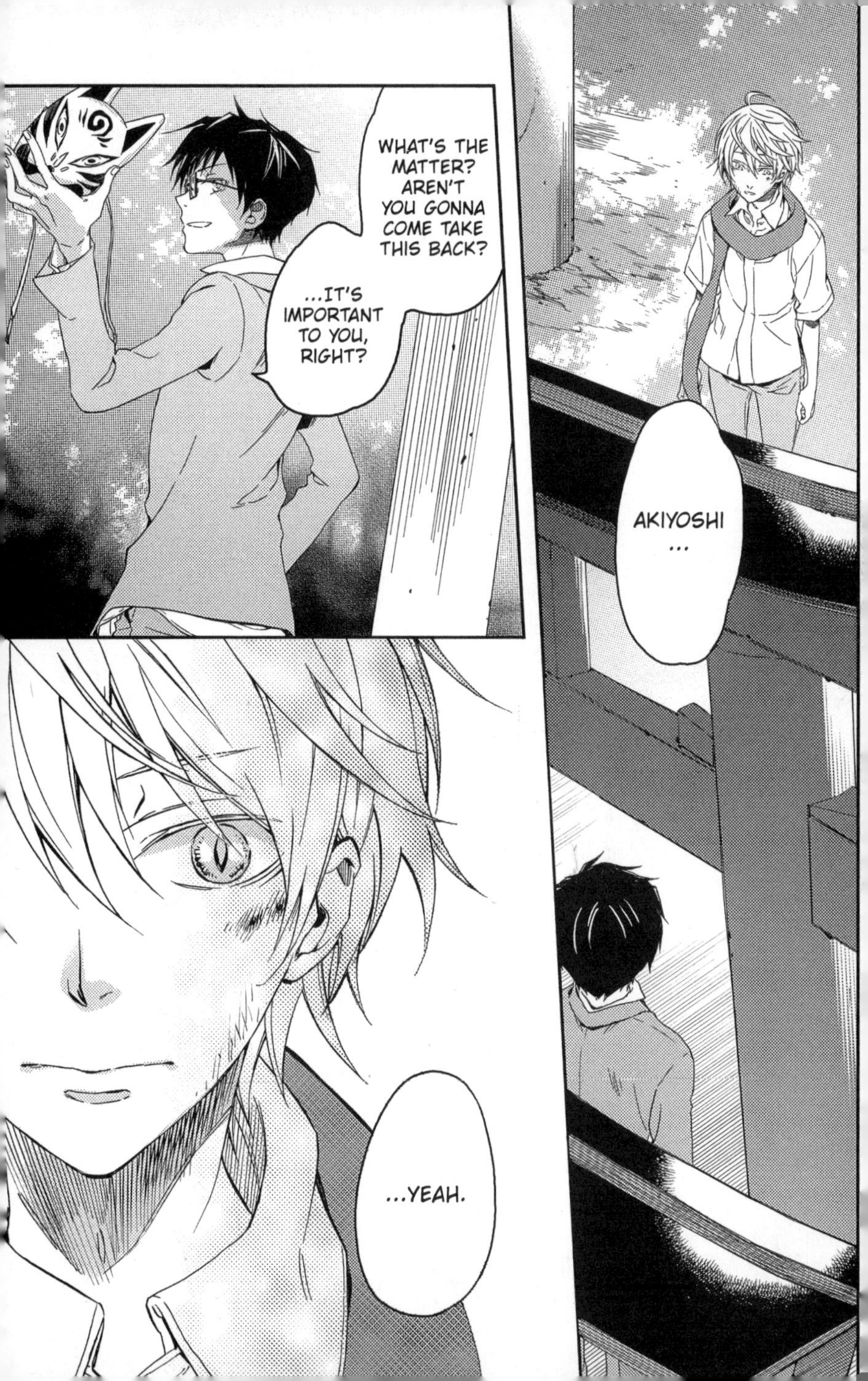
AKIYOSHI ...
WHAT'S THE MATTER? AREN'T YOU GONNA COME TAKE THIS BACK?
...IT'S IMPORTANT TO YOU, RIGHT?
...YEAH.

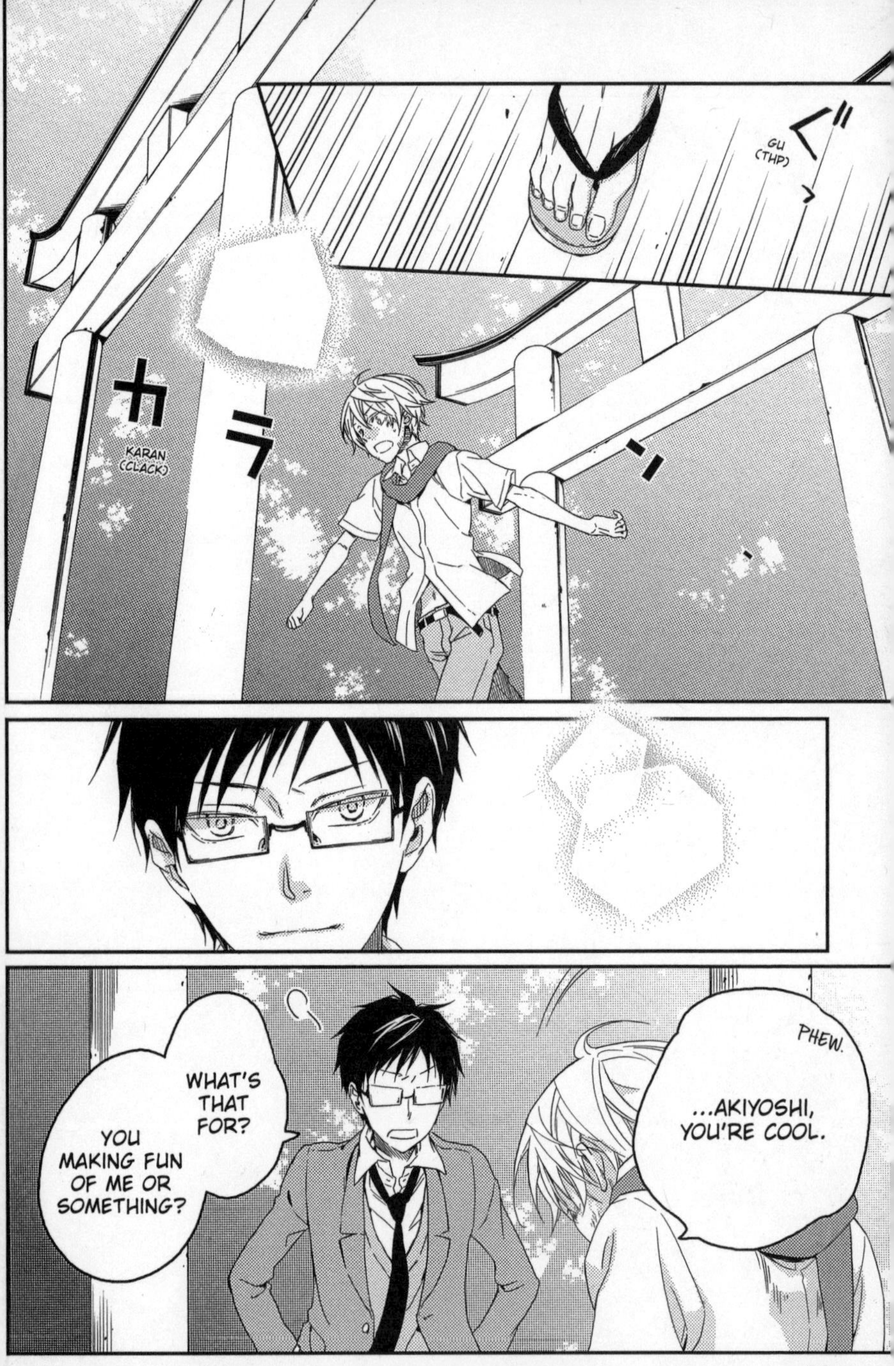
GU (THP)
KARAN (CLACK)
...AKIYOSHI, YOU'RE COOL.
PHEW.
WHAT'S THAT FOR?
YOU MAKING FUN OF ME OR SOMETHING?

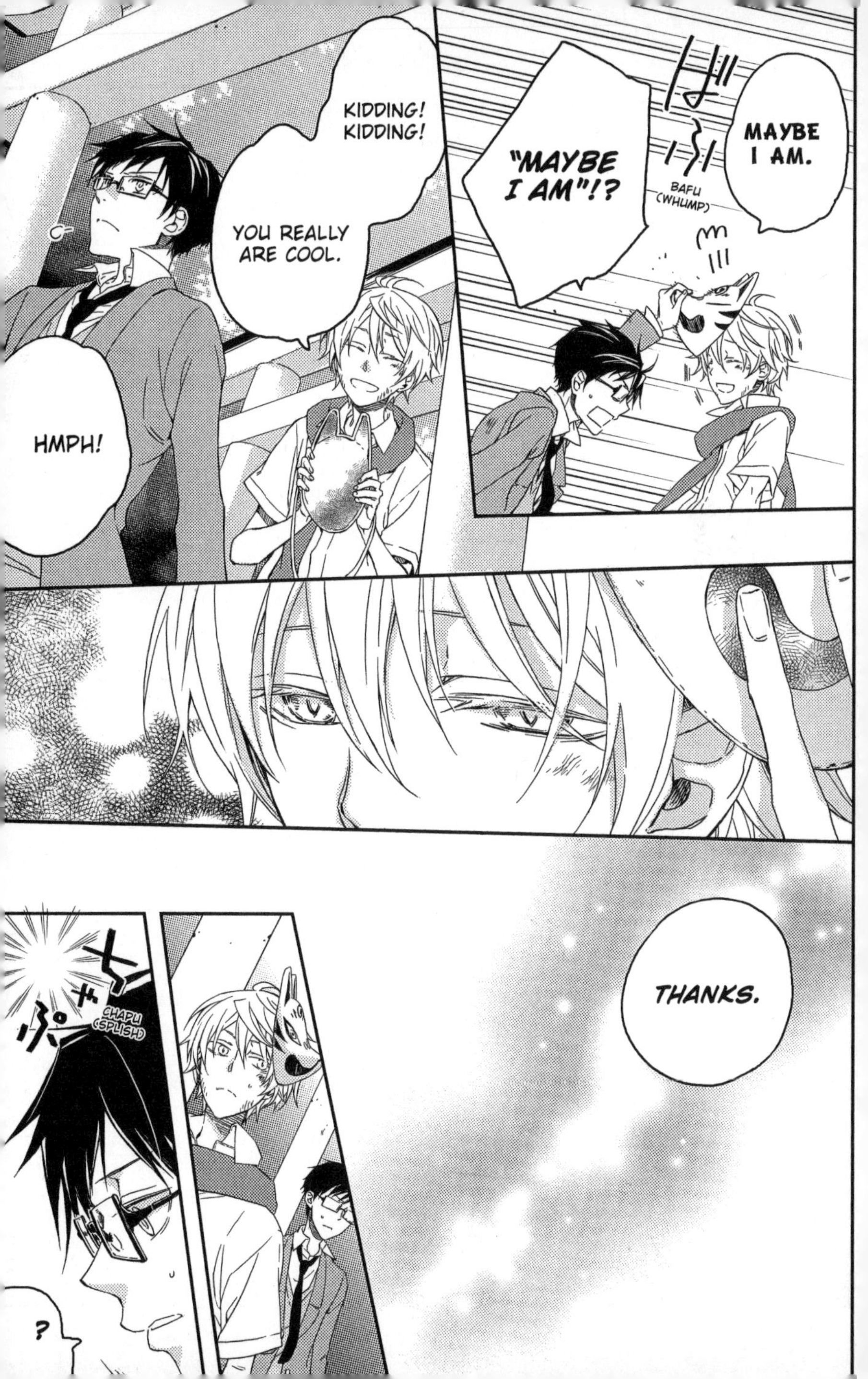
MAYBE I AM.
BAFU (WHUMP)
"MAYBE I AM"!?
KIDDING! KIDDING!
YOU REALLY ARE COOL.
HMPH!
THANKS.
CHAPU (SPLISH)
?

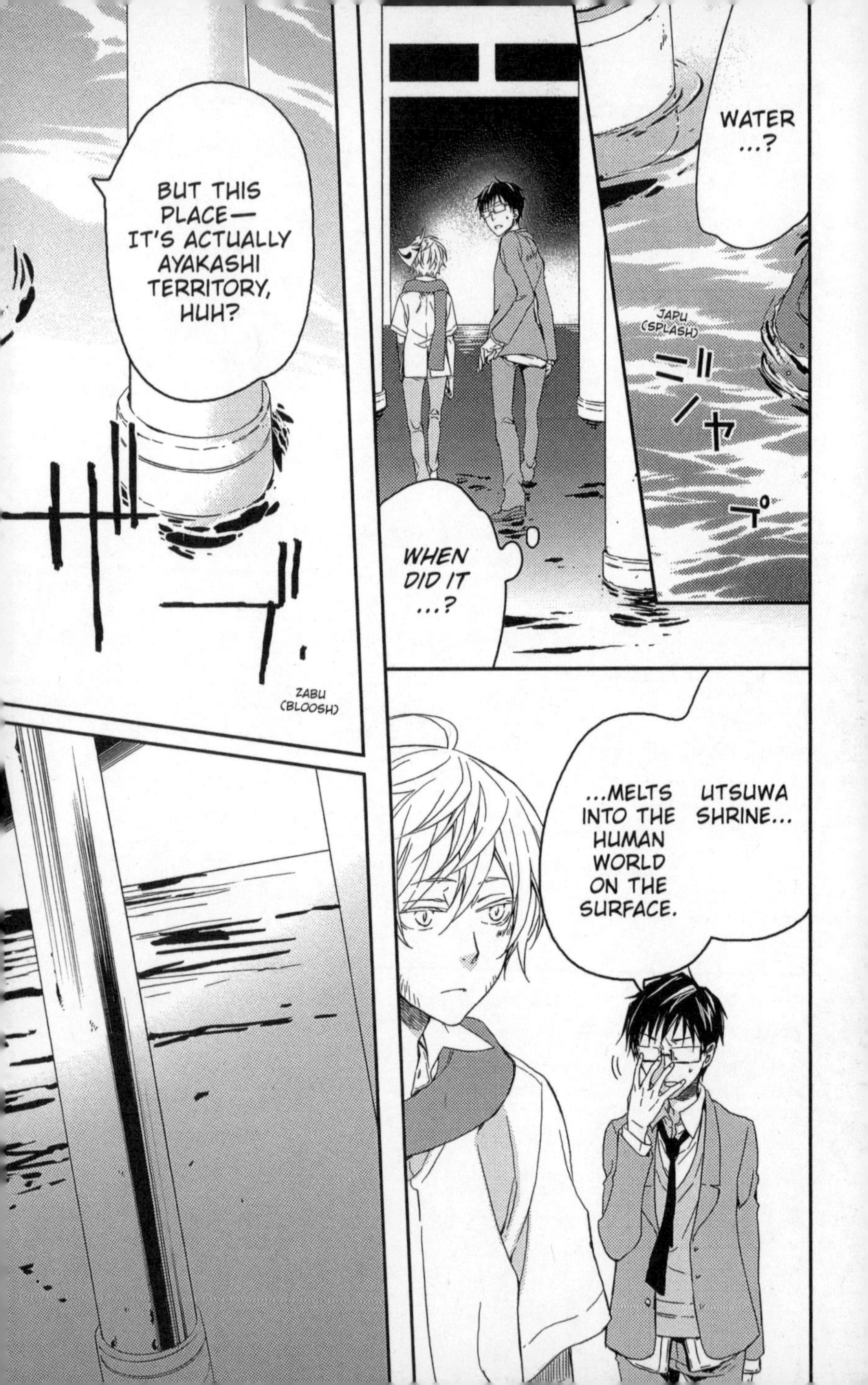
WATER ...?
JAPU (SPLASH)
WHEN DID IT ...?
BUT THIS PLACE— IT'S ACTUALLY AYAKASHI TERRITORY, HUH?
ZABU (BLOOSH)
UTSUWA SHRINE...
...MELTS INTO THE HUMAN WORLD ON THE SURFACE.

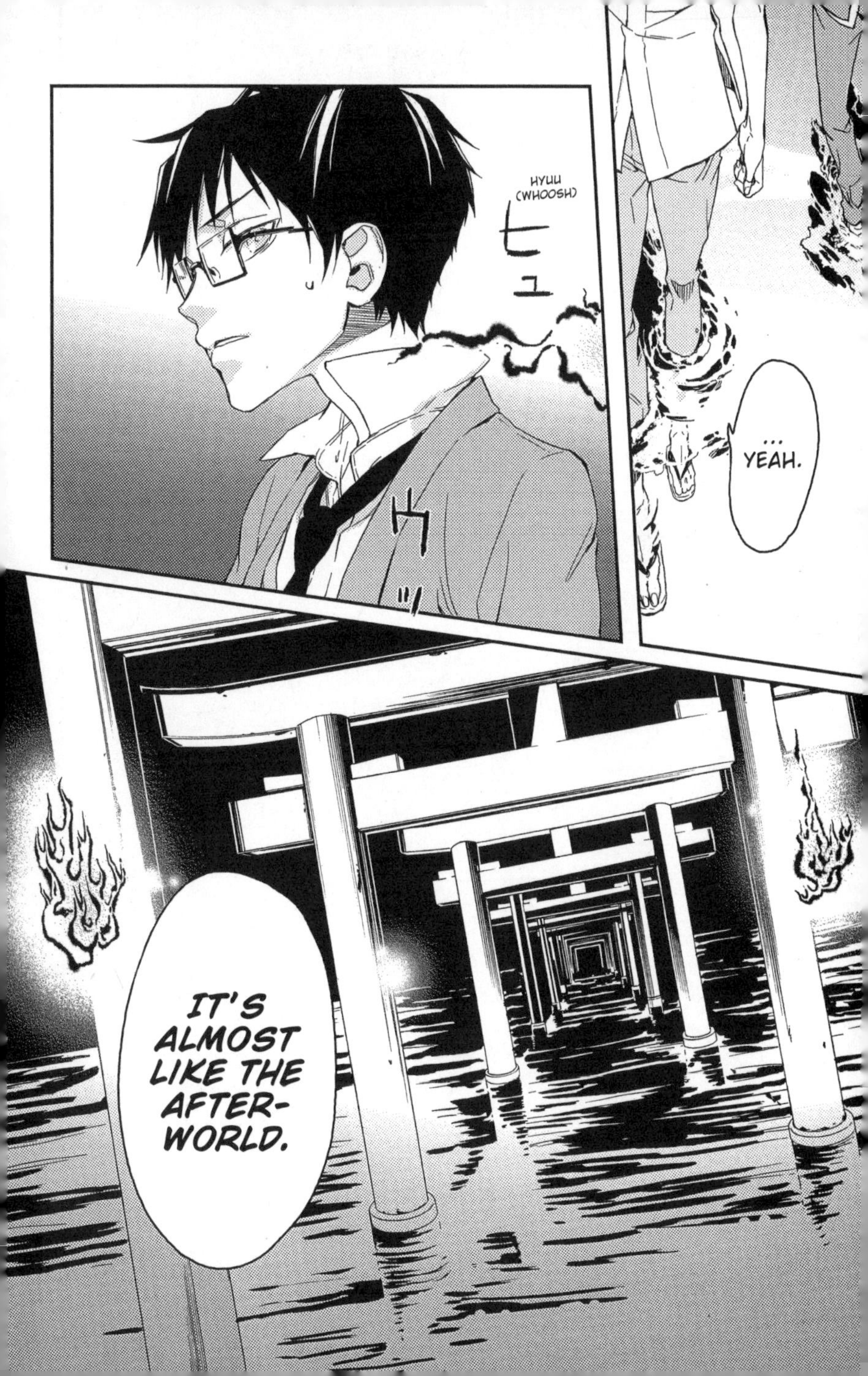
... YEAH.
HYUU (WHOOSH)
ヒュ
IT'S ALMOST LIKE THE AFTER-WORLD.

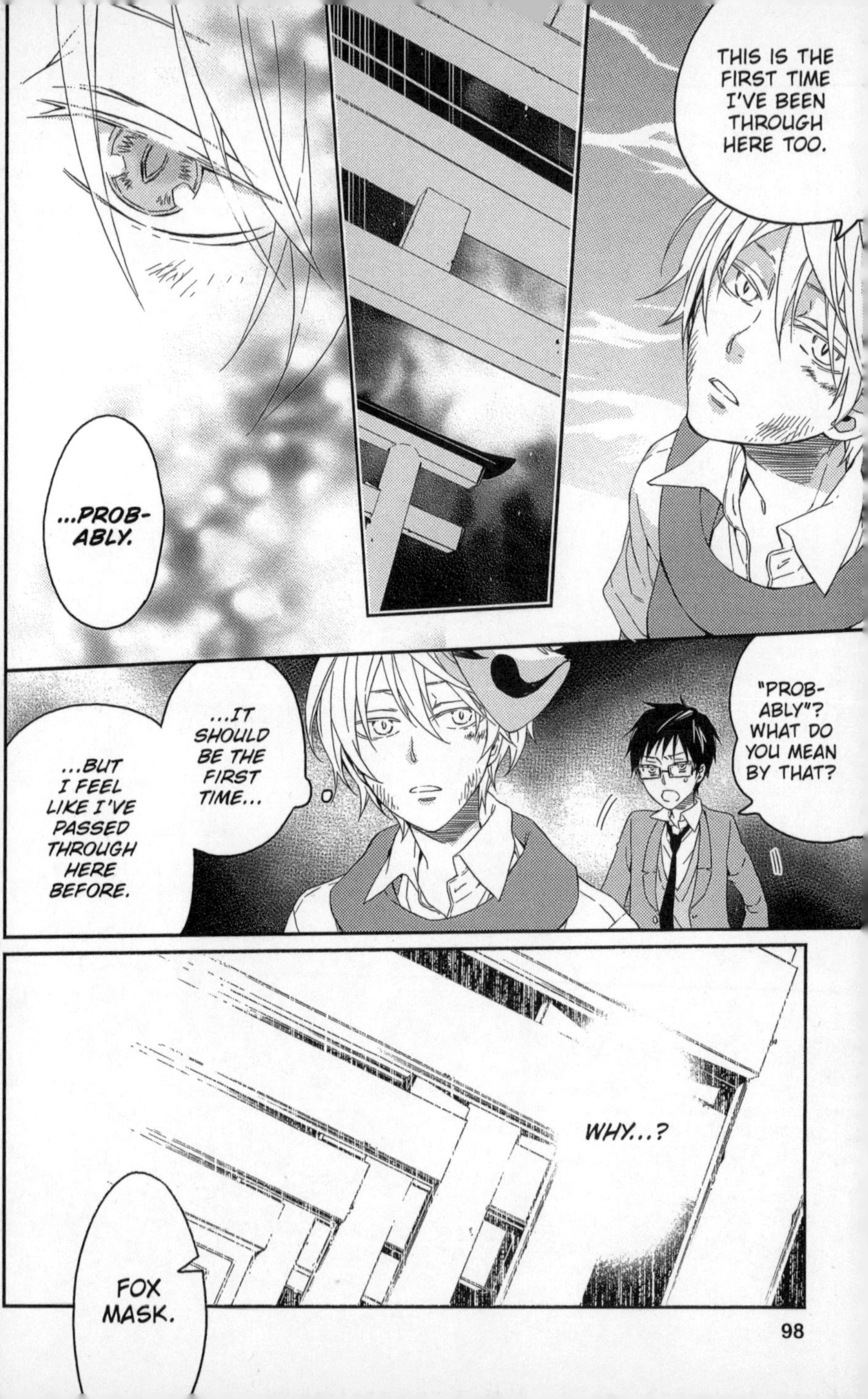
THIS IS THE FIRST TIME I'VE BEEN THROUGH HERE TOO.
...PROB-ABLY.
"PROB-ABLY"? WHAT DO YOU MEAN BY THAT?
...IT SHOULD BE THE FIRST TIME...
...BUT I FEEL LIKE I'VE PASSED THROUGH HERE BEFORE.
WHY...?
FOX MASK.

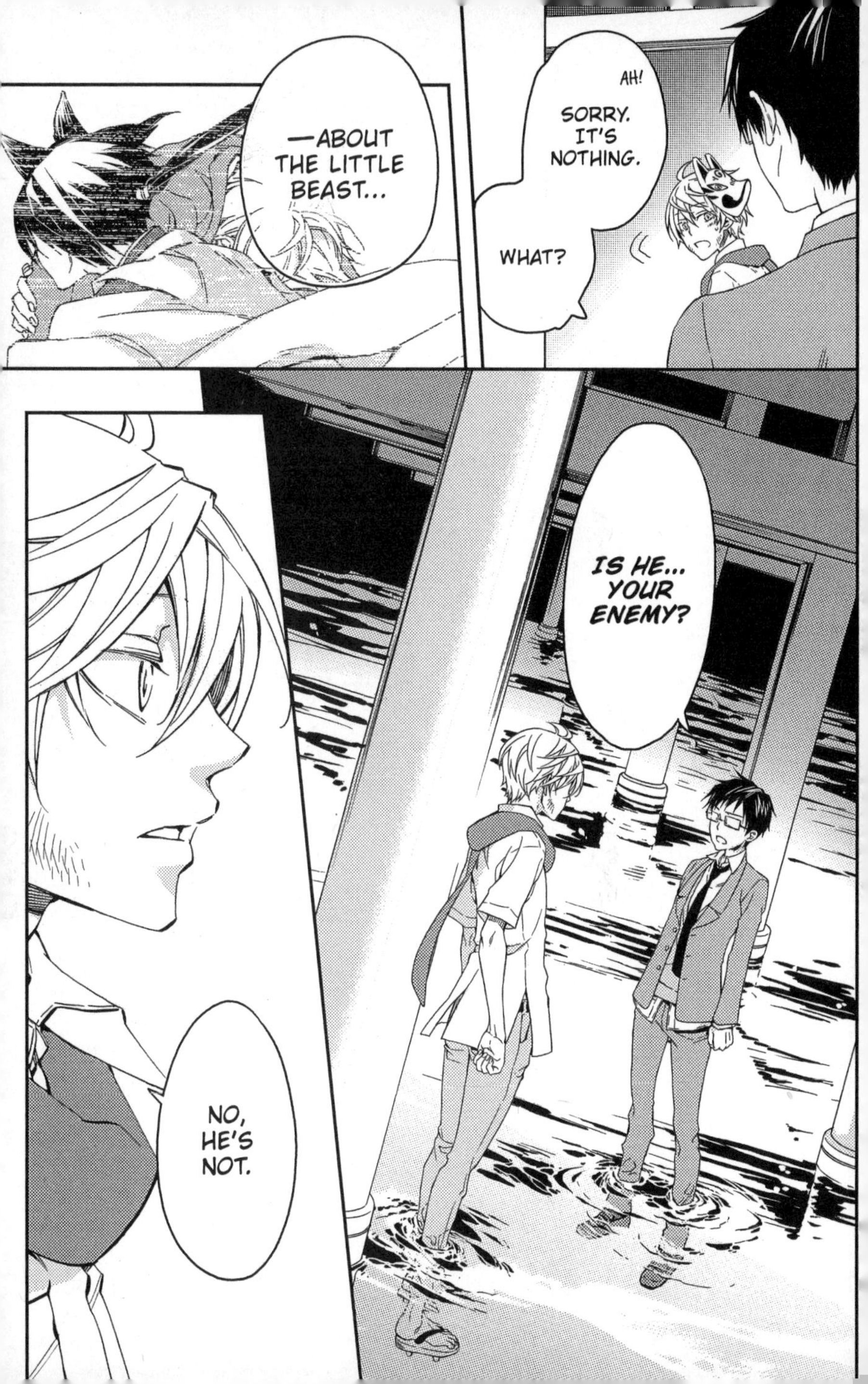

AH!
SORRY. IT'S NOTHING.
WHAT?
—ABOUT THE LITTLE BEAST...
IS HE... YOUR ENEMY?
NO, HE'S NOT.

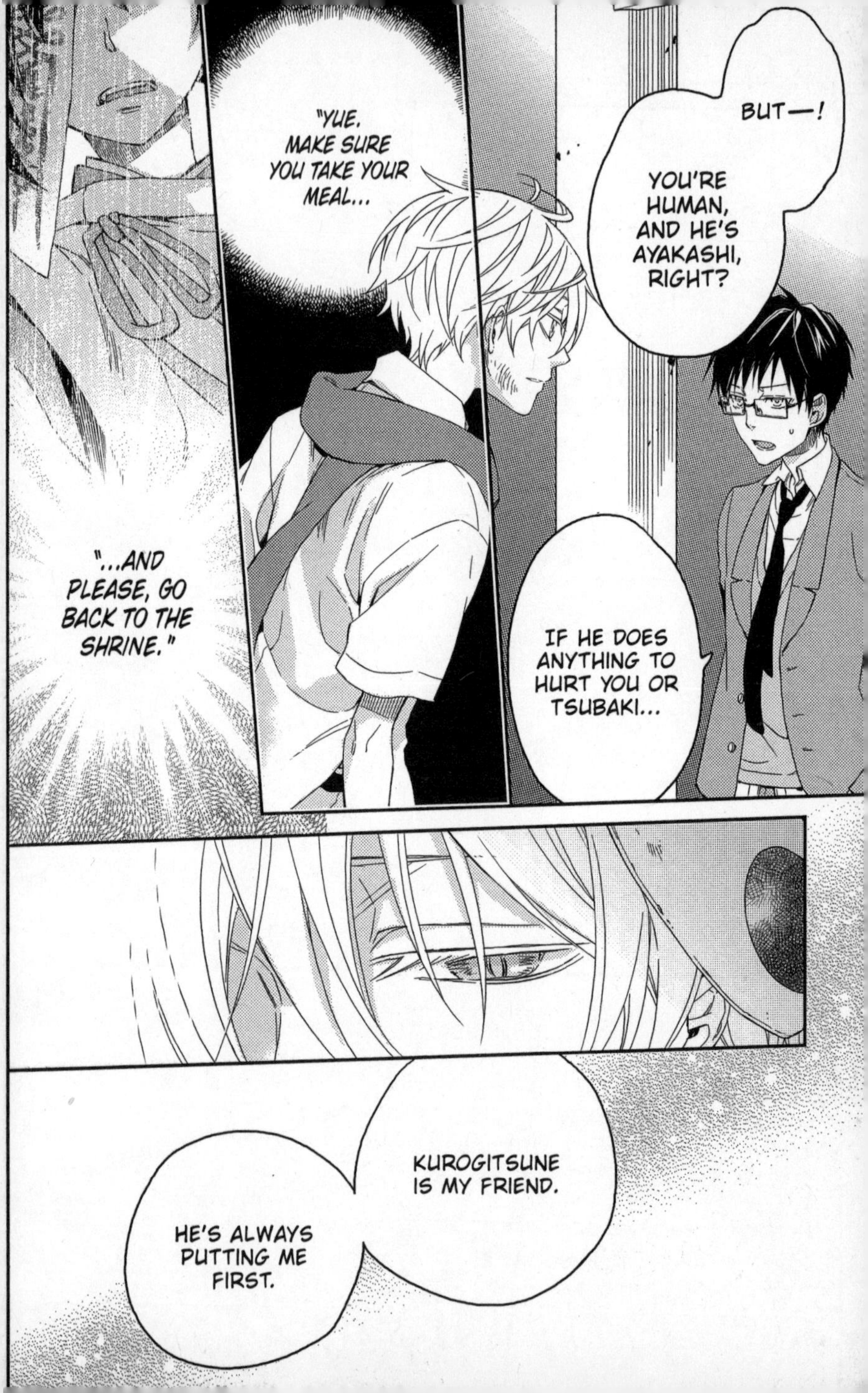
BUT—!
YOU'RE HUMAN, AND HE'S AYAKASHI, RIGHT?
IF HE DOES ANYTHING TO HURT YOU OR TSUBAKI...
"YUE. MAKE SURE YOU TAKE YOUR MEAL...
"...AND PLEASE, GO BACK TO THE SHRINE."
KUROGITSUNE IS MY FRIEND.
HE'S ALWAYS PUTTING ME FIRST.

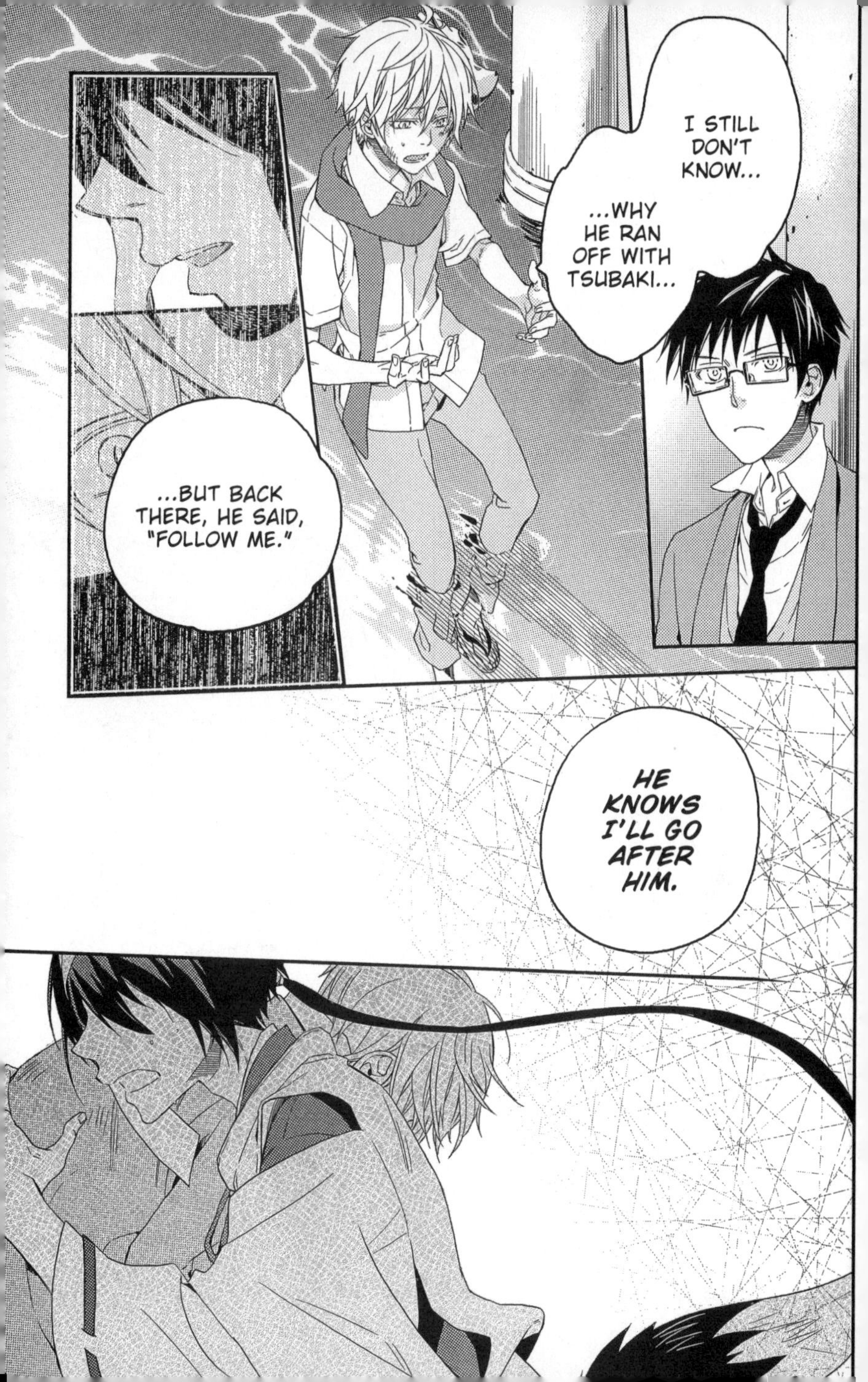
I STILL DON'T KNOW...
...WHY HE RAN OFF WITH TSUBAKI...
...BUT BACK THERE, HE SAID, "FOLLOW ME."
HE KNOWS I'LL GO AFTER HIM.

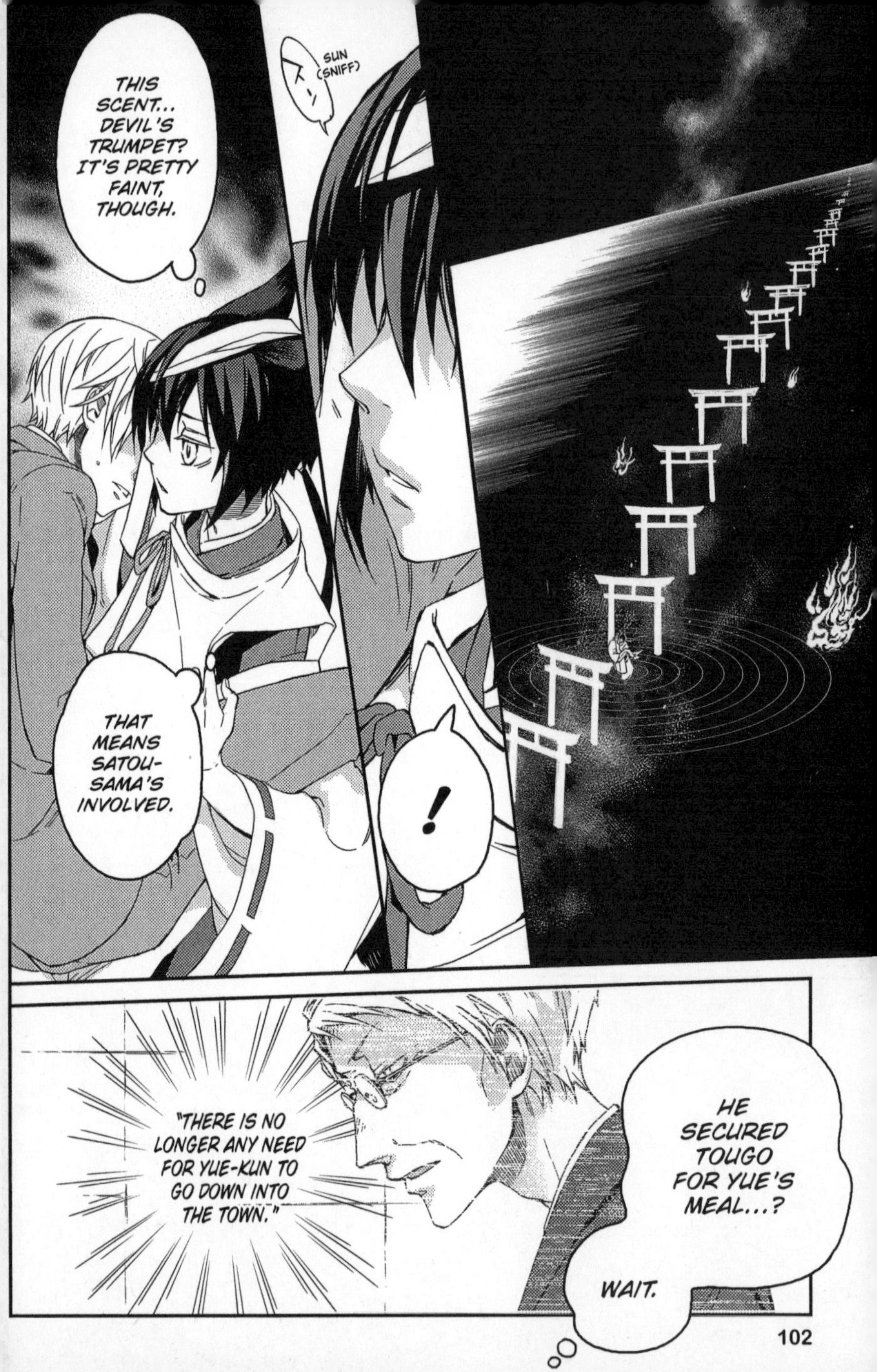
SUN (SNIFF)
!
THIS SCENT... DEVIL'S TRUMPET? IT'S PRETTY FAINT, THOUGH.
THAT MEANS SATOU-SAMA'S INVOLVED.
HE SECURED TOUGO FOR YUE'S MEAL...?
WAIT.
"THERE IS NO LONGER ANY NEED FOR YUE-KUN TO GO DOWN INTO THE TOWN."

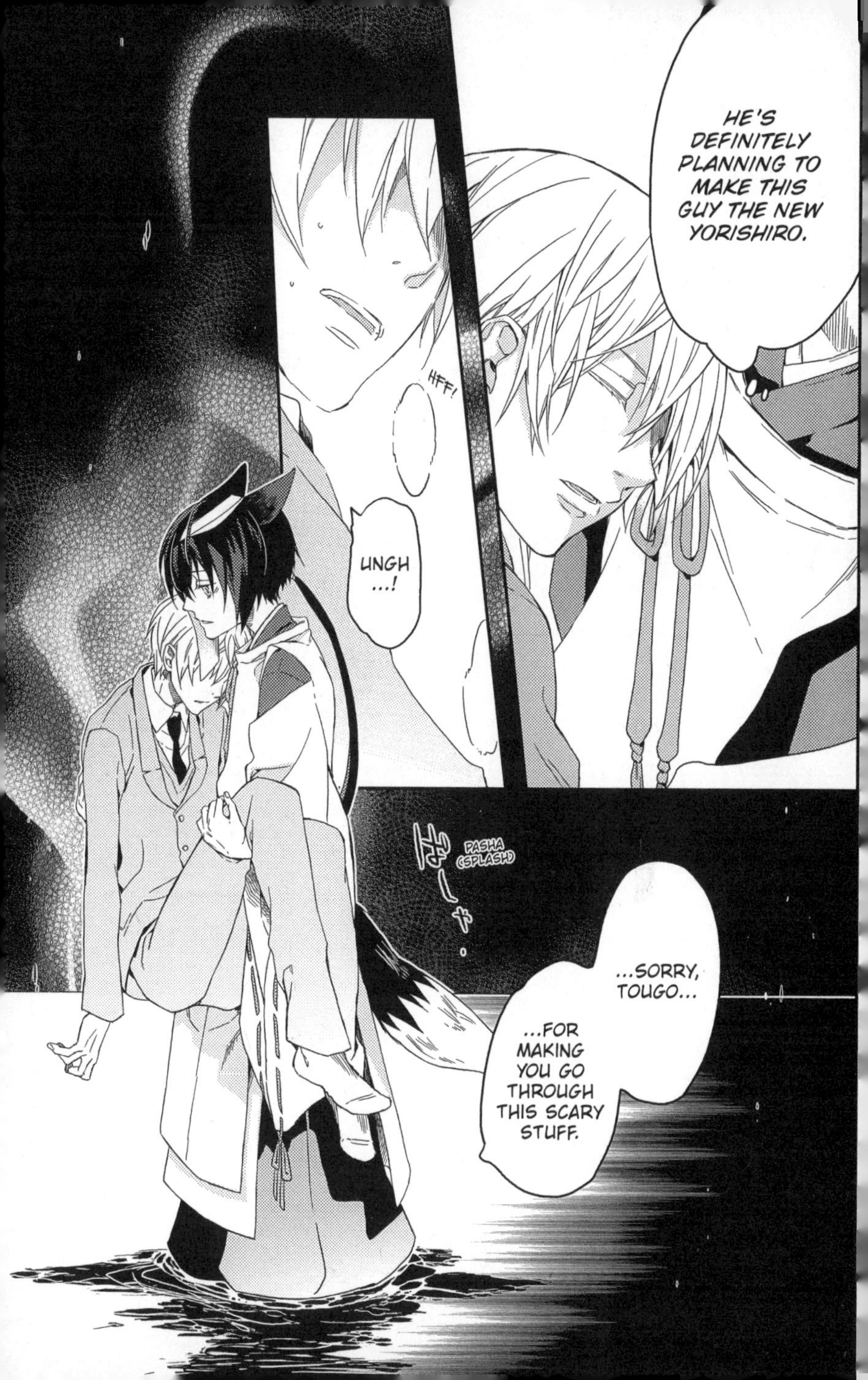
HE'S DEFINITELY PLANNING TO MAKE THIS GUY THE NEW YORISHIRO.
HFF!
UNGH ...!
ぱしゃ
PASHA (SPLASH)
...SORRY, TOUGO...
...FOR MAKING YOU GO THROUGH THIS SCARY STUFF.

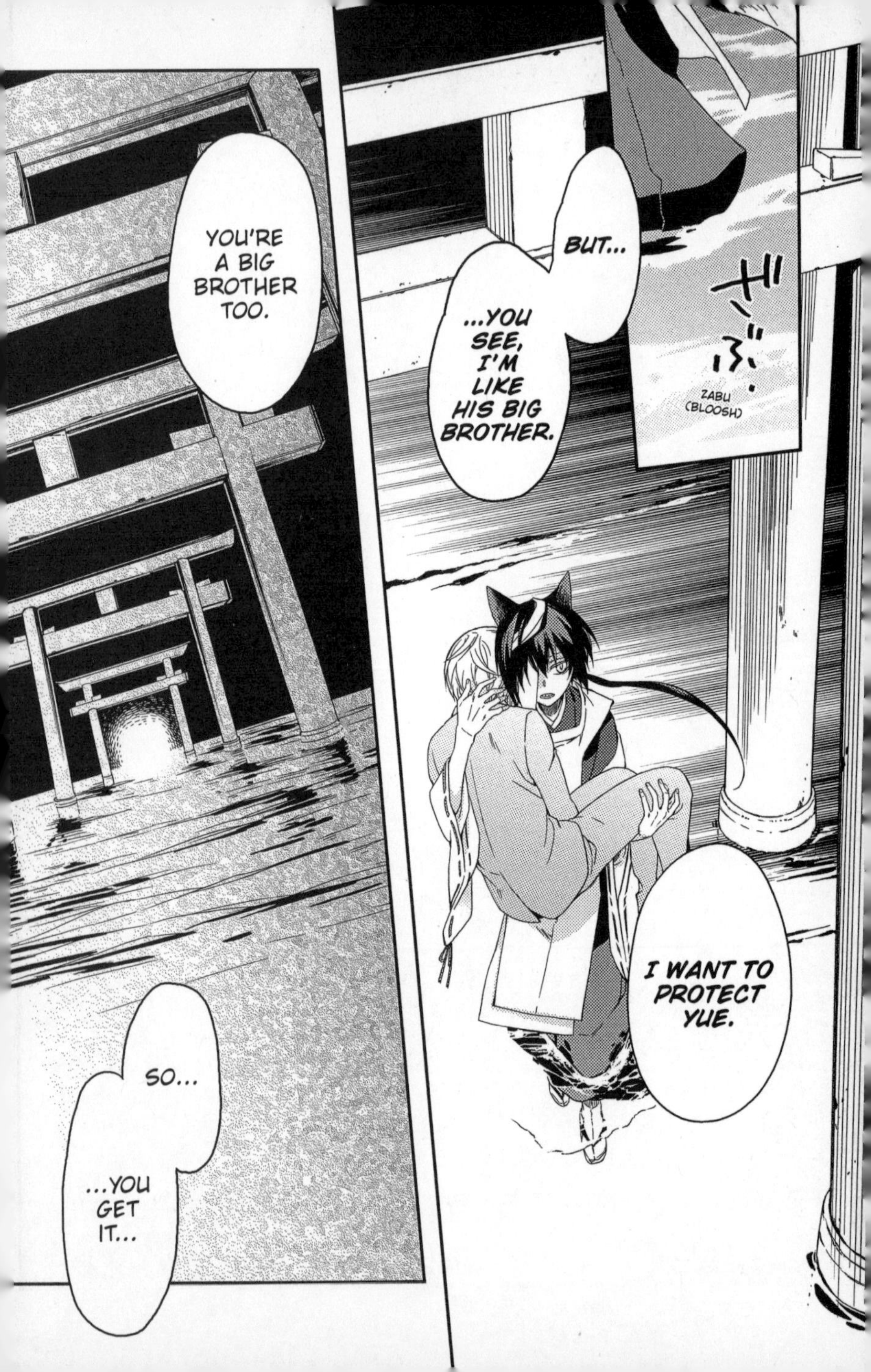
BUT...
...YOU SEE, I'M LIKE HIS BIG BROTHER.
ザぶ
ZABU (BLOOSH)
I WANT TO PROTECT YUE.
YOU'RE A BIG BROTHER TOO.
SO...
...YOU GET IT...

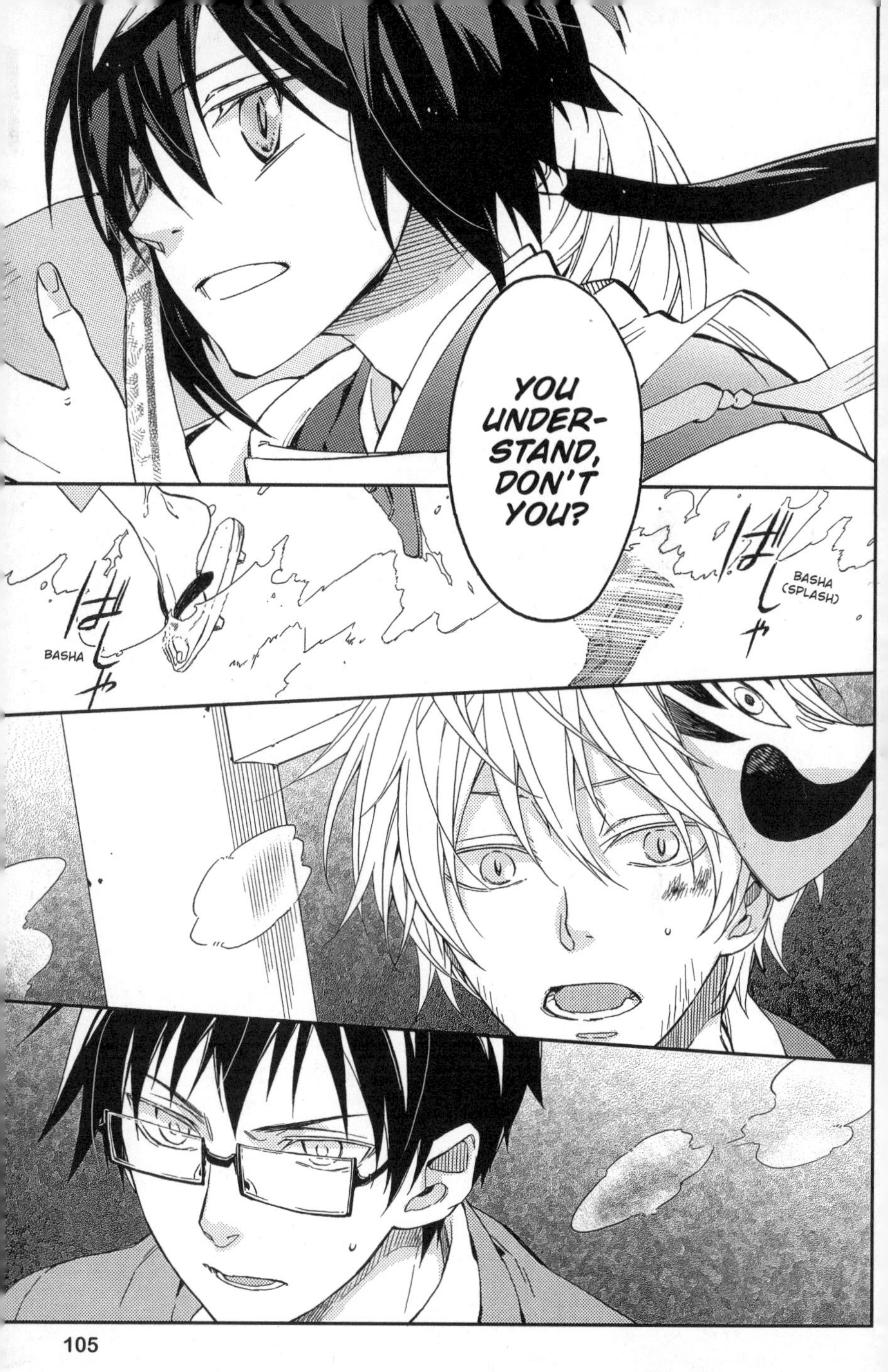
YOU UNDER-STAND, DON'T YOU?
ばしゃ
BASHA (SPLASH)
ばしゃ
BASHA

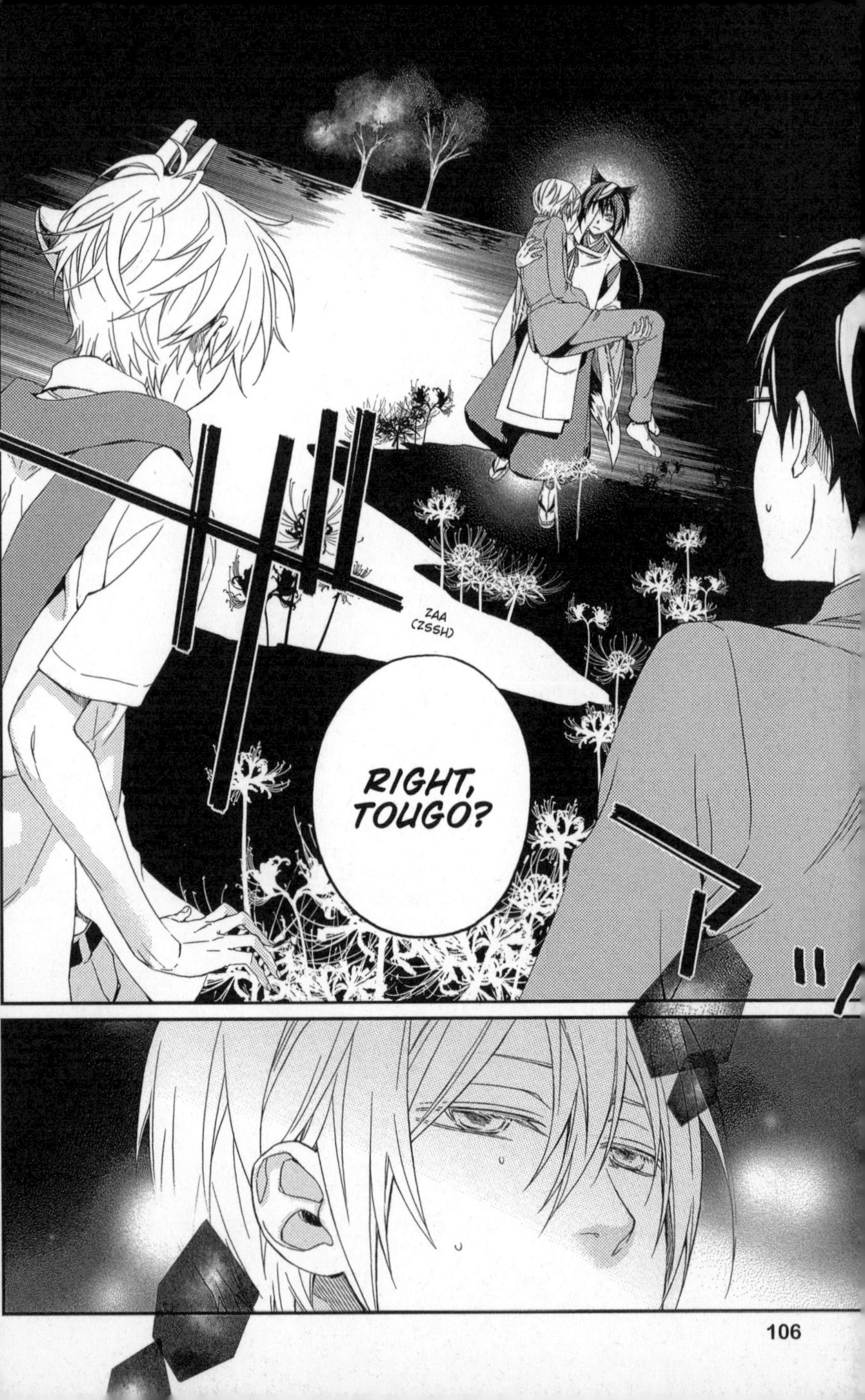
ZAA
(ZSSH)
RIGHT, TOUGO?

Of the Red,
the Light,
and the
Ayakashi

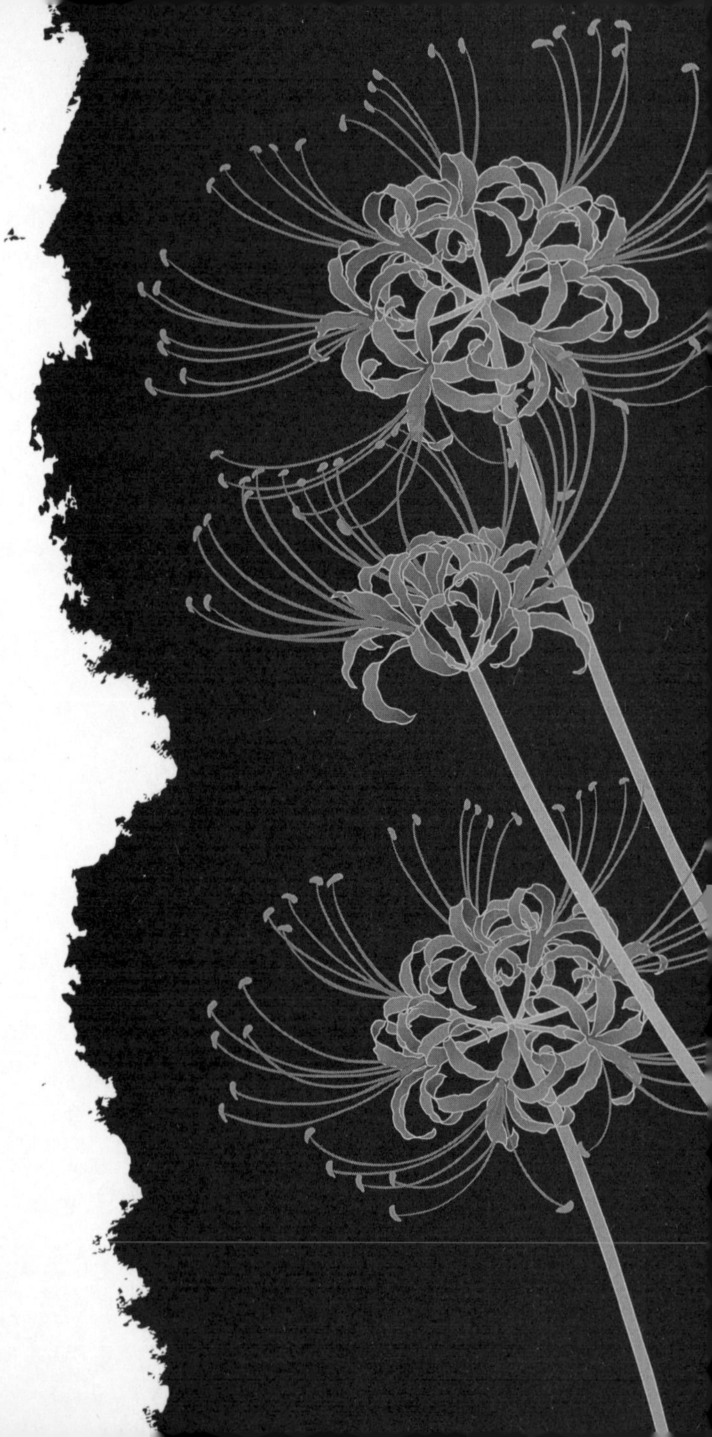

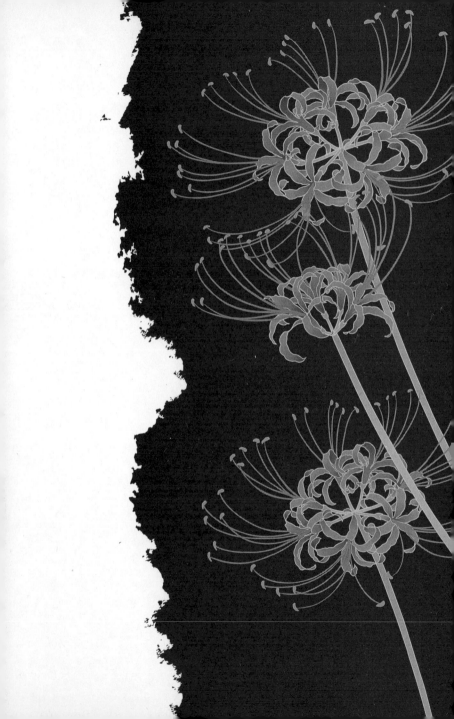

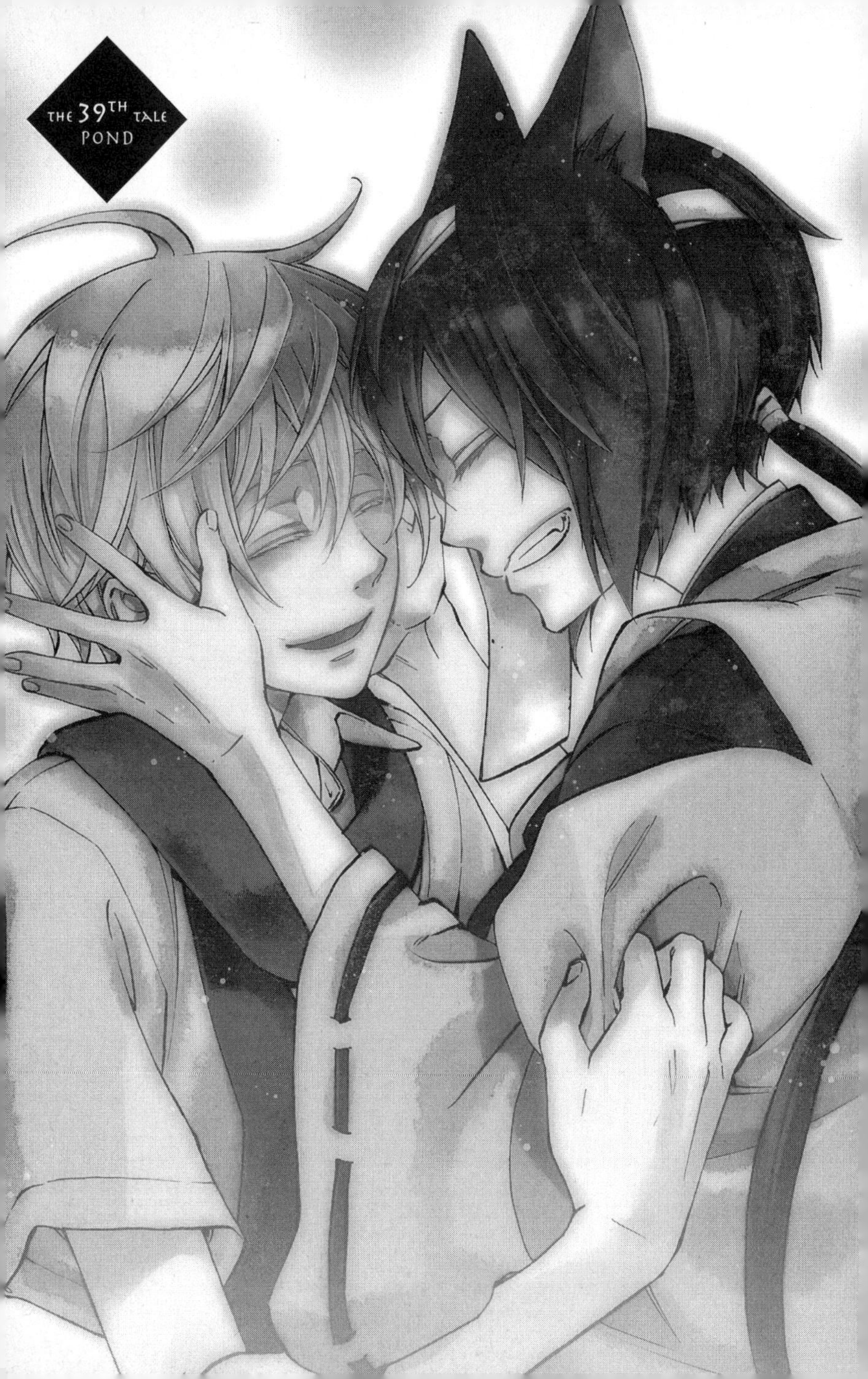
THE 39TH TALE
POND

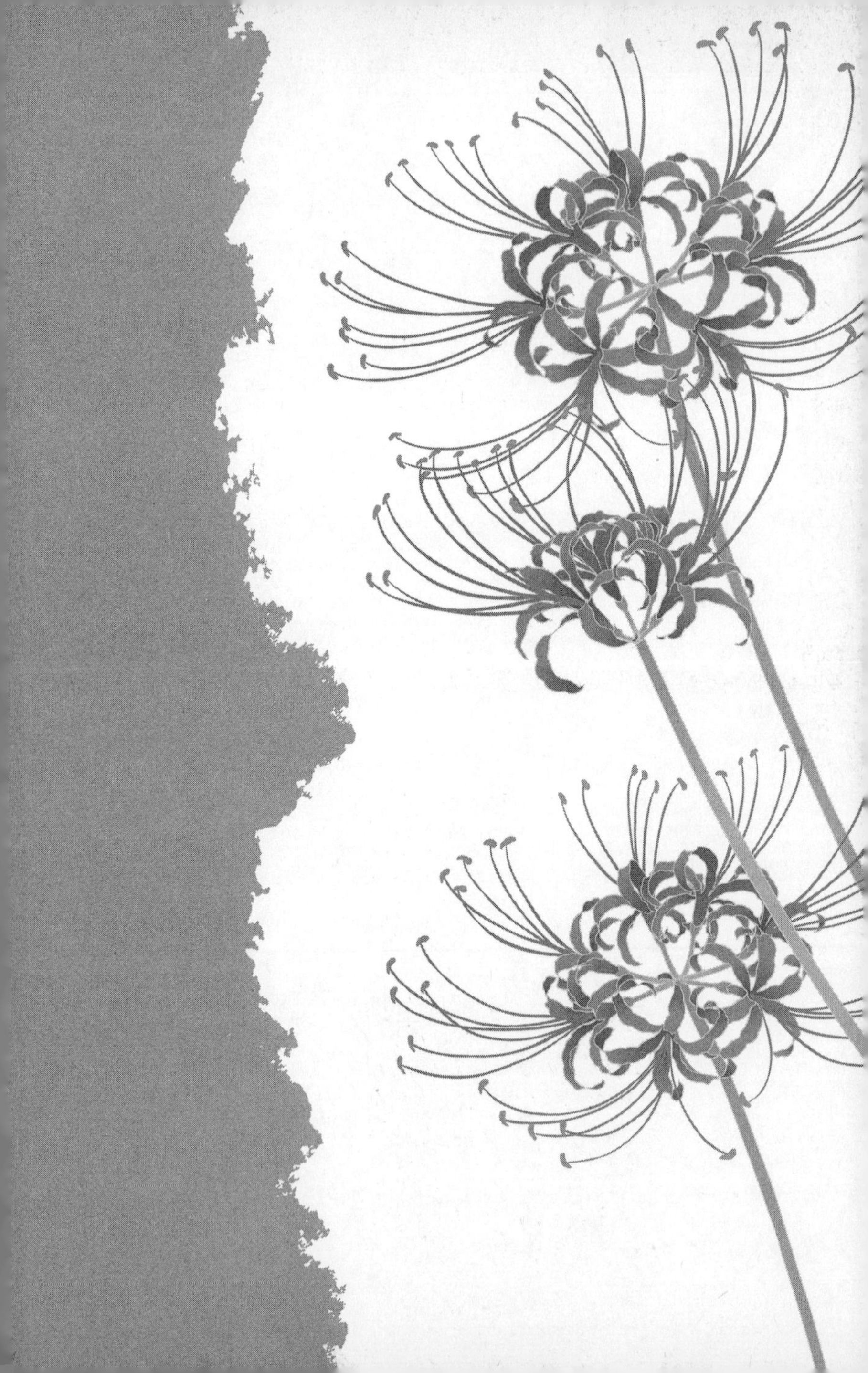

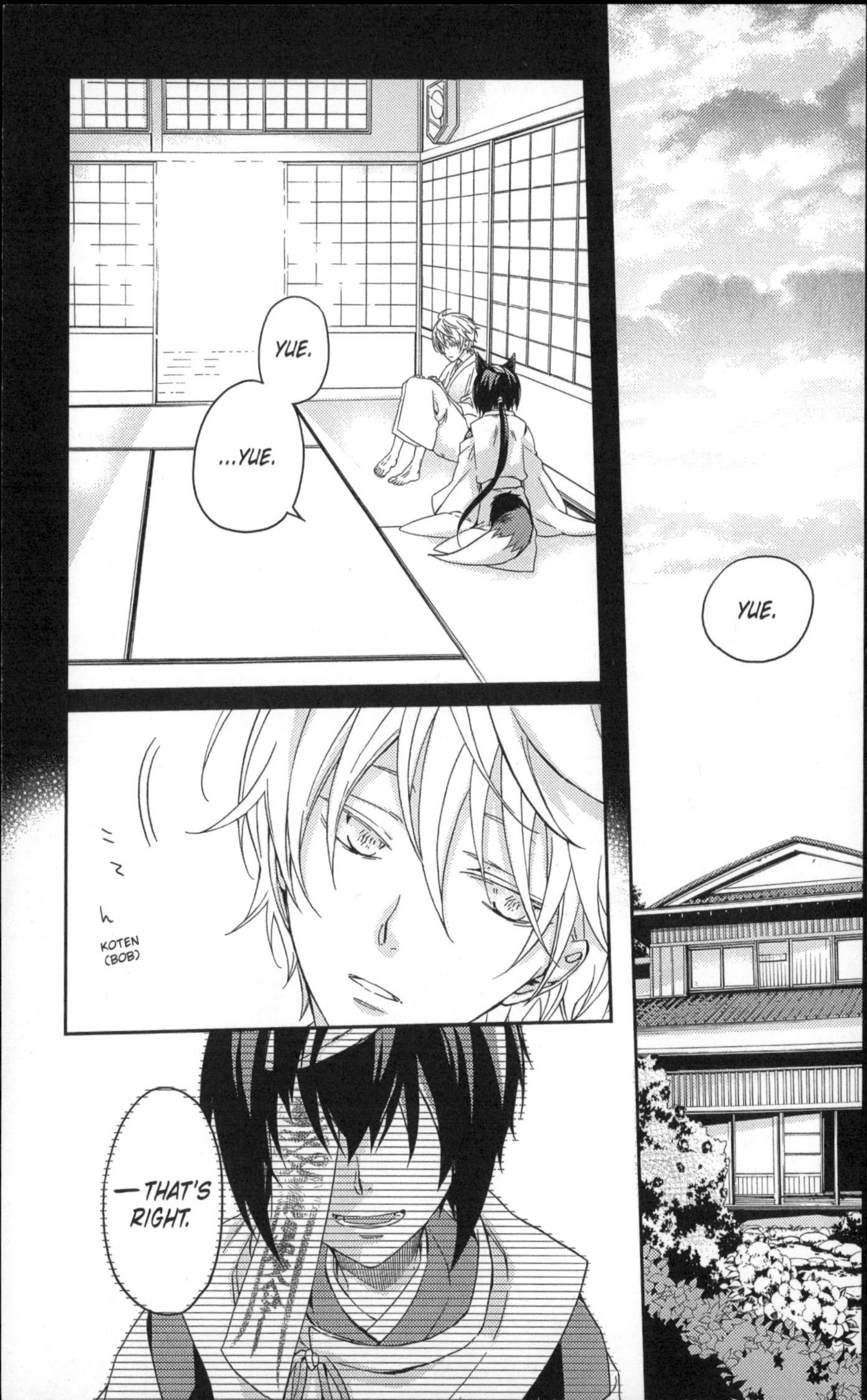
YUE.
YUE.
...YUE.
KOTEN (BOB)
—THAT'S RIGHT.

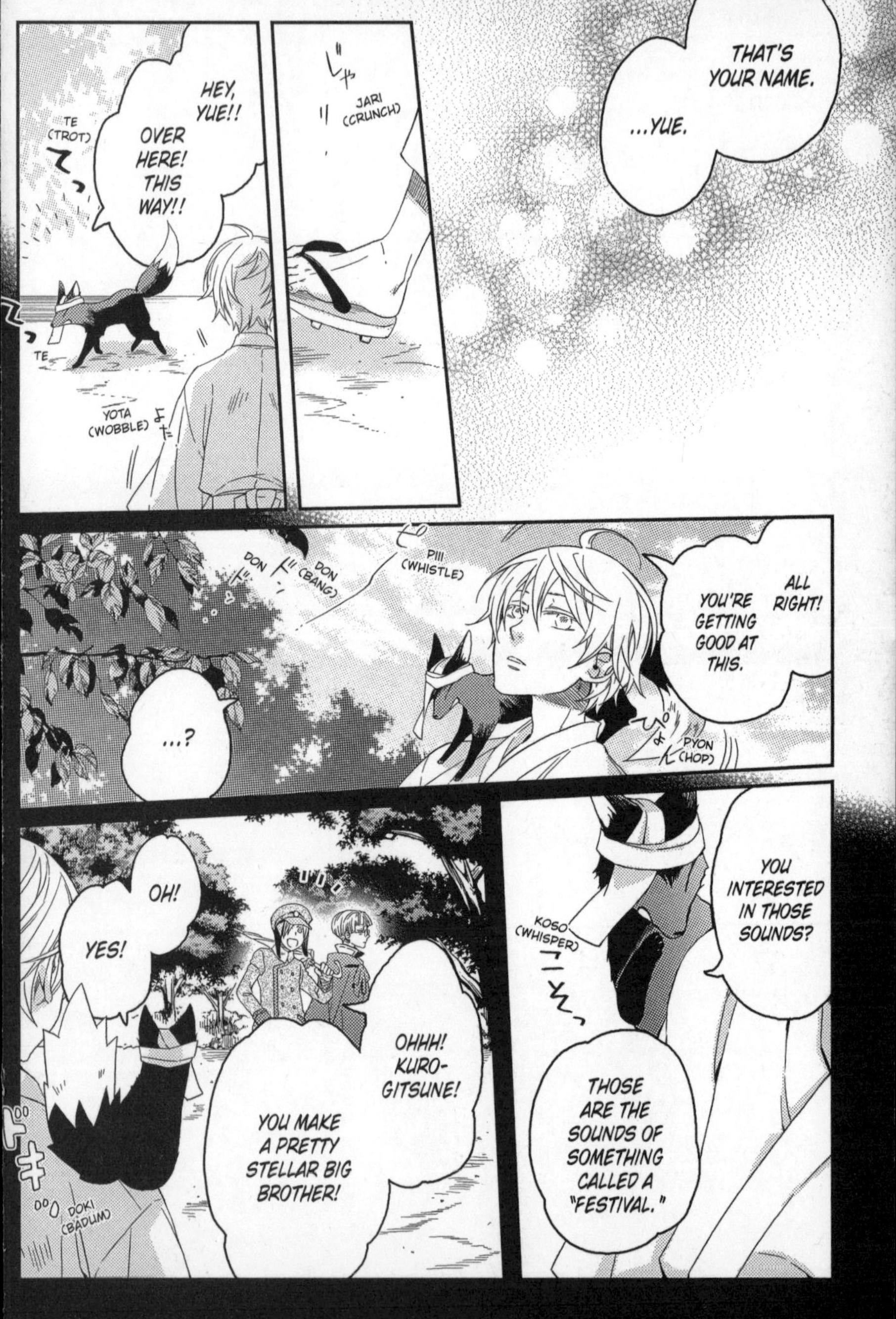
THAT'S YOUR NAME.
...YUE.
JARI (CRUNCH)
HEY, YUE!!
OVER HERE! THIS WAY!!
TE (TROT)
TE
YOTA (WOBBLE)
ALL RIGHT!
YOU'RE GETTING GOOD AT THIS.
PYON (HOP)
PIII (WHISTLE)
DON (BANG)
DON
...?
YOU INTERESTED IN THOSE SOUNDS?
KOSO (WHISPER)
THOSE ARE THE SOUNDS OF SOMETHING CALLED A "FESTIVAL."
OH!
YES!
OHHH! KURO-GITSUNE!
YOU MAKE A PRETTY STELLAR BIG BROTHER!
DOKI (BADUM)

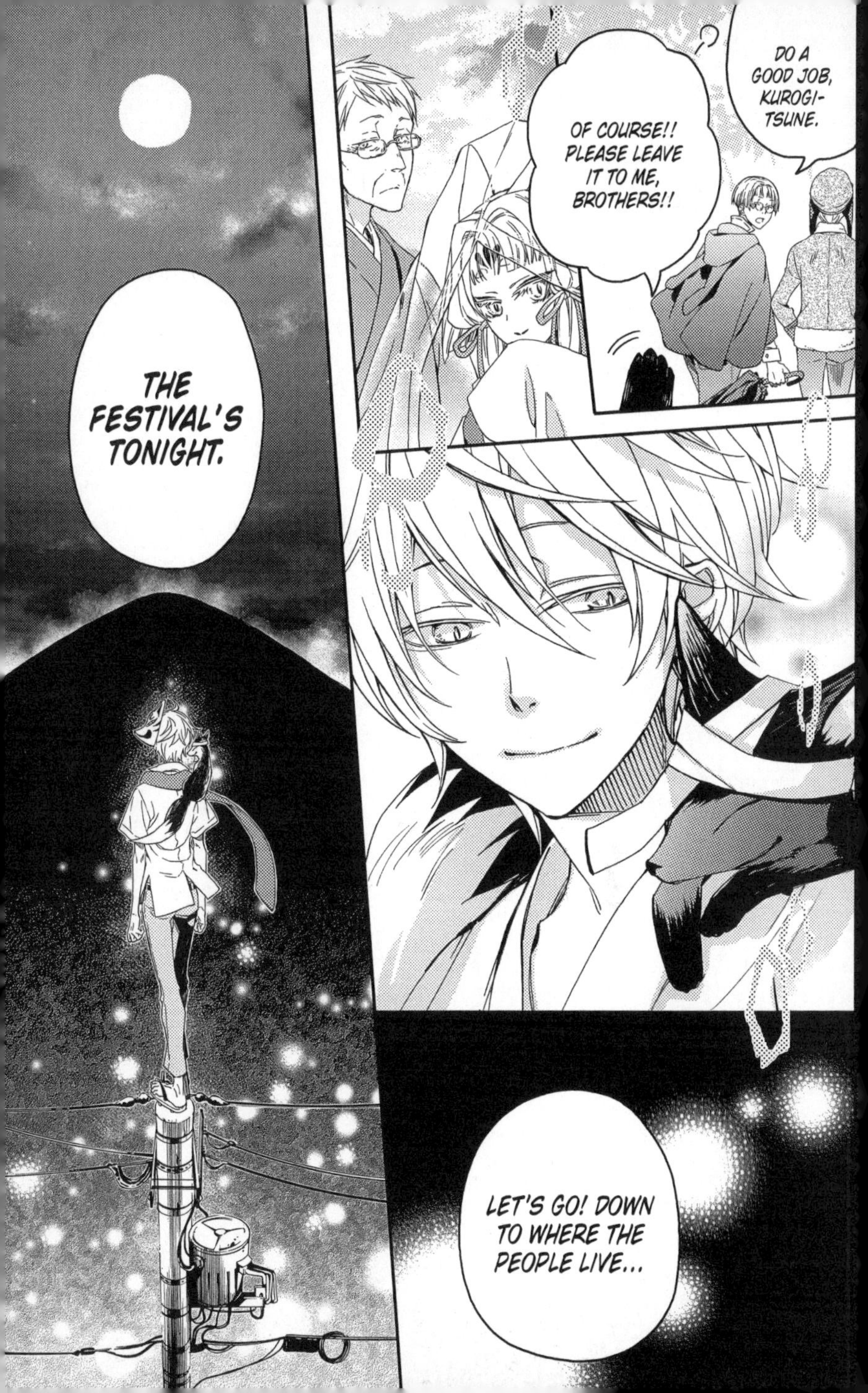
DO A GOOD JOB, KUROGI-TSUNE.
OF COURSE!! PLEASE LEAVE IT TO ME, BROTHERS!!
LET'S GO! DOWN TO WHERE THE PEOPLE LIVE...
THE FESTIVAL'S TONIGHT.

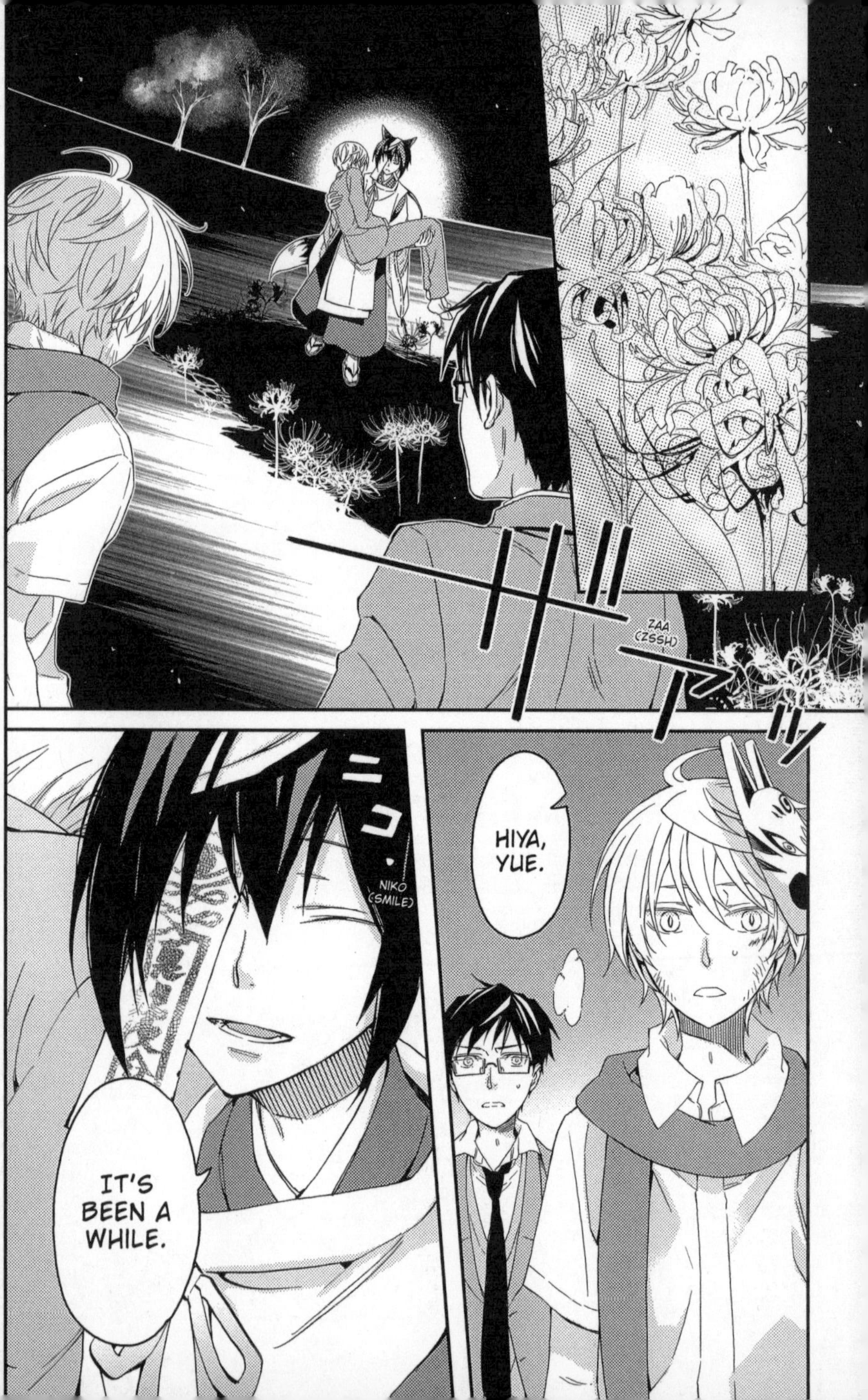
ZAA
(ZSSH)
HIYA, YUE.
NIKO
(SMILE)
IT'S BEEN A WHILE.

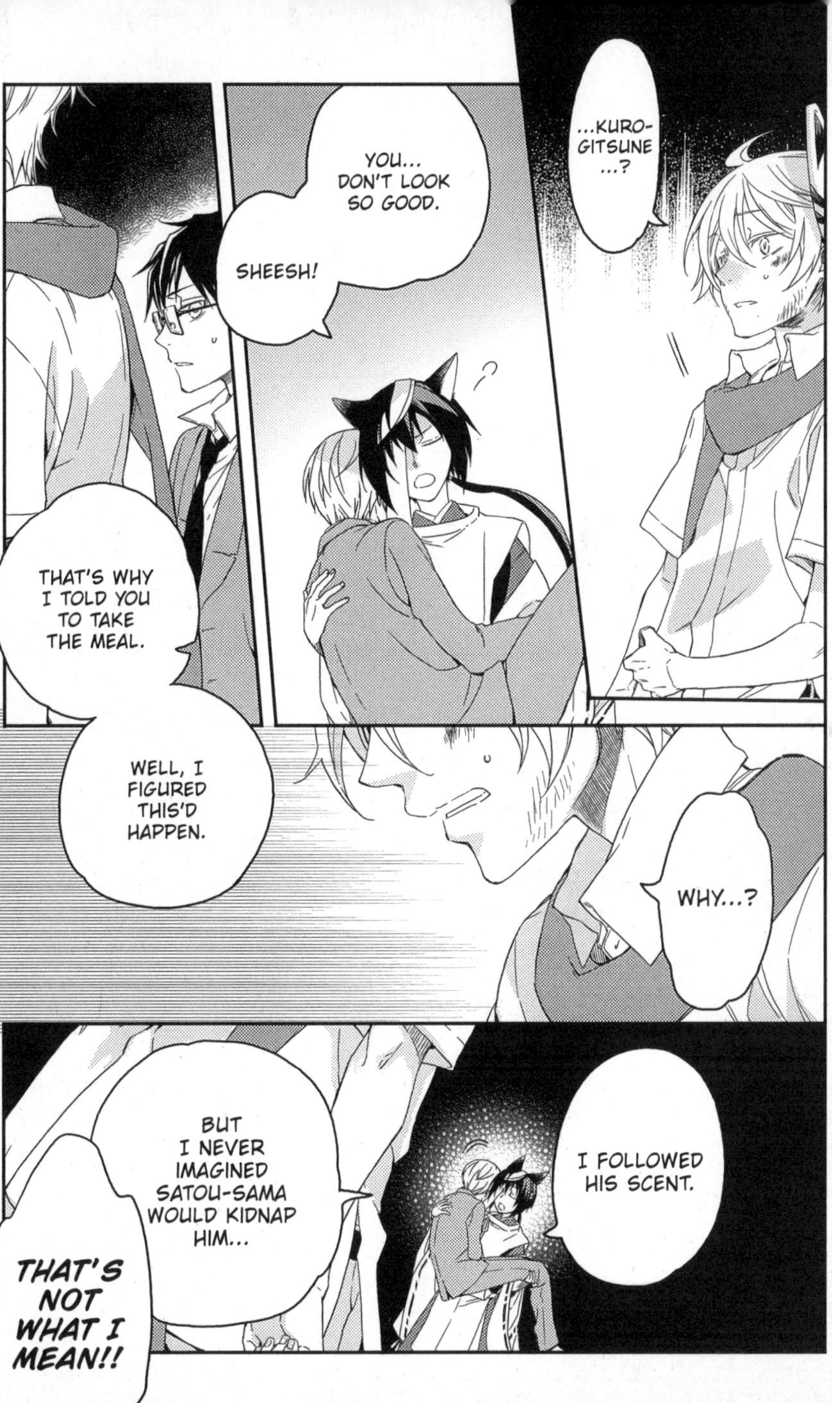
...KURO-GITSUNE ...?
YOU... DON'T LOOK SO GOOD.
SHEESH!
THAT'S WHY I TOLD YOU TO TAKE THE MEAL.
WHY...?
WELL, I FIGURED THIS'D HAPPEN.
I FOLLOWED HIS SCENT.
BUT I NEVER IMAGINED SATOU-SAMA WOULD KIDNAP HIM...
THAT'S NOT WHAT I MEAN!!

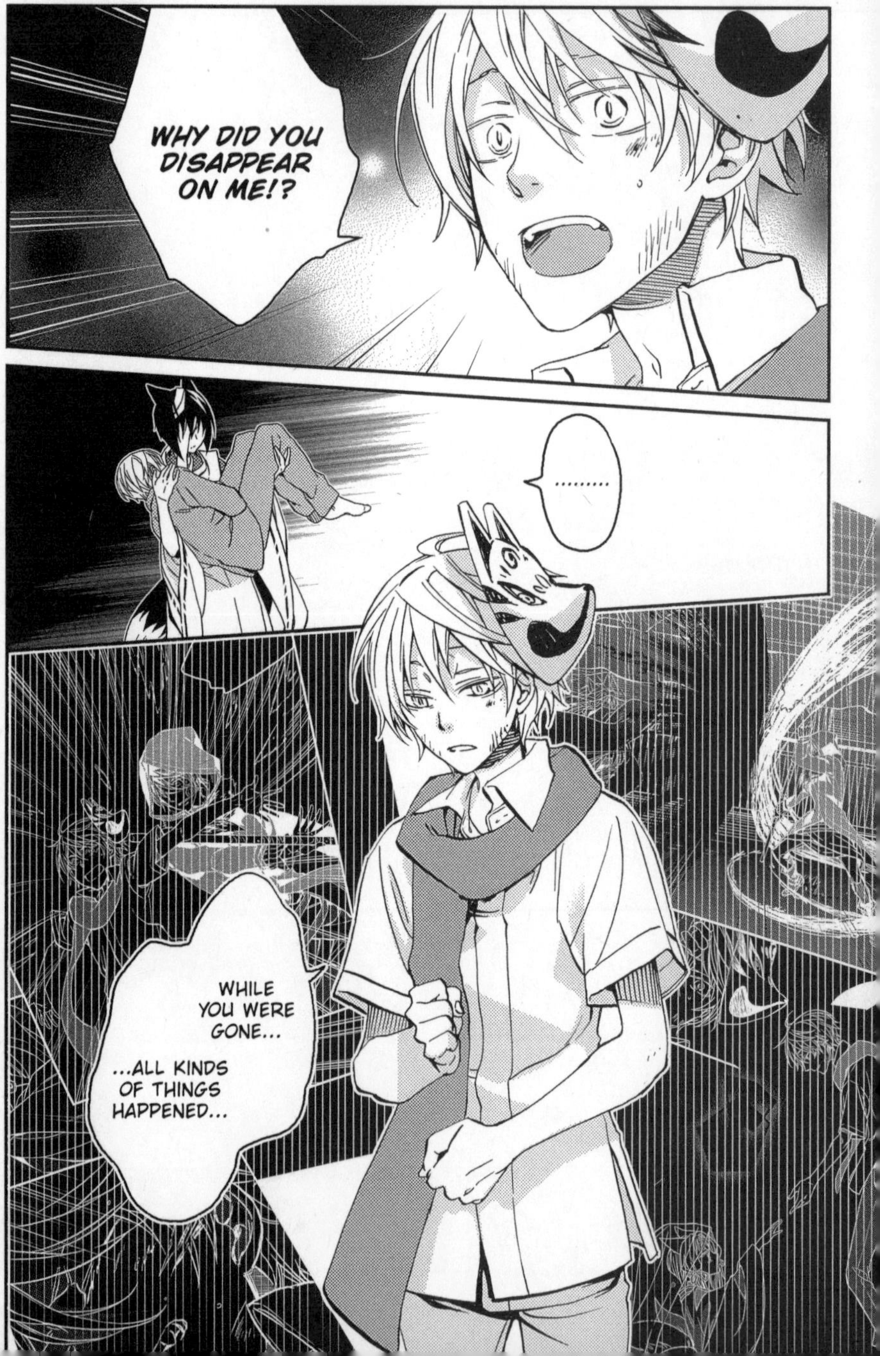
WHY DID YOU DISAPPEAR ON ME!?
....
WHILE YOU WERE GONE...
...ALL KINDS OF THINGS HAPPENED...

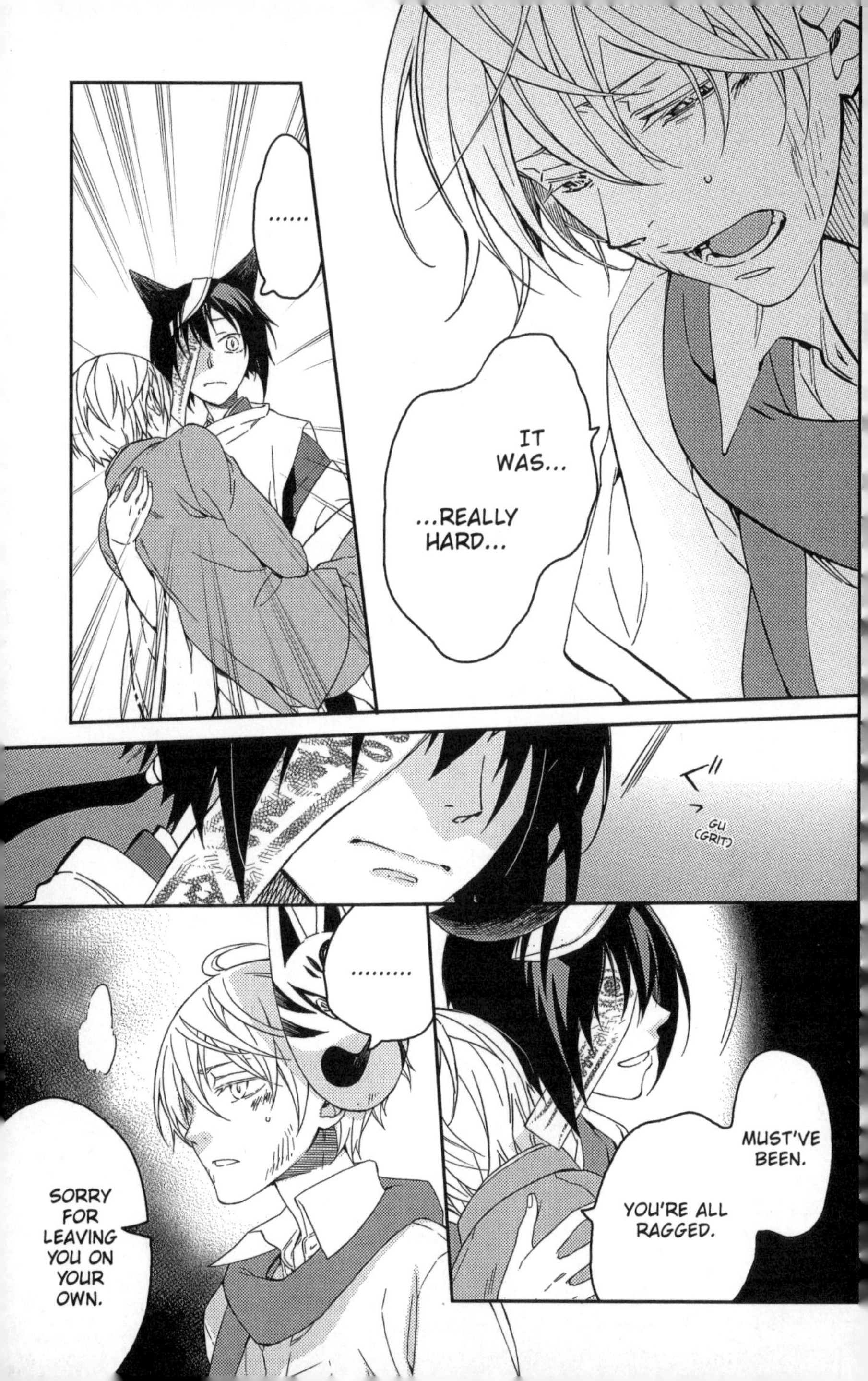
IT WAS...
...REALLY HARD...
......
GU (GRIT)
MUST'VE BEEN.
YOU'RE ALL RAGGED.
....
SORRY FOR LEAVING YOU ON YOUR OWN.

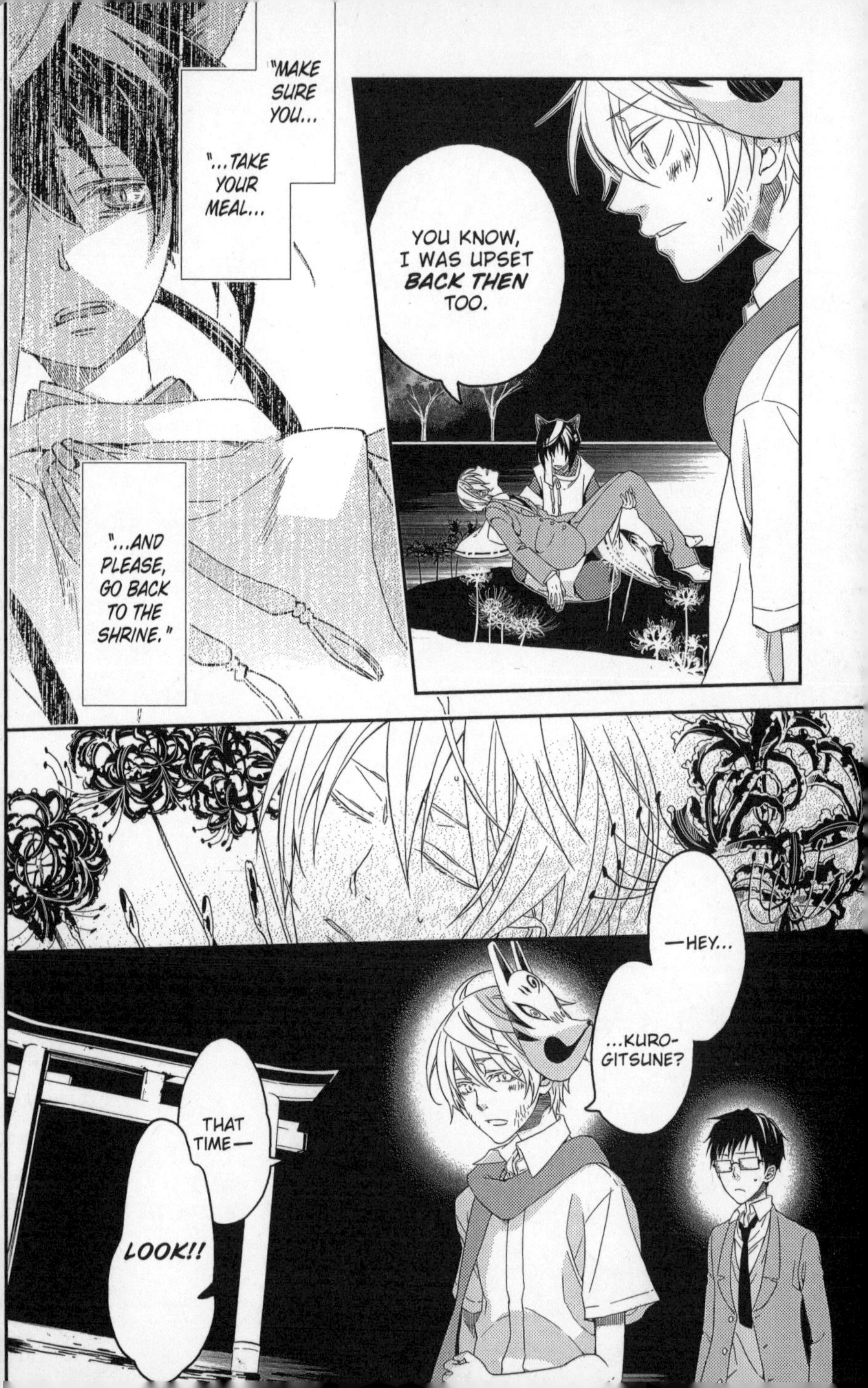
YOU KNOW, I WAS UPSET BACK THEN TOO.
"MAKE SURE YOU...
"...TAKE YOUR MEAL...
"...AND PLEASE, GO BACK TO THE SHRINE."
—HEY...
...KURO-GITSUNE?
THAT TIME—
LOOK!!

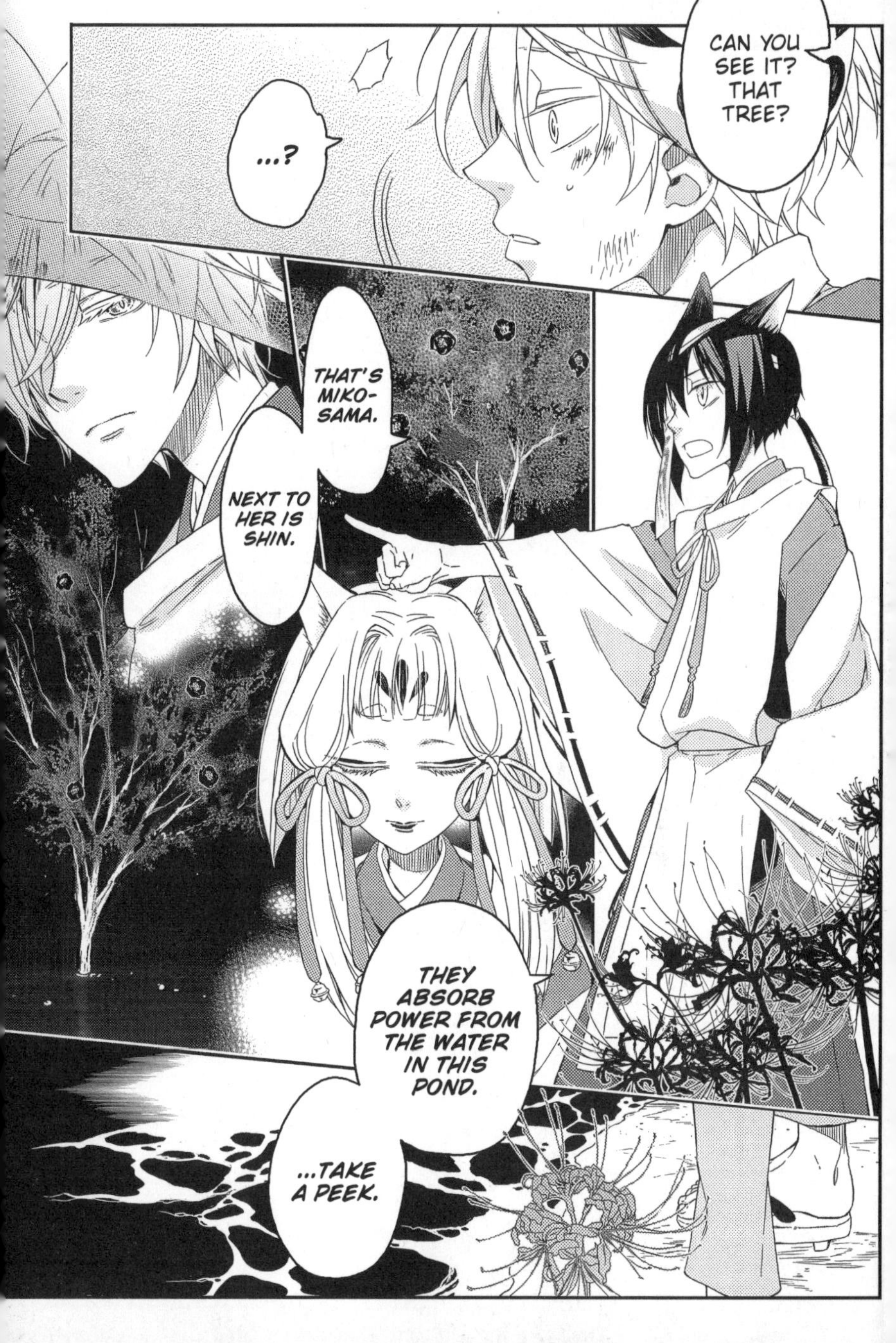
CAN YOU SEE IT? THAT TREE?
...?
THAT'S MIKO-SAMA.
NEXT TO HER IS SHIN.
THEY ABSORB POWER FROM THE WATER IN THIS POND.
...TAKE A PEEK.

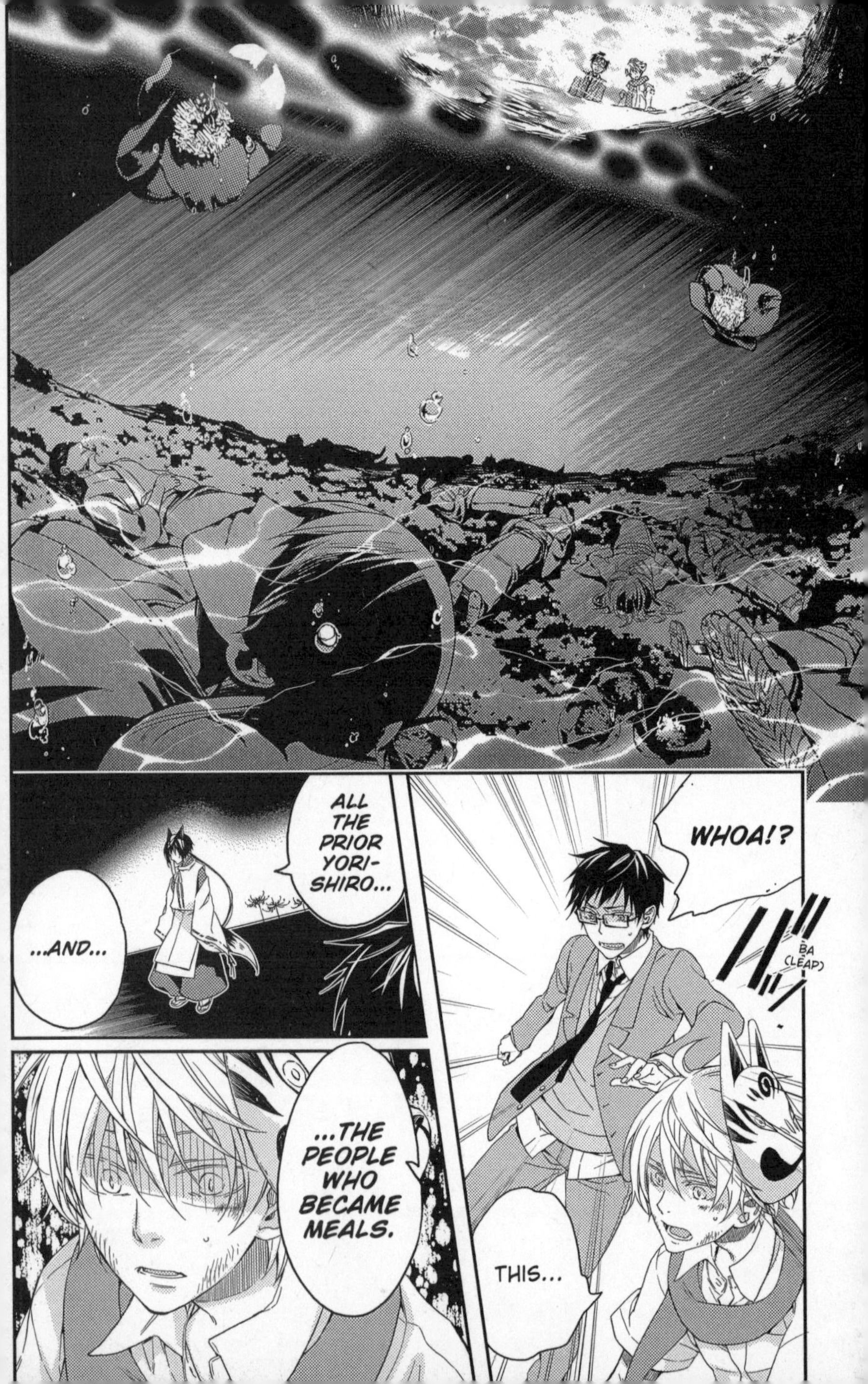
WHOA!?
BA (LEAP)
THIS...
ALL THE PRIOR YORI-SHIRO...
...AND...
...THE PEOPLE WHO BECAME MEALS.

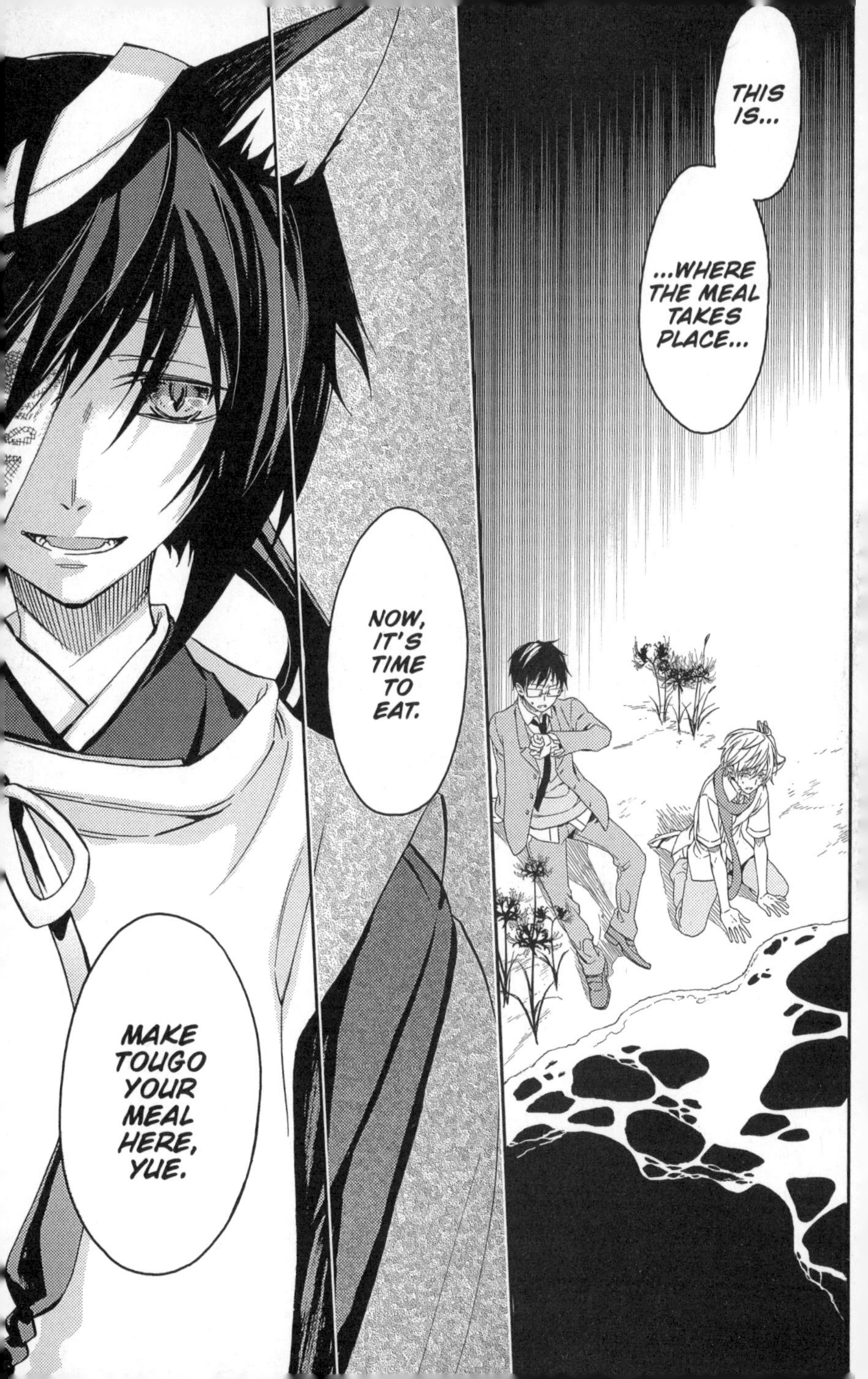
THIS IS...
...WHERE THE MEAL TAKES PLACE...
NOW, IT'S TIME TO EAT.
MAKE TOUGO YOUR MEAL HERE, YUE.

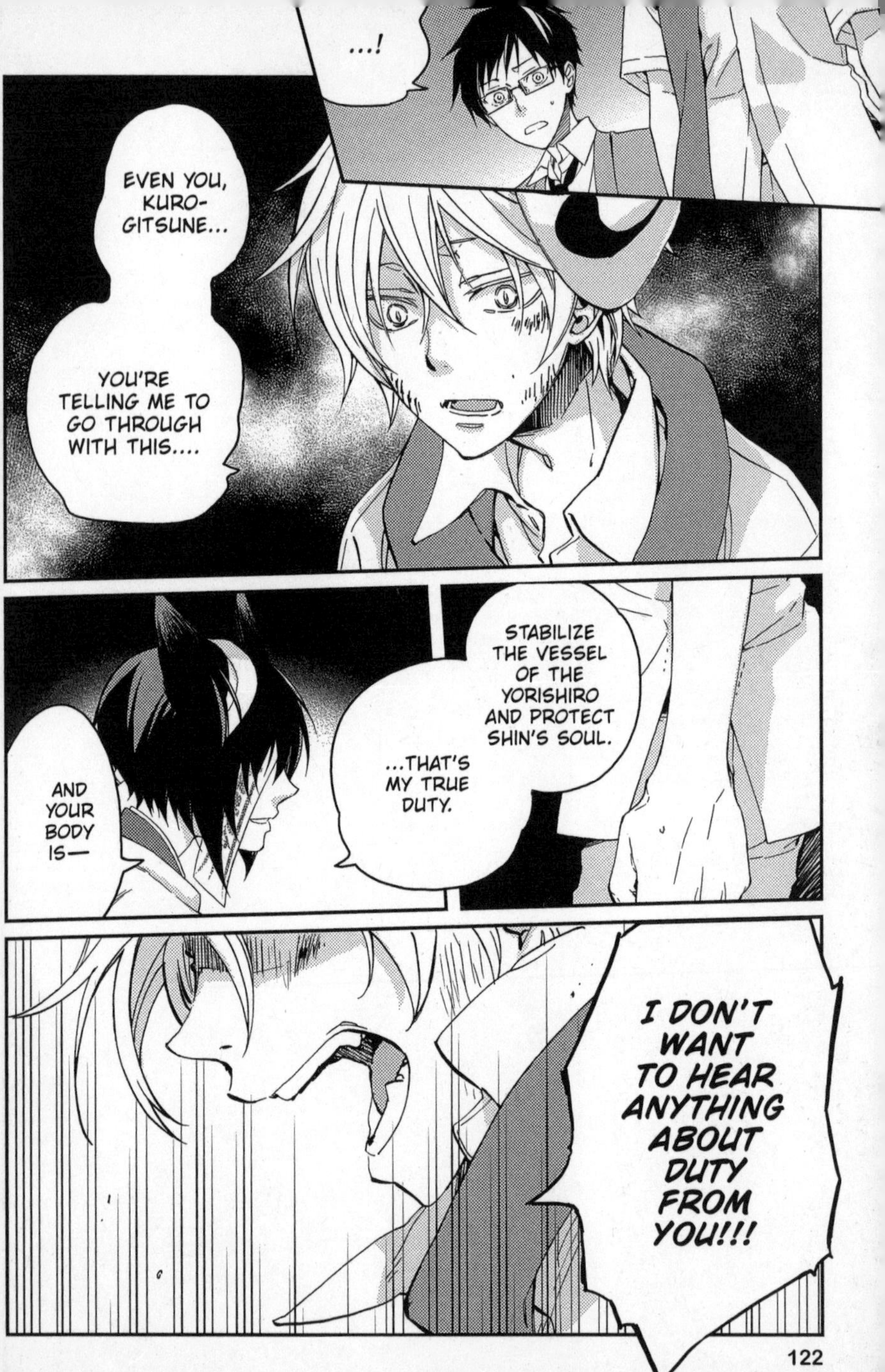
...!
EVEN YOU, KURO-GITSUNE...
YOU'RE TELLING ME TO GO THROUGH WITH THIS....
STABILIZE THE VESSEL OF THE YORISHIRO AND PROTECT SHIN'S SOUL.
...THAT'S MY TRUE DUTY.
AND YOUR BODY IS—
I DON'T WANT TO HEAR ANYTHING ABOUT DUTY FROM YOU!!!

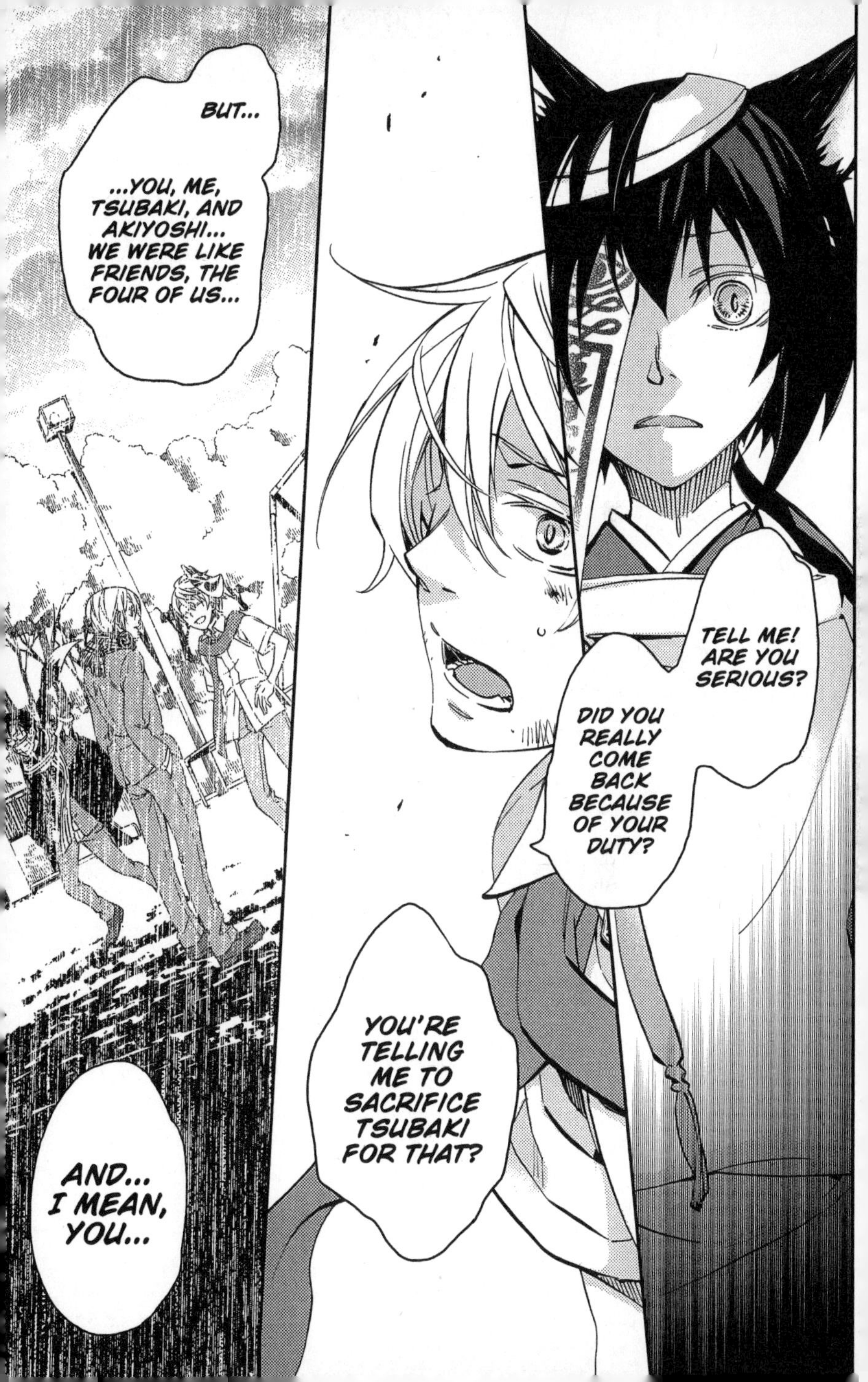
TELL ME! ARE YOU SERIOUS?
DID YOU REALLY COME BACK BECAUSE OF YOUR DUTY?
YOU'RE TELLING ME TO SACRIFICE TSUBAKI FOR THAT?
BUT...
...YOU, ME, TSUBAKI, AND AKIYOSHI... WE WERE LIKE FRIENDS, THE FOUR OF US...
AND... I MEAN, YOU...

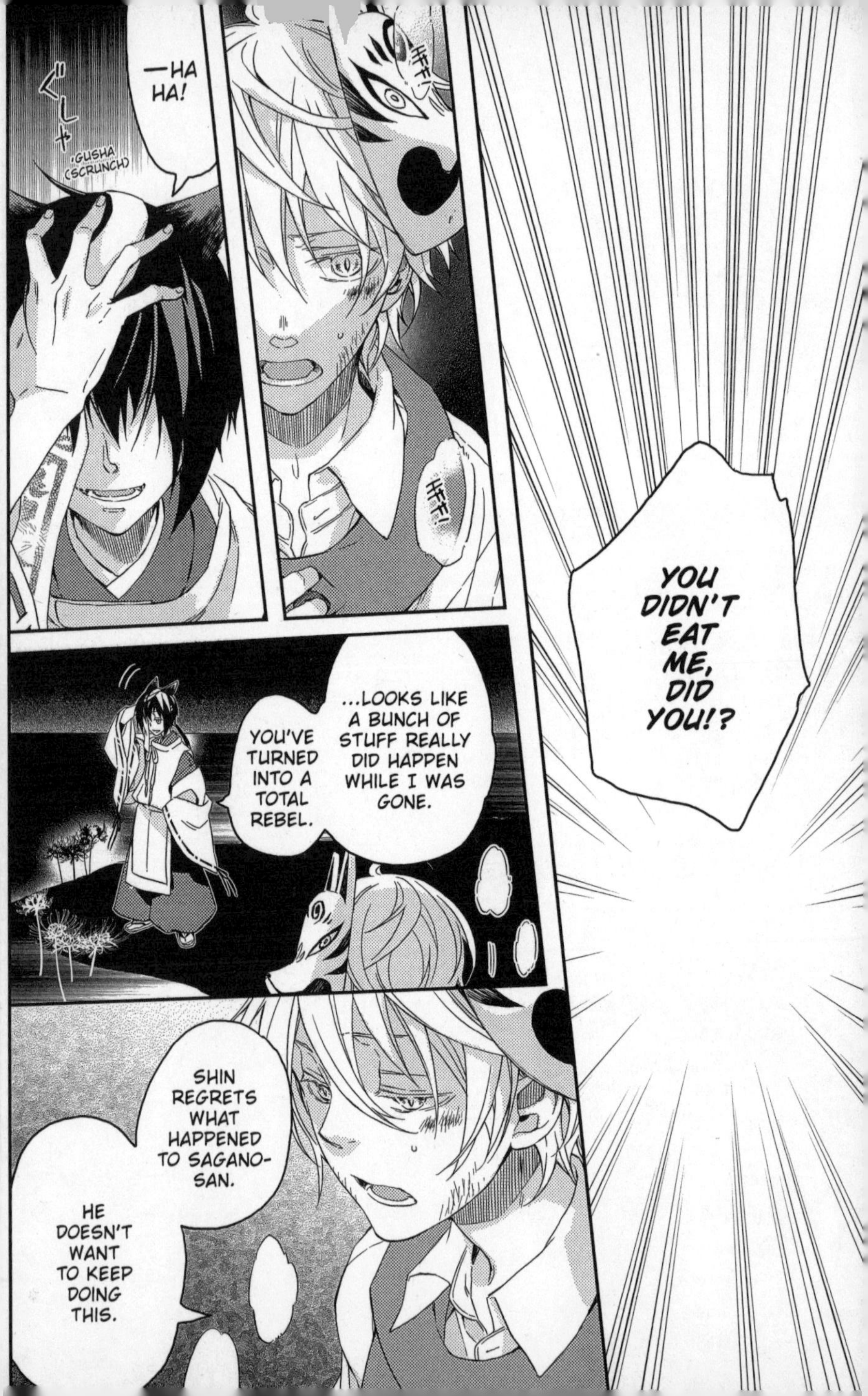
YOU DIDN'T EAT ME, DID YOU!?
HFF!
HFF!
—HA HA!
ぐしゃ
GUSHA (SCRUNCH)
...LOOKS LIKE A BUNCH OF STUFF REALLY DID HAPPEN WHILE I WAS GONE.
YOU'VE TURNED INTO A TOTAL REBEL.
SHIN REGRETS WHAT HAPPENED TO SAGANO-SAN.
HE DOESN'T WANT TO KEEP DOING THIS.

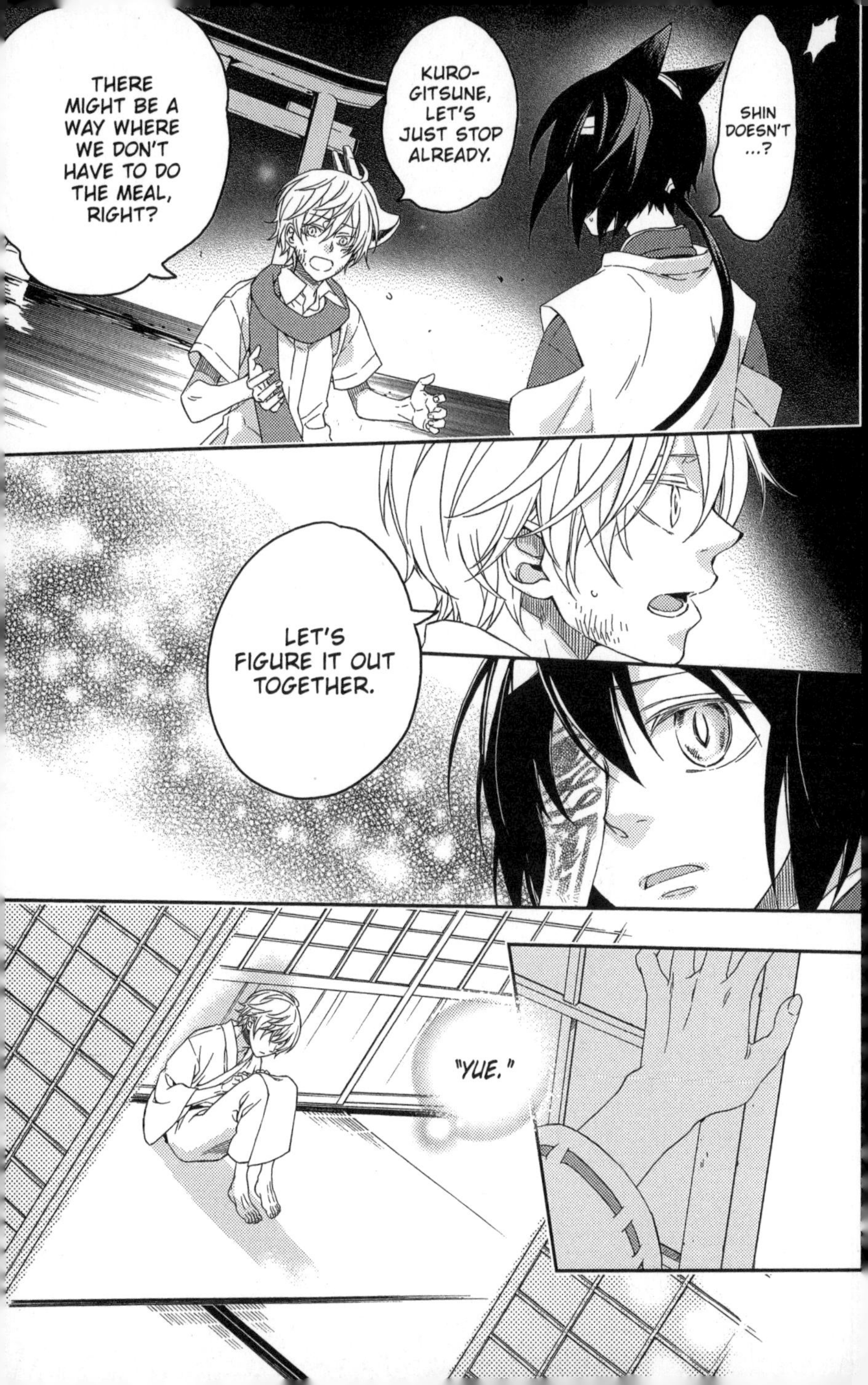
SHIN DOESN'T ...?
KURO-GITSUNE, LET'S JUST STOP ALREADY.
THERE MIGHT BE A WAY WHERE WE DON'T HAVE TO DO THE MEAL, RIGHT?
LET'S FIGURE IT OUT TOGETHER.
"YUE."

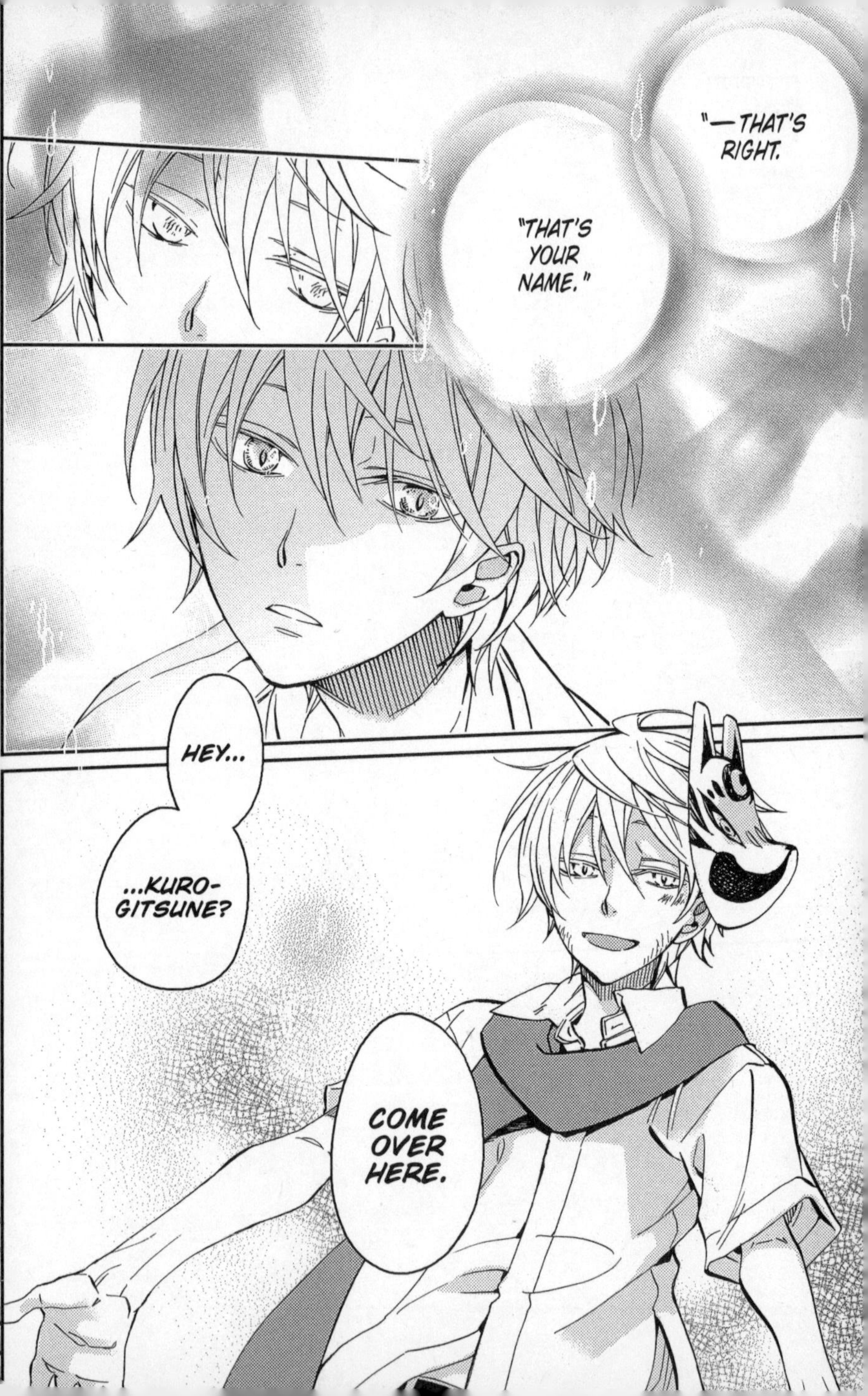
"—THAT'S RIGHT.
"THAT'S YOUR NAME."
HEY...
...KURO-GITSUNE?
COME OVER HERE.

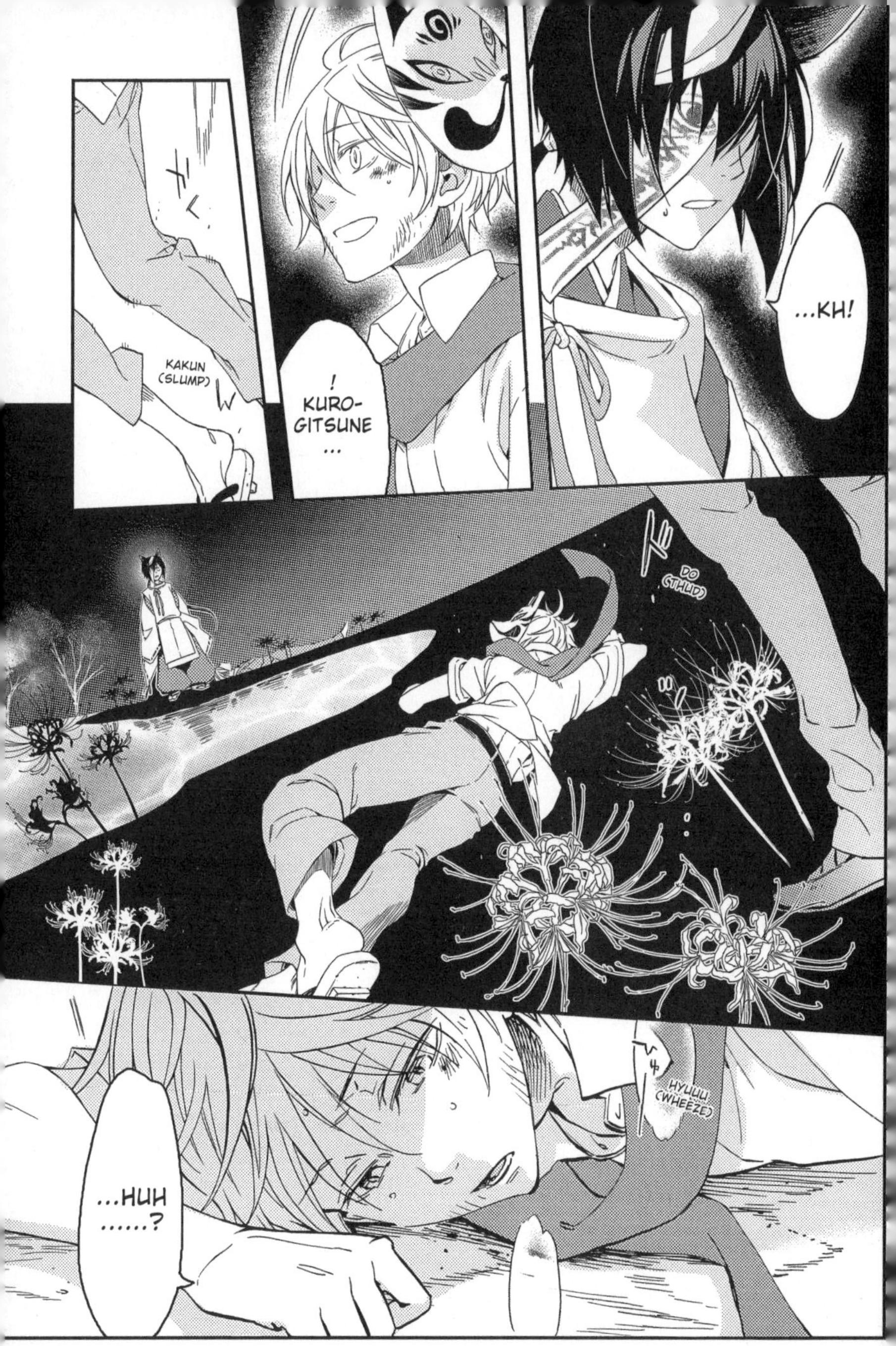
...KH!
! KURO-GITSUNE ...
KAKUN (SLUMP)
DO (THUD)
HYUUU (WHEEZE)
...HUH ......?

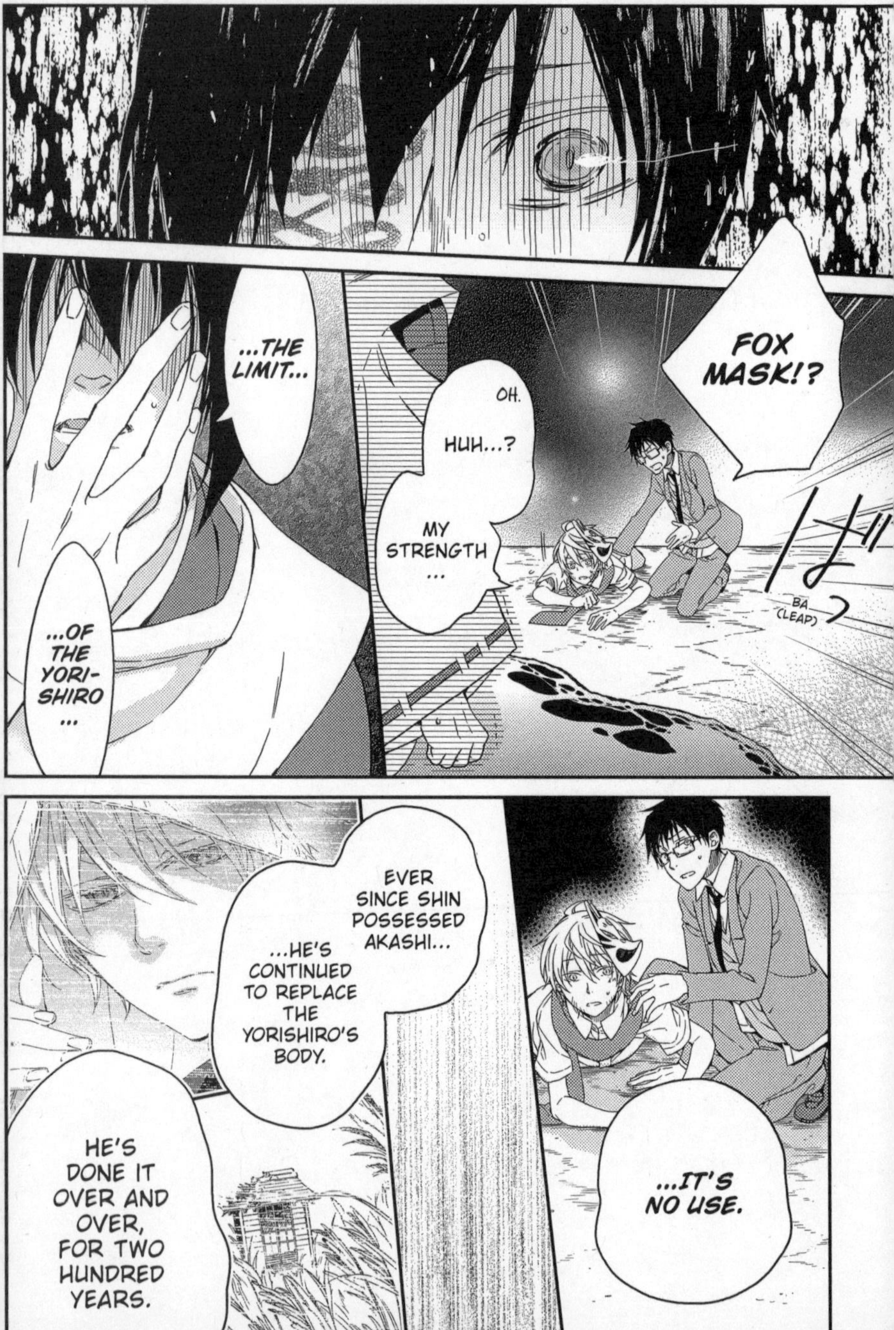
FOX MASK!?
BA (LEAP)
OH.
HUH...?
MY STRENGTH ...
...THE LIMIT...
...OF THE YORI-SHIRO ...
...IT'S NO USE.
EVER SINCE SHIN POSSESSED AKASHI...
...HE'S CONTINUED TO REPLACE THE YORISHIRO'S BODY.
HE'S DONE IT OVER AND OVER, FOR TWO HUNDRED YEARS.

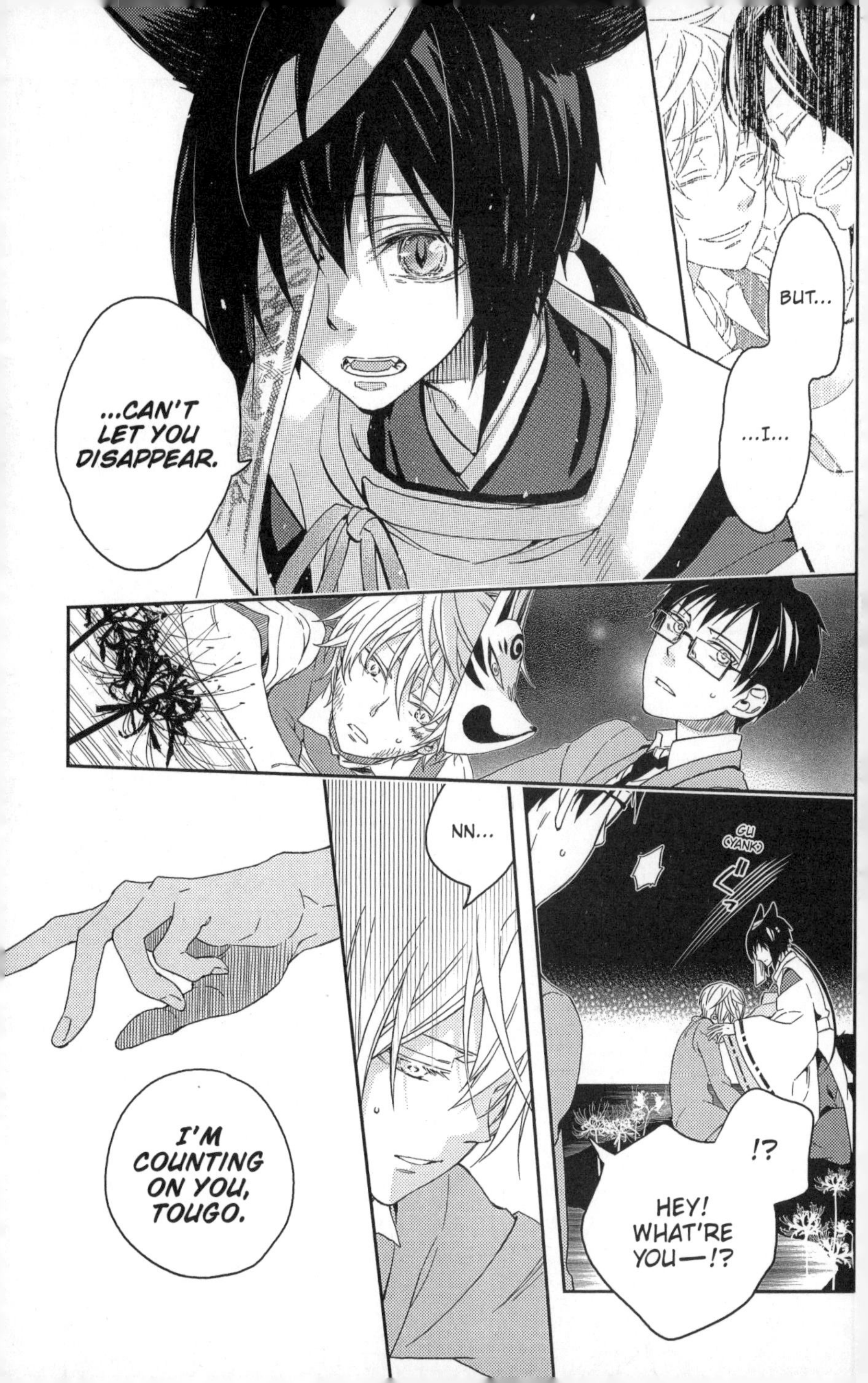
BUT...
...I...
...CAN'T LET YOU DISAPPEAR.
GU (YANK)
!?
HEY! WHAT'RE YOU—!?
NN...
I'M COUNTING ON YOU, TOUGO.

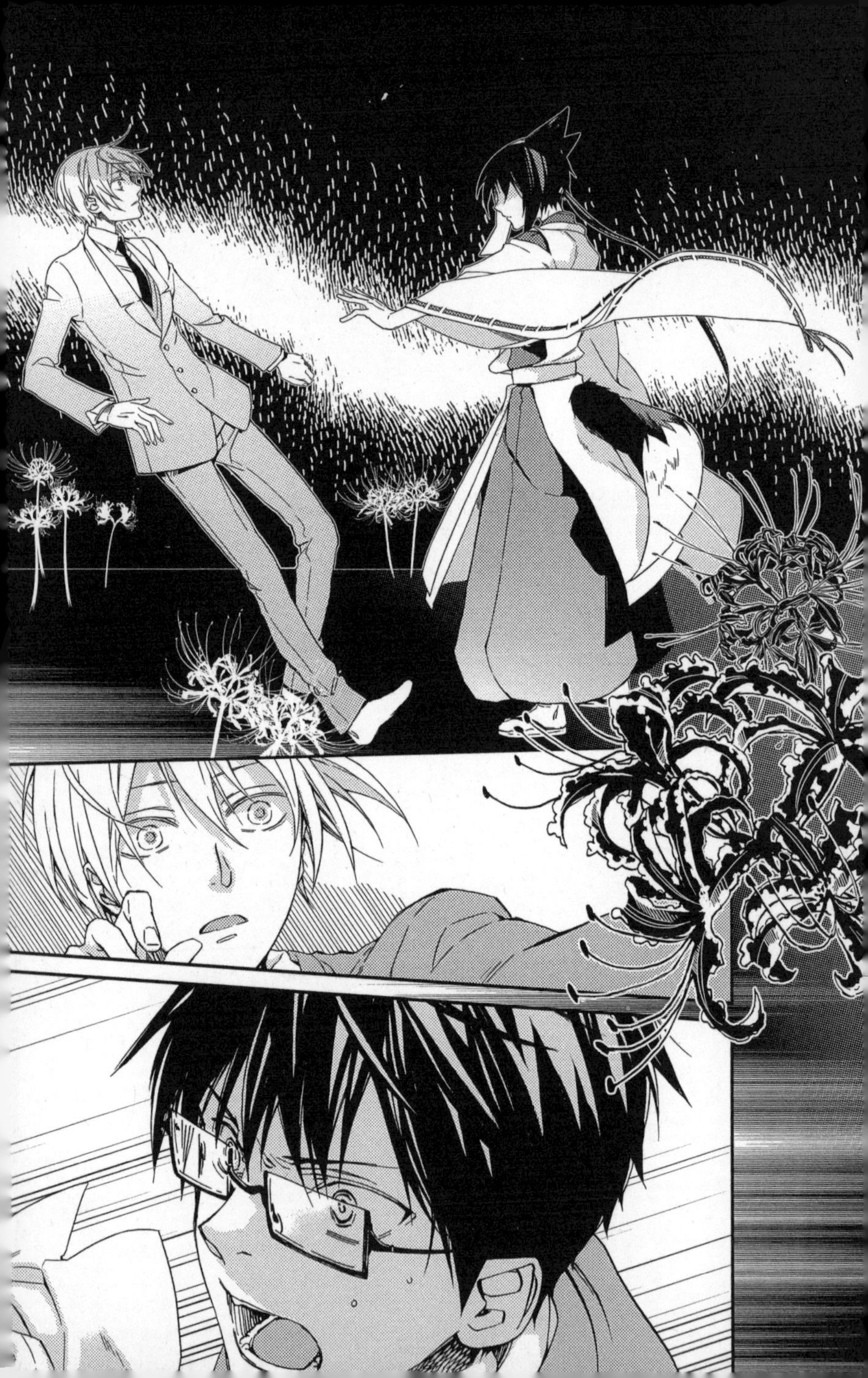

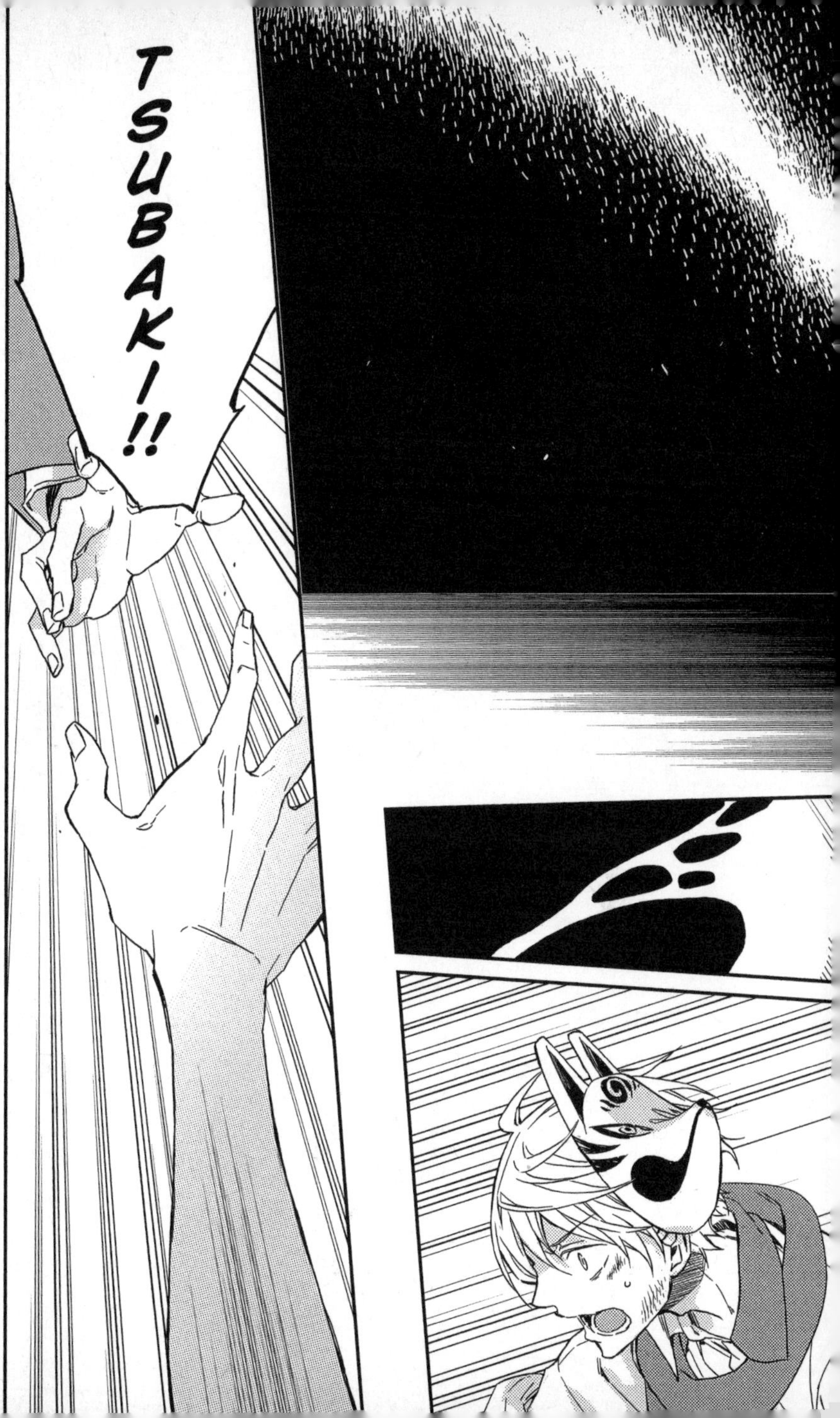
TSUBAKI!!

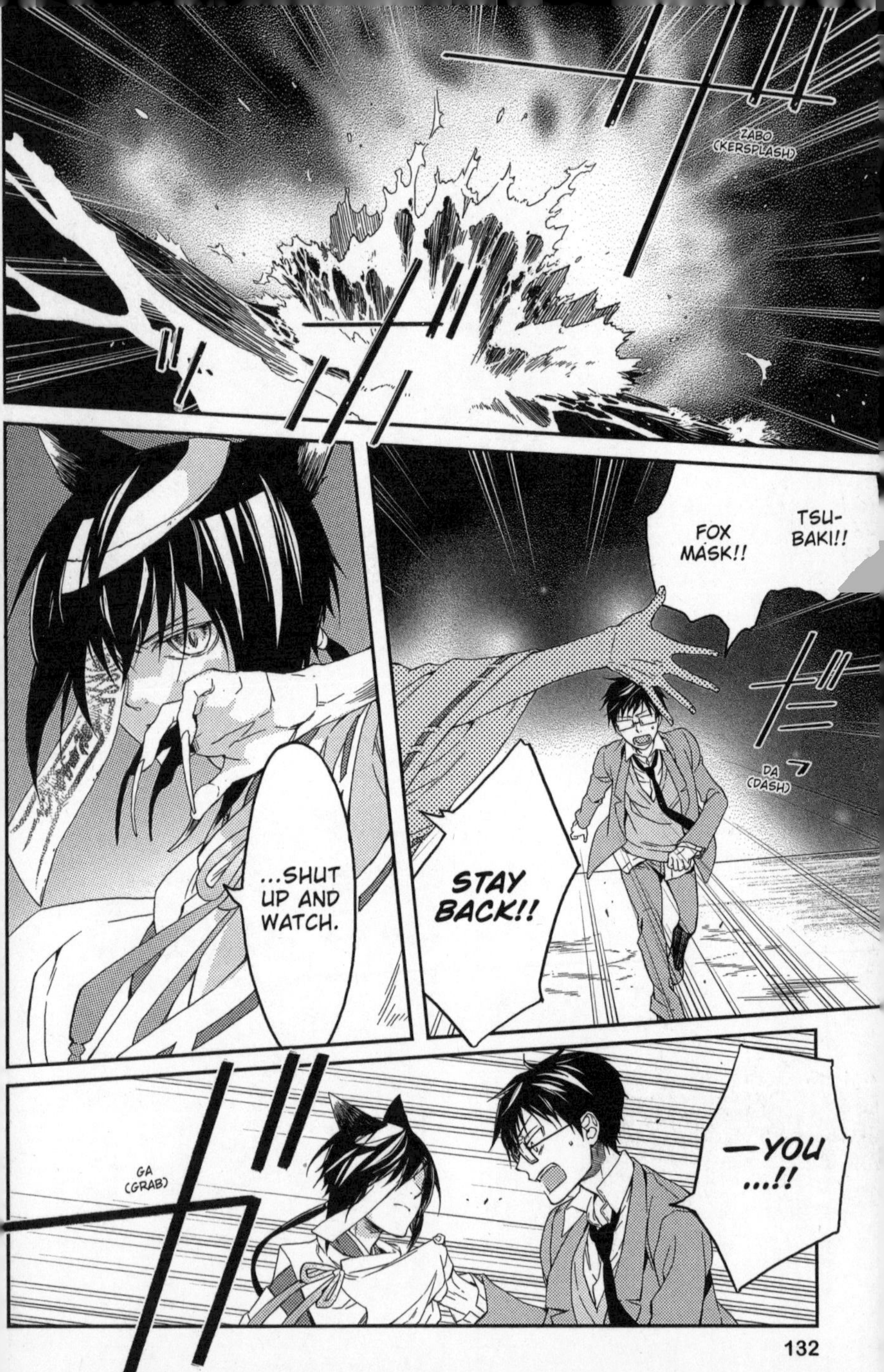
ZABO
(KERSPLASH)
TSU-
BAKI!!
FOX
MASK!!
DA
(DASH)
STAY
BACK!!
...SHUT
UP AND
WATCH.
—YOU
...!!
GA
(GRAB)

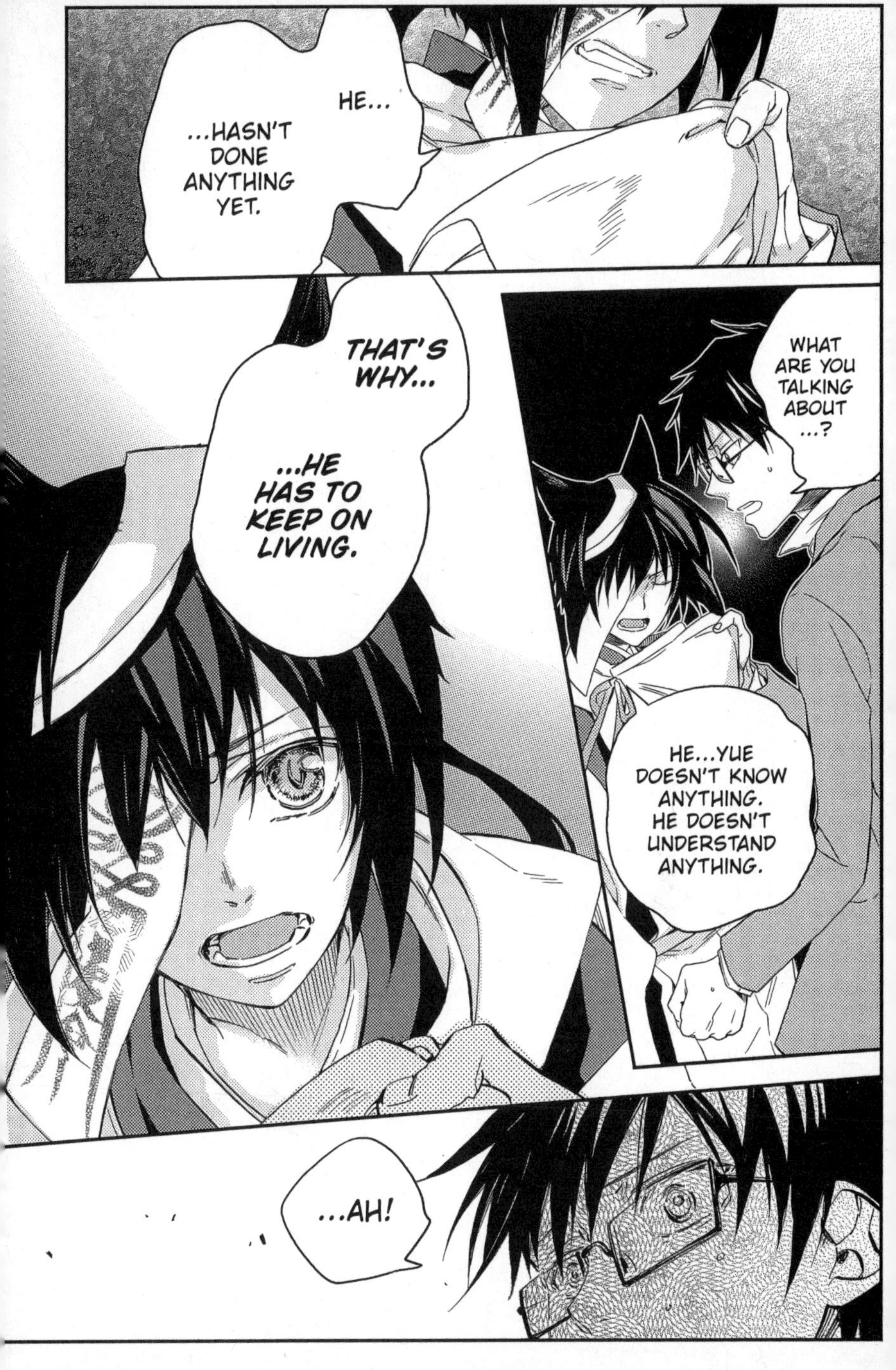
HE...
...HASN'T DONE ANYTHING YET.
WHAT ARE YOU TALKING ABOUT ...?
HE...YUE DOESN'T KNOW ANYTHING. HE DOESN'T UNDERSTAND ANYTHING.
THAT'S WHY...
...HE HAS TO KEEP ON LIVING.
...AH!

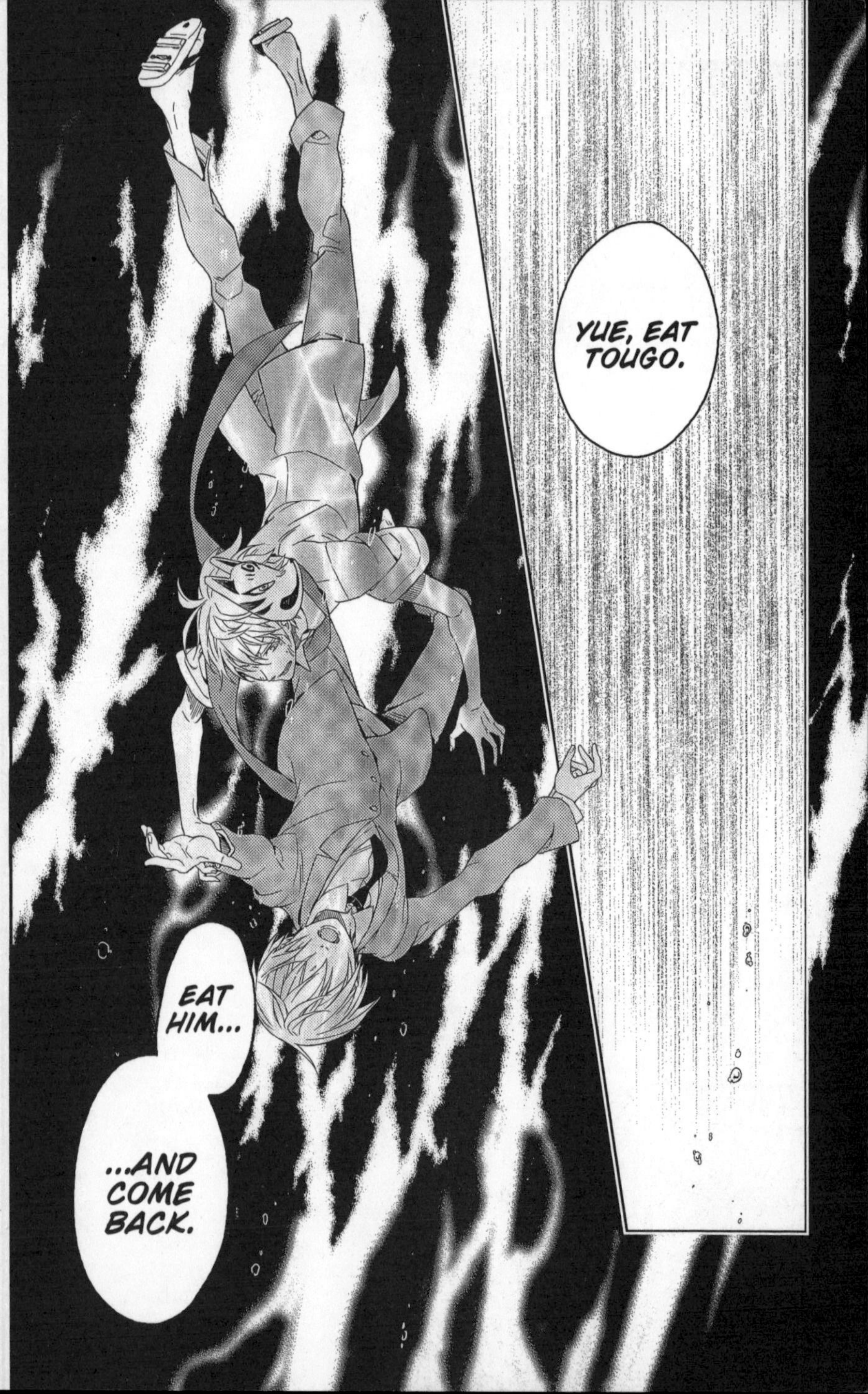
YUE, EAT TOUGO.
EAT HIM...
...AND COME BACK.

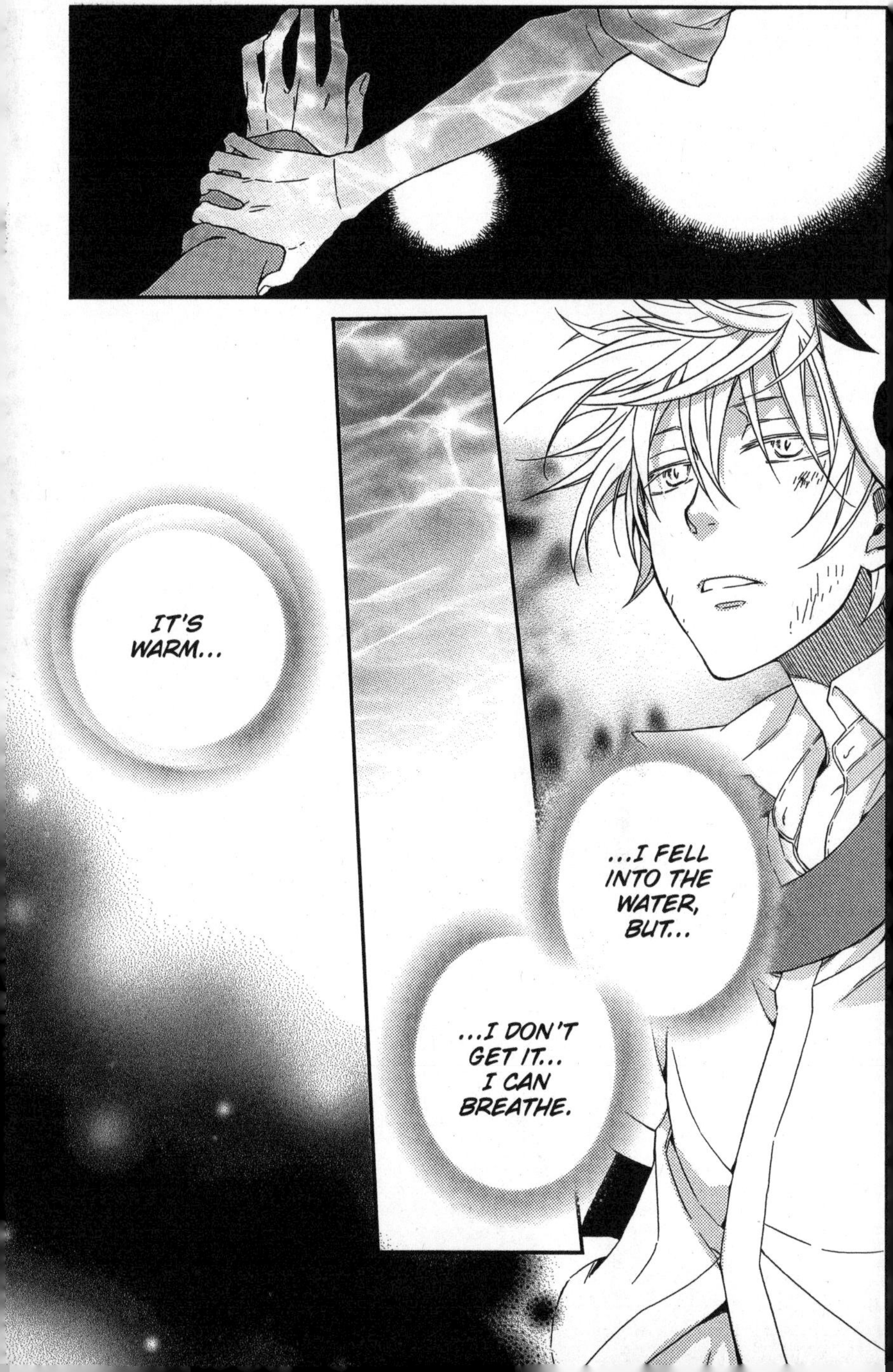
IT'S WARM...
...I FELL INTO THE WATER, BUT...
...I DON'T GET IT... I CAN BREATHE.

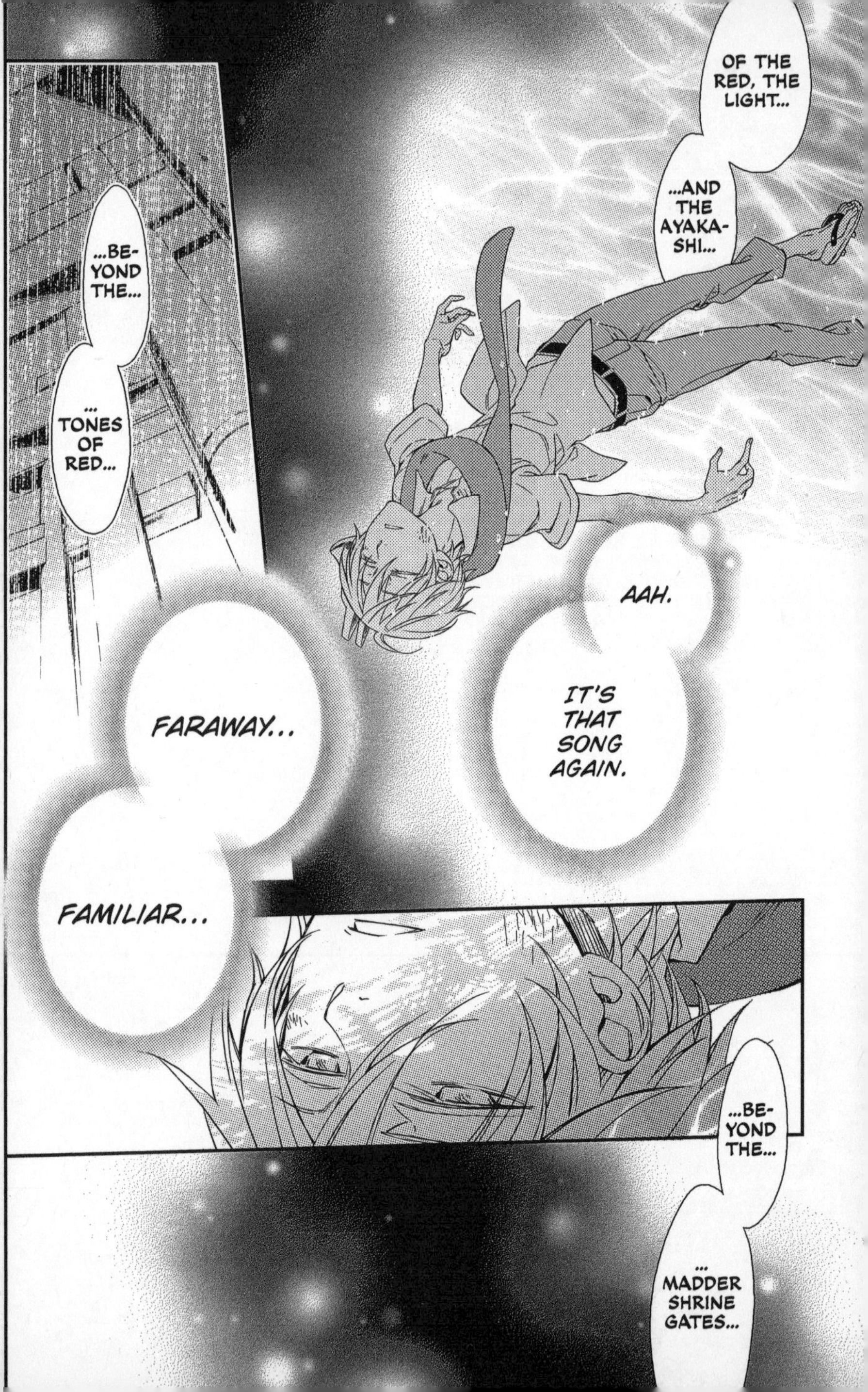
OF THE RED, THE LIGHT...
...AND THE AYAKASHI...
...BEYOND THE...
...TONES OF RED...
AAH.
IT'S THAT SONG AGAIN.
FARAWAY...
FAMILIAR...
...BEYOND THE...
...MADDER SHRINE GATES...

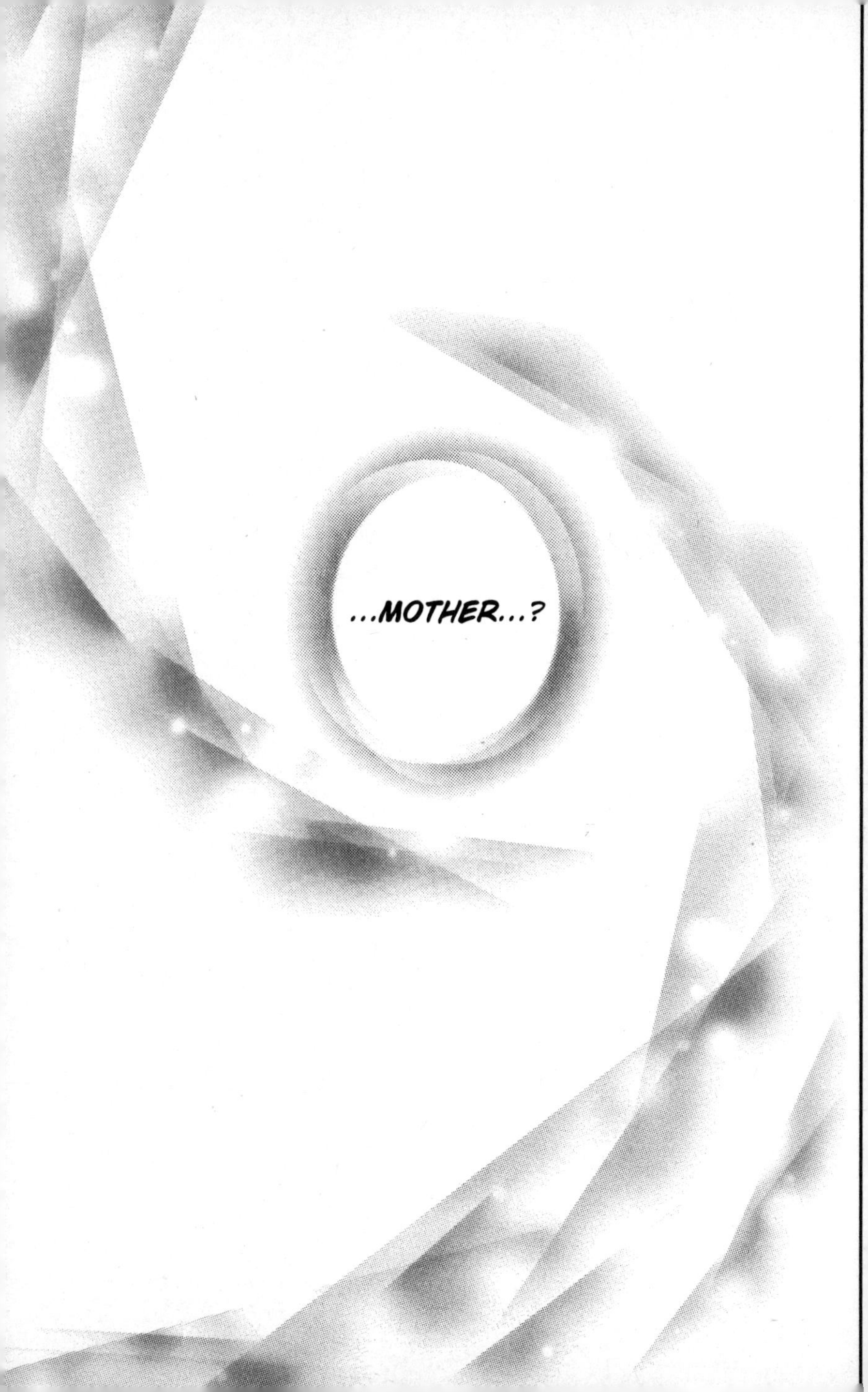
...MOTHER...?

TO BE CONTINUED
IN VOLUME 9

SPECIAL EXTRA
MOMIJI-SAN'S DINNER

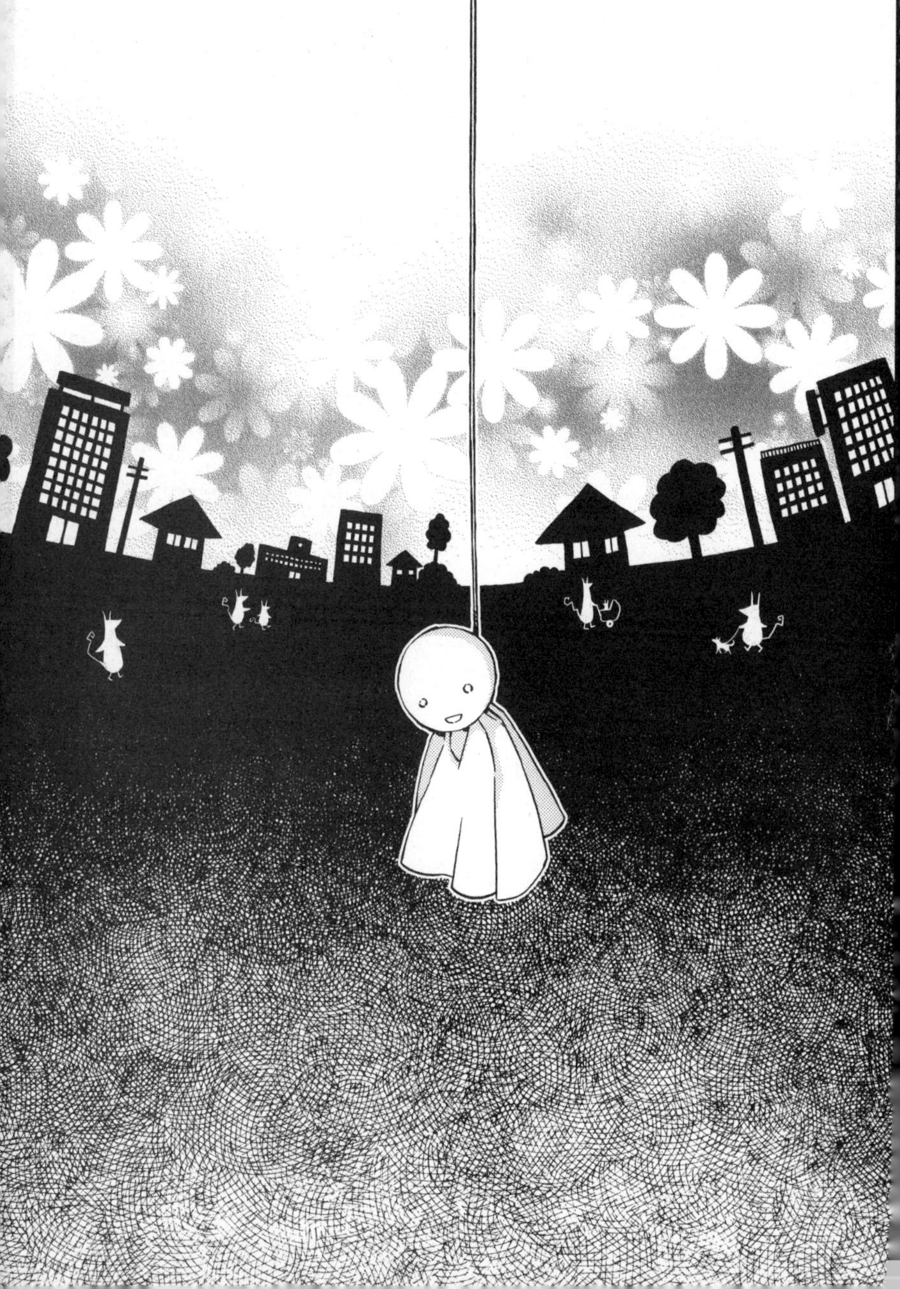

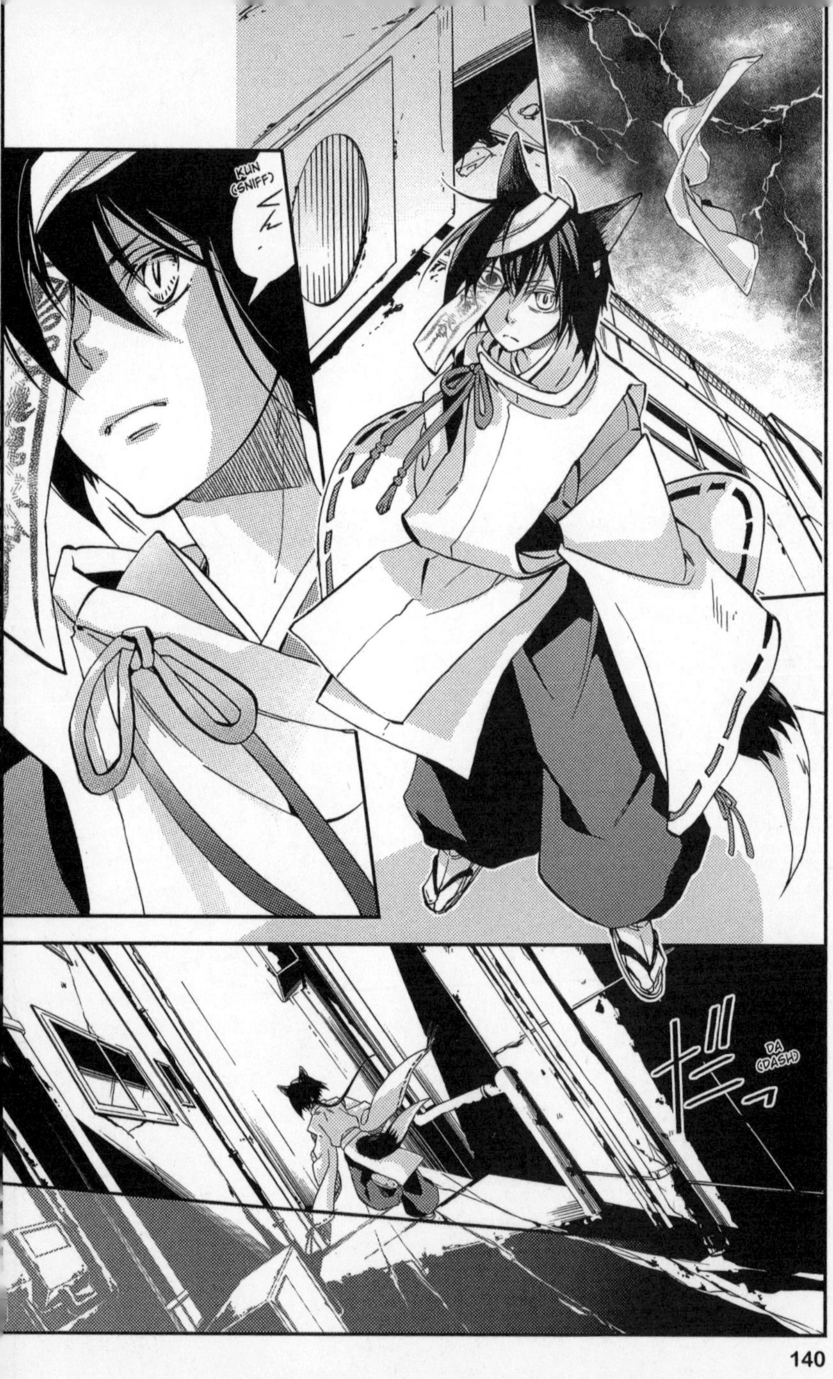
KUN (SNIFF)
DA (DASH)

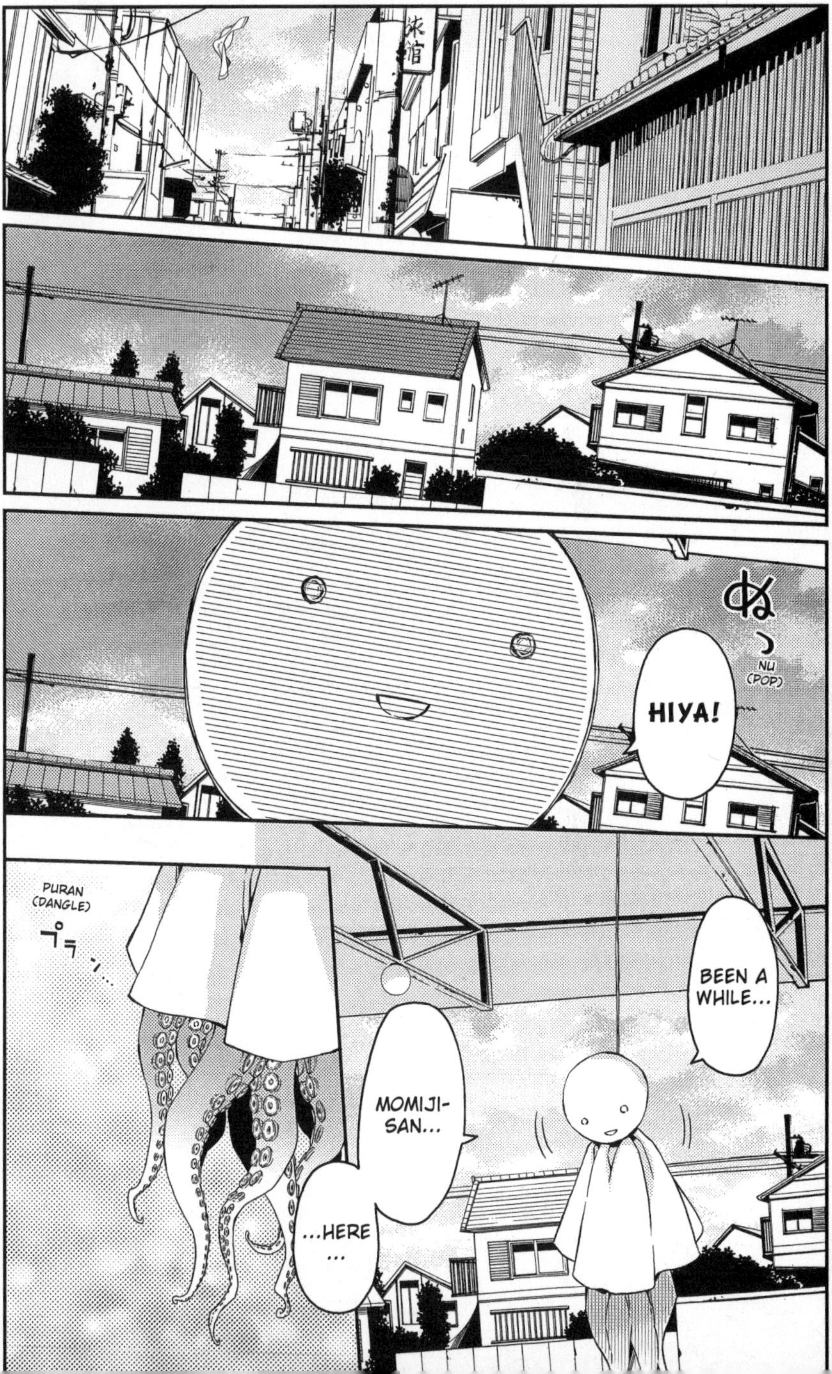
ぬっ
NU (POP)
HIYA!
BEEN A WHILE...
MOMIJI-SAN...
...HERE...
PURAN (DANGLE)
プラン...

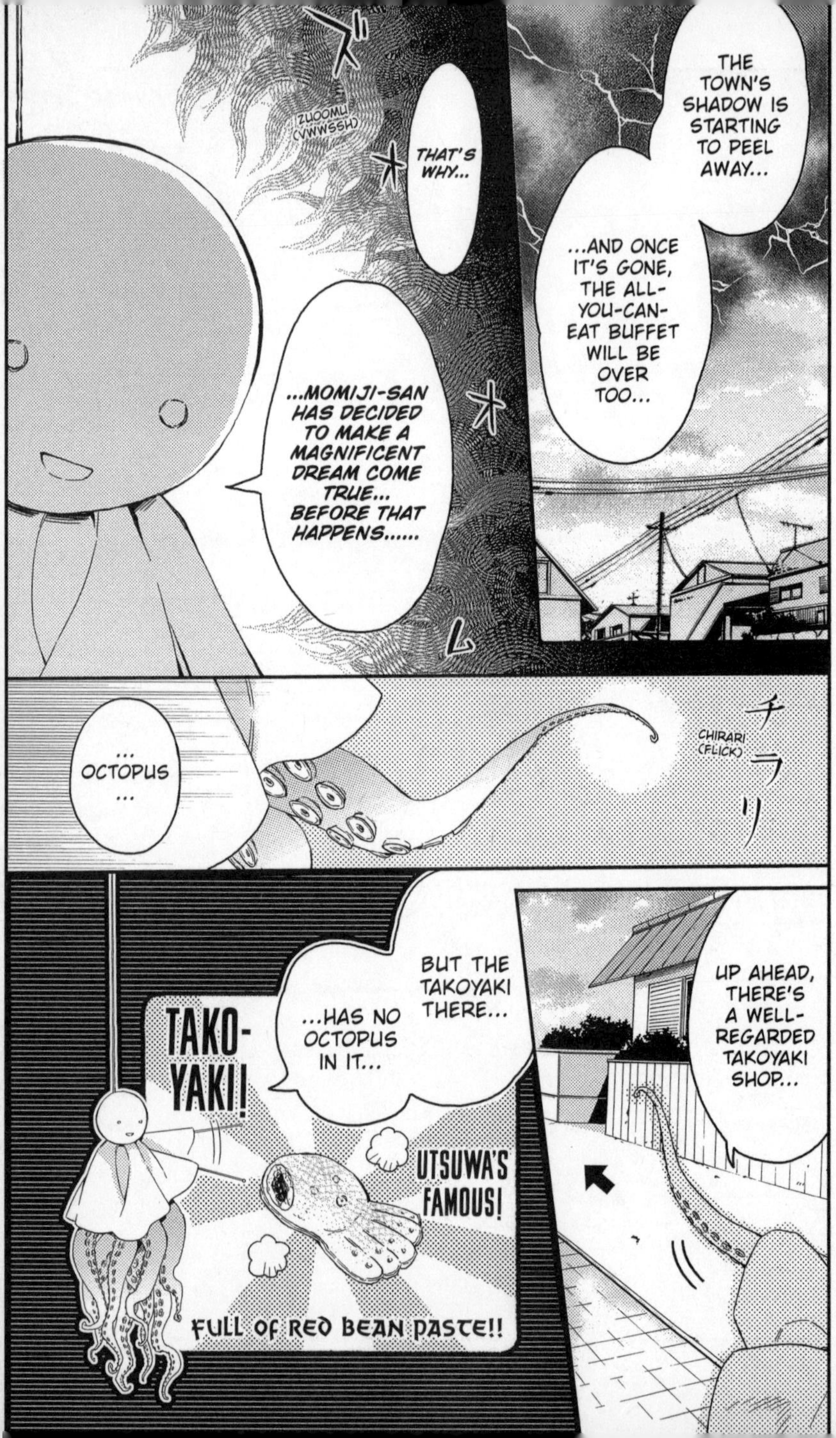
THE TOWN'S SHADOW IS STARTING TO PEEL AWAY...
...AND ONCE IT'S GONE, THE ALL-YOU-CAN-EAT BUFFET WILL BE OVER TOO...
ZUOOMU (VWWSSH)
THAT'S WHY...
...MOMIJI-SAN HAS DECIDED TO MAKE A MAGNIFICENT DREAM COME TRUE... BEFORE THAT HAPPENS......
CHIRARI (FLICK)
...OCTOPUS...
UP AHEAD, THERE'S A WELL-REGARDED TAKOYAKI SHOP...
BUT THE TAKOYAKI THERE...
...HAS NO OCTOPUS IN IT...
TAKO-YAKI!
UTSUWA'S FAMOUS!
FULL OF RED BEAN PASTE!!

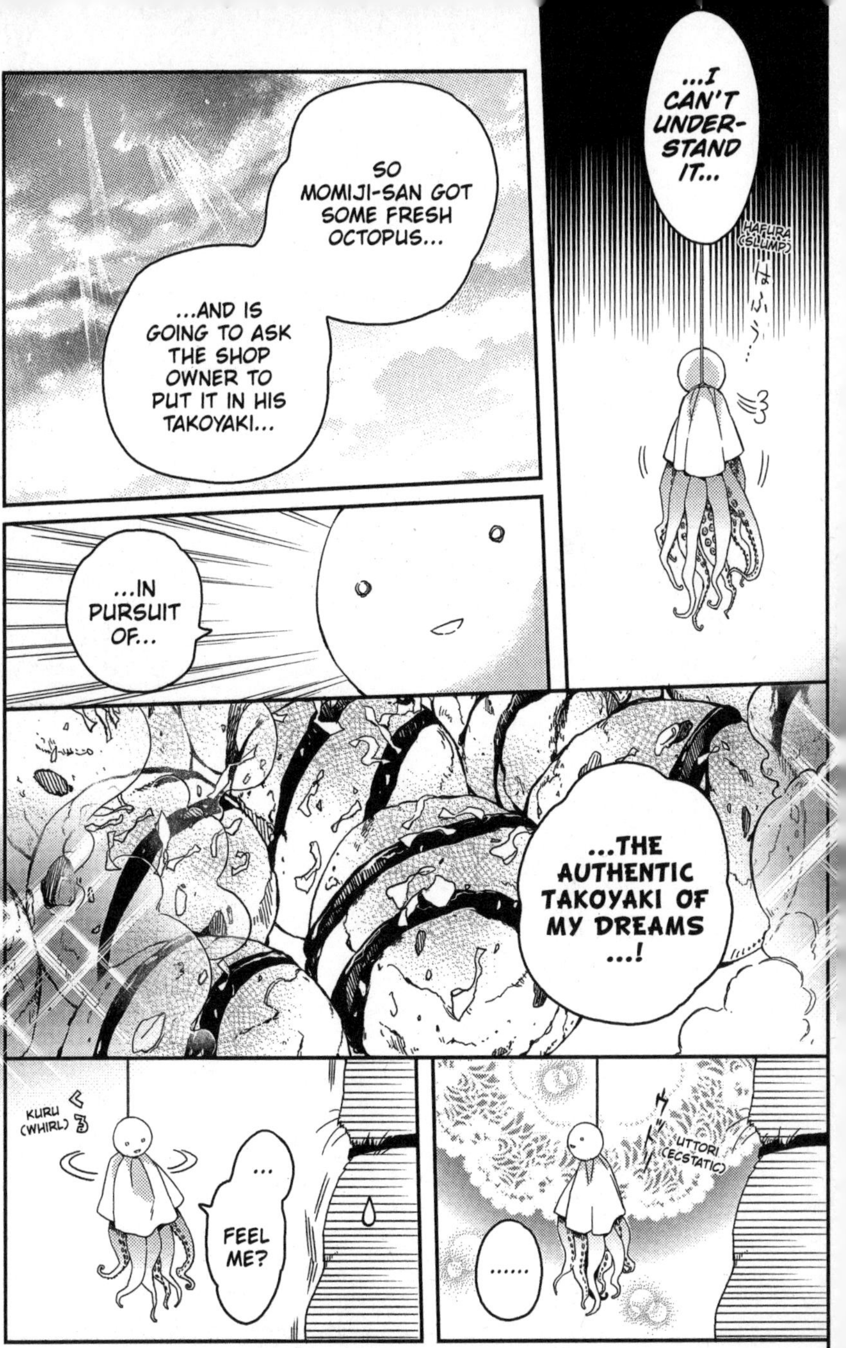
...I CAN'T UNDER-STAND IT...
HAFURA (SLUMP)
SO MOMIJI-SAN GOT SOME FRESH OCTOPUS...
...AND IS GOING TO ASK THE SHOP OWNER TO PUT IT IN HIS TAKOYAKI...
...IN PURSUIT OF...
...THE AUTHENTIC TAKOYAKI OF MY DREAMS ...!
UTTORI (ECSTATIC)
......
KURU (WHIRL)
... FEEL ME?

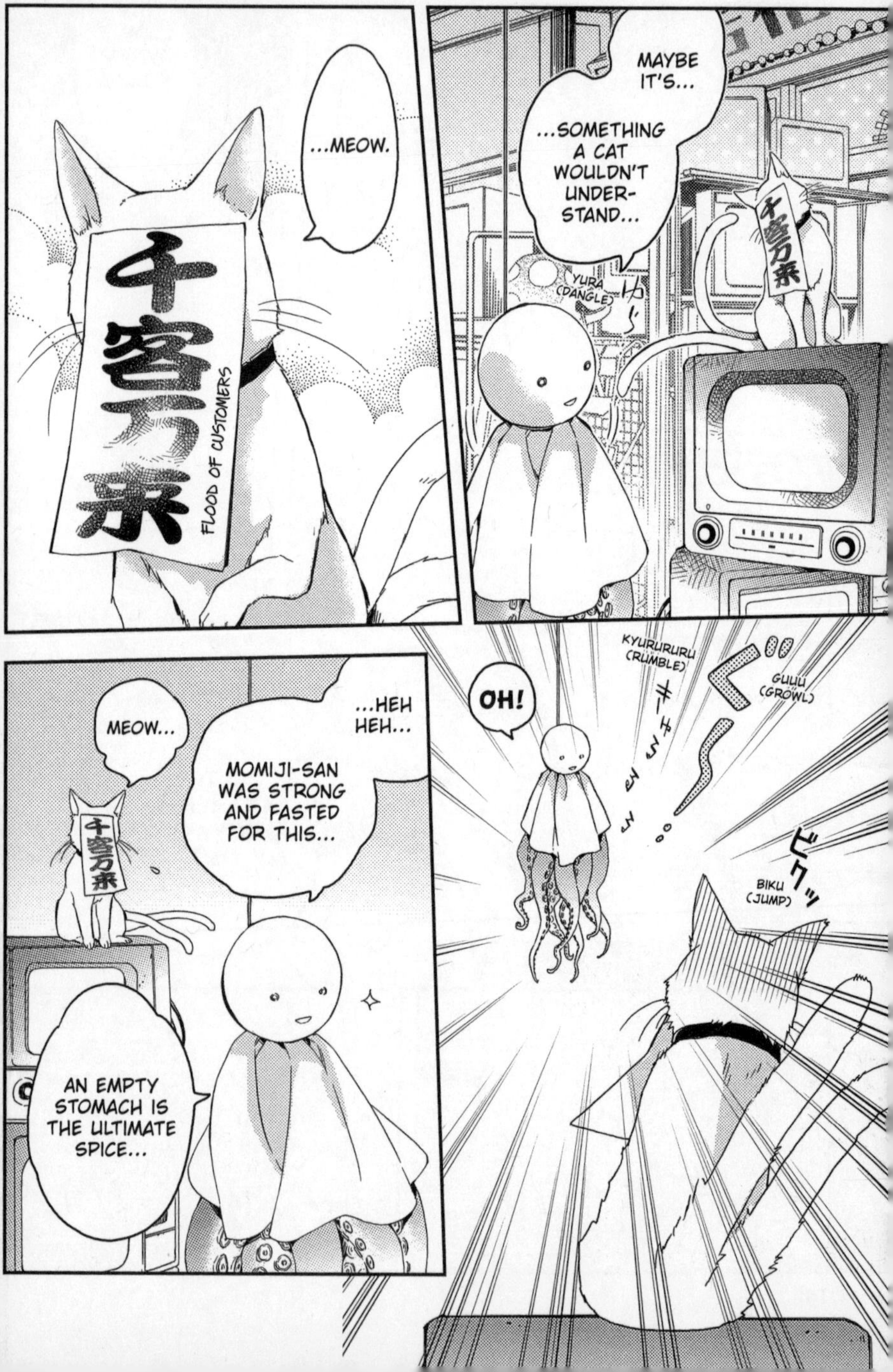
MAYBE IT'S...
...SOMETHING A CAT WOULDN'T UNDER-STAND...
YURA (DANGLE)
...MEOW.
FLOOD OF CUSTOMERS
KYURURURU (RUMBLE)
GUUU (GROWL)
OH!
BIKU (JUMP)
...HEH HEH...
MOMIJI-SAN WAS STRONG AND FASTED FOR THIS...
MEOW...
AN EMPTY STOMACH IS THE ULTIMATE SPICE...

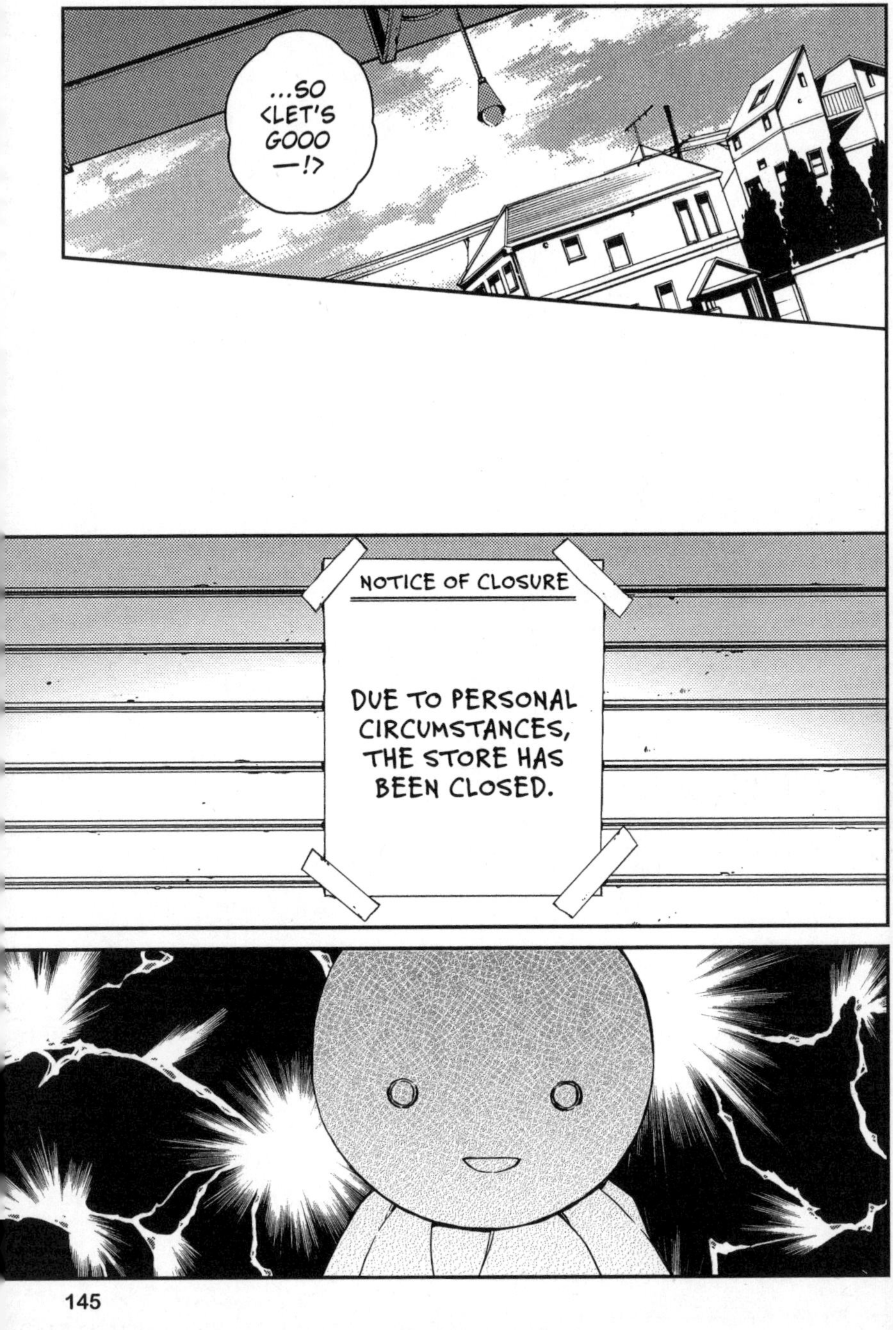
...SO <LET'S GOOO—!>
NOTICE OF CLOSURE
DUE TO PERSONAL CIRCUMSTANCES, THE STORE HAS BEEN CLOSED.

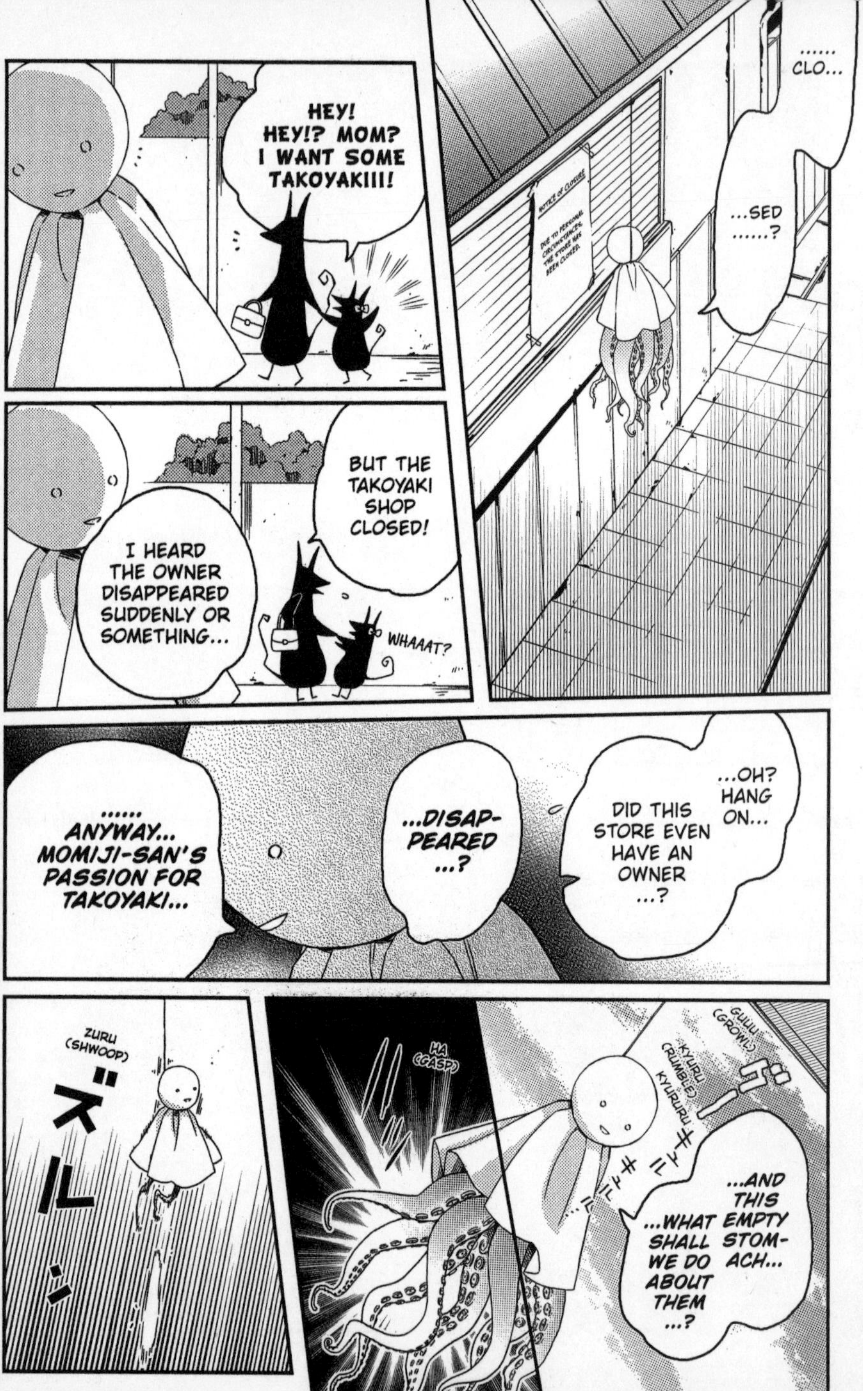
......CLO...
...SED ......?
NOTICE OF CLOSURE
DUE TO PERSONAL CIRCUMSTANCES, THE STORE HAS BEEN CLOSED.
HEY! HEY!? MOM? I WANT SOME TAKOYAKIII!
BUT THE TAKOYAKI SHOP CLOSED!
WHAAAT?
I HEARD THE OWNER DISAPPEARED SUDDENLY OR SOMETHING...
...OH? HANG ON...
DID THIS STORE EVEN HAVE AN OWNER ...?
...DISAP-PEARED ...?
...... ANYWAY... MOMIJI-SAN'S PASSION FOR TAKOYAKI...
GUUU (GROWL)
KYURURU (RUMBLE) KYURURU
...AND THIS EMPTY STOM-ACH...
...WHAT SHALL WE DO ABOUT THEM ...?
HA (GASP)
ZURU (SHWOOP)

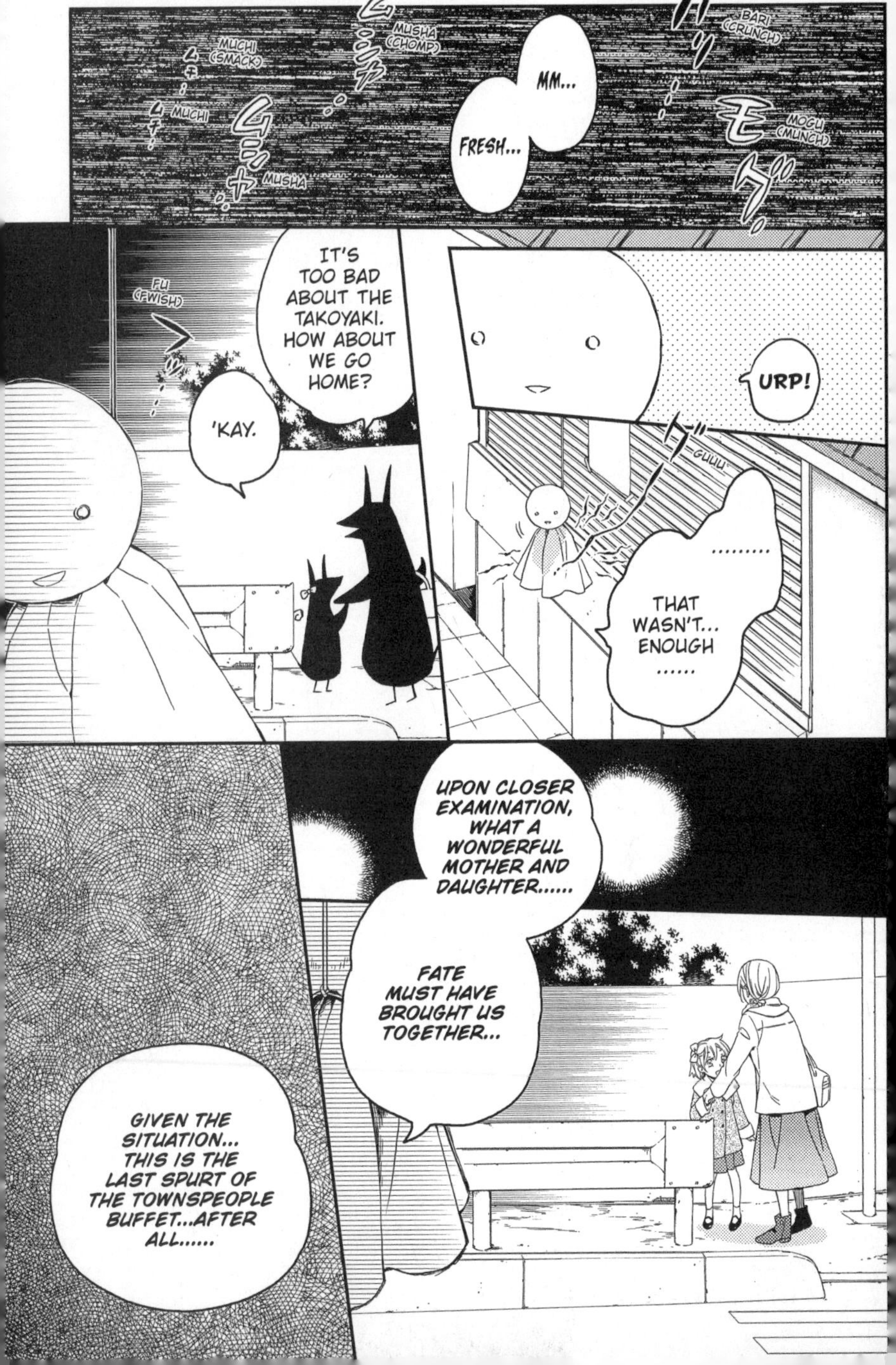
BARI (CRUNCH)
MOGU (MUNCH)
MM...
FRESH...
MUSHA (CHOMP)
MUSHA
MUCHI (SMACK)
MUCHI
URP!
GUUU
....
THAT WASN'T... ENOUGH ......
IT'S TOO BAD ABOUT THE TAKOYAKI. HOW ABOUT WE GO HOME?
'KAY.
FU (FWISH)
UPON CLOSER EXAMINATION, WHAT A WONDERFUL MOTHER AND DAUGHTER......
FATE MUST HAVE BROUGHT US TOGETHER...
GIVEN THE SITUATION... THIS IS THE LAST SPURT OF THE TOWNSPEOPLE BUFFET...AFTER ALL......

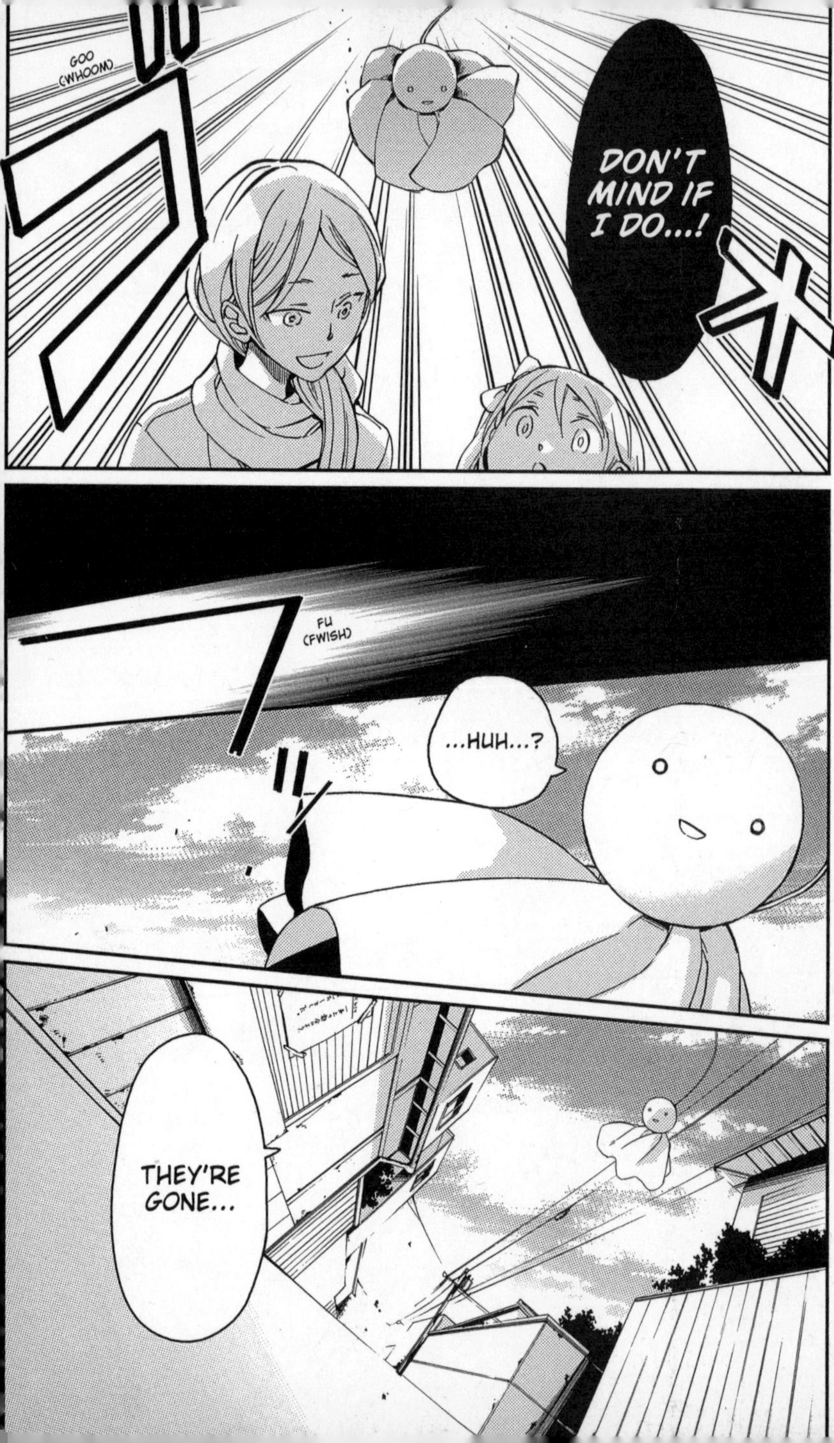
DON'T MIND IF I DO...!
GOO (WHOOM)
FU (FWISH)
...HUH...?
THEY'RE GONE...

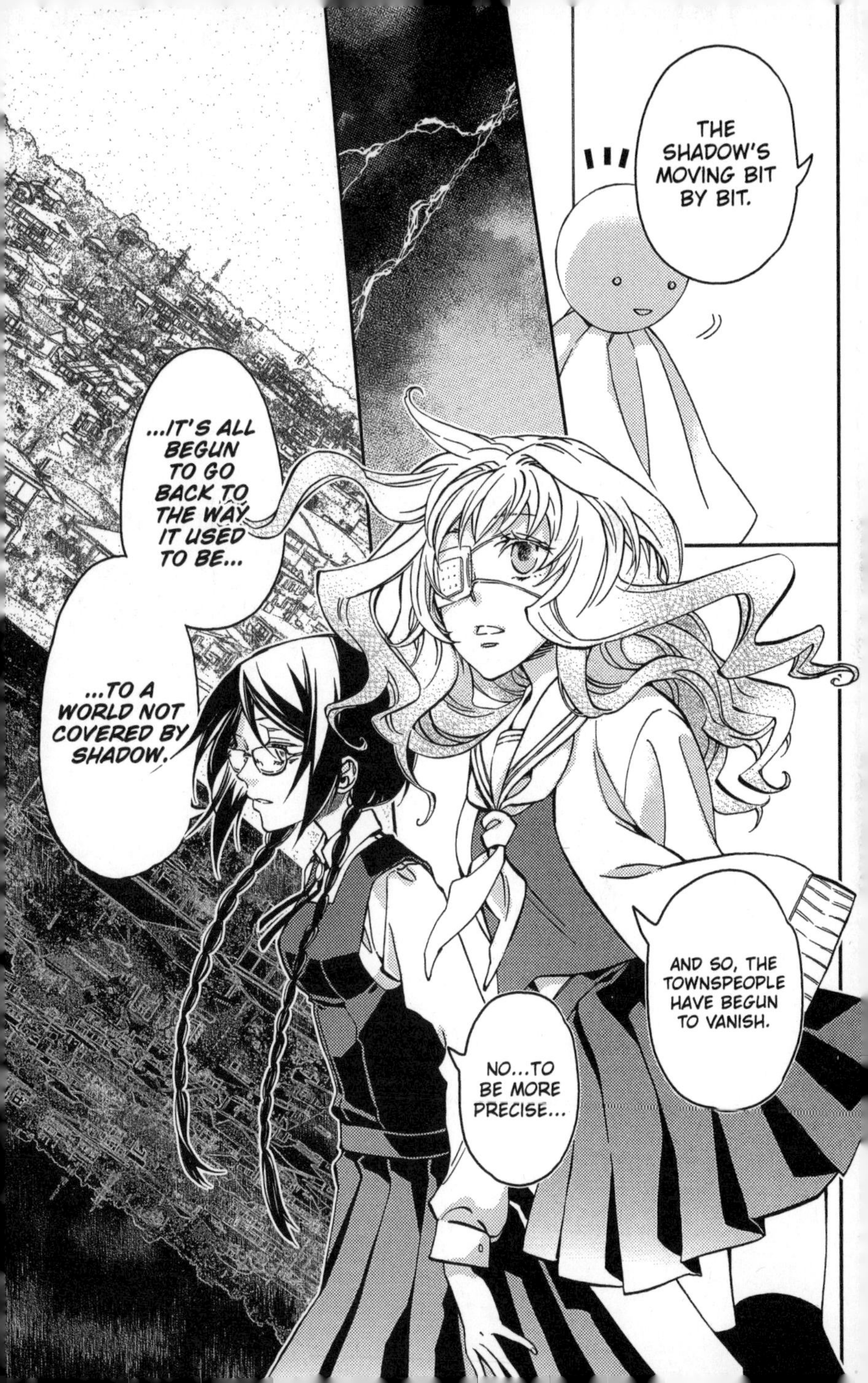
THE SHADOW'S MOVING BIT BY BIT.
AND SO, THE TOWNSPEOPLE HAVE BEGUN TO VANISH.
NO...TO BE MORE PRECISE...
...IT'S ALL BEGUN TO GO BACK TO THE WAY IT USED TO BE...
...TO A WORLD NOT COVERED BY SHADOW.

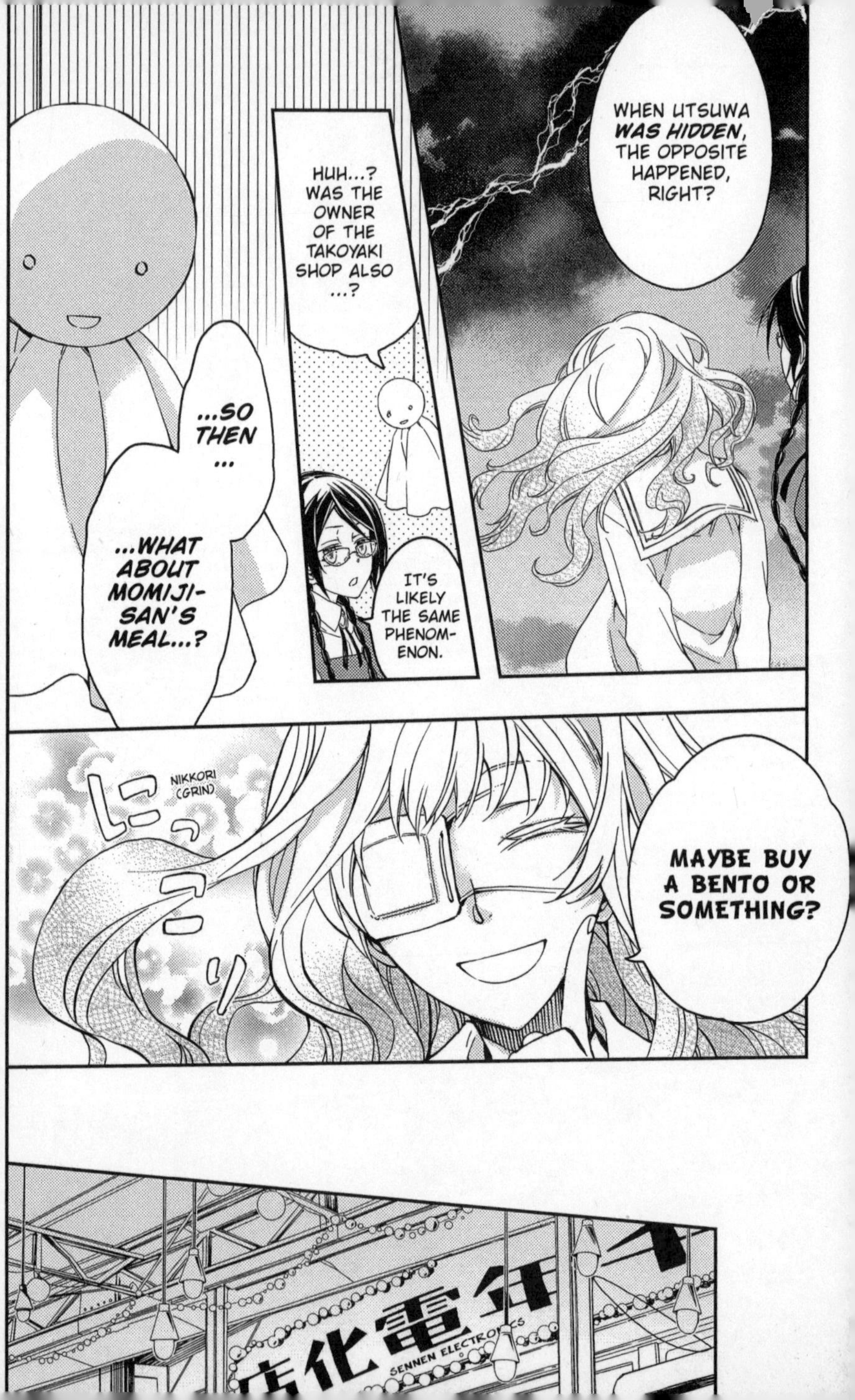
WHEN UTSUWA *WAS HIDDEN*, THE OPPOSITE HAPPENED, RIGHT?
HUH...? WAS THE OWNER OF THE TAKOYAKI SHOP ALSO ...?
IT'S LIKELY THE SAME PHENOMENON.
...SO THEN ...
...WHAT ABOUT MOMIJI-SAN'S MEAL...?
MAYBE BUY A BENTO OR SOMETHING?
NIKKORI (GRIN)
SENNEN ELECTRONICS

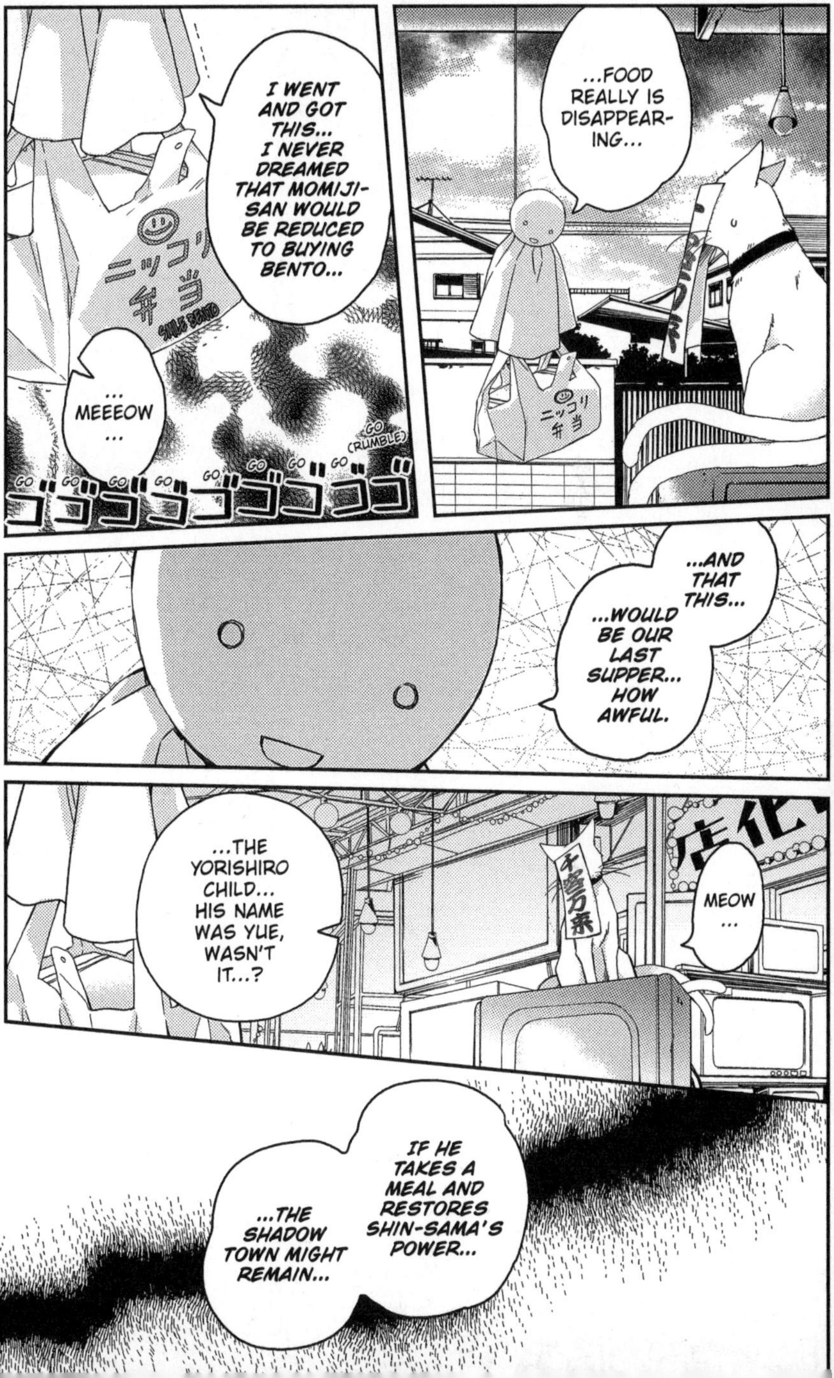
...FOOD REALLY IS DISAPPEARING...
ニッコリ弁当
I WENT AND GOT THIS... I NEVER DREAMED THAT MOMIJI-SAN WOULD BE REDUCED TO BUYING BENTO...
ニッコリ弁当
SMILE BENTO
...MEEEOW...
GO GO GO GO GO GO GO GO (RUMBLE)
...AND THAT THIS... ...WOULD BE OUR LAST SUPPER... HOW AWFUL.
MEOW...
...THE YORISHIRO CHILD... HIS NAME WAS YUE, WASN'T IT...?
IF HE TAKES A MEAL AND RESTORES SHIN-SAMA'S POWER...
...THE SHADOW TOWN MIGHT REMAIN...

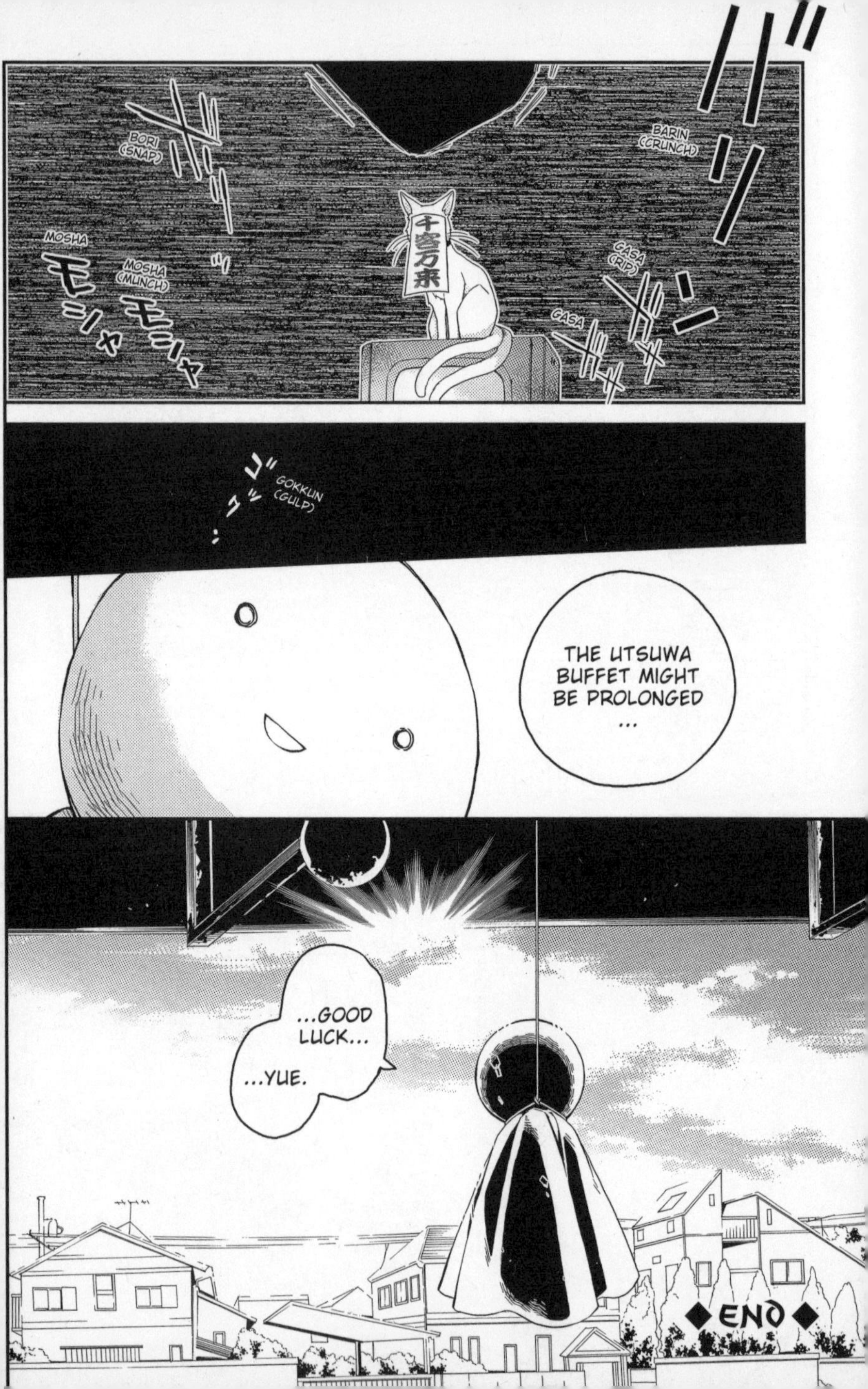
BARIN (CRUNCH)
BORI (SNAP)
GASA (RIP)
GASA
MOSHA (MUNCH)
MOSHA
千客万来
GOKKUN (GULP)
THE UTSUWA BUFFET MIGHT BE PROLONGED ...
...GOOD LUCK...
...YUE.
END

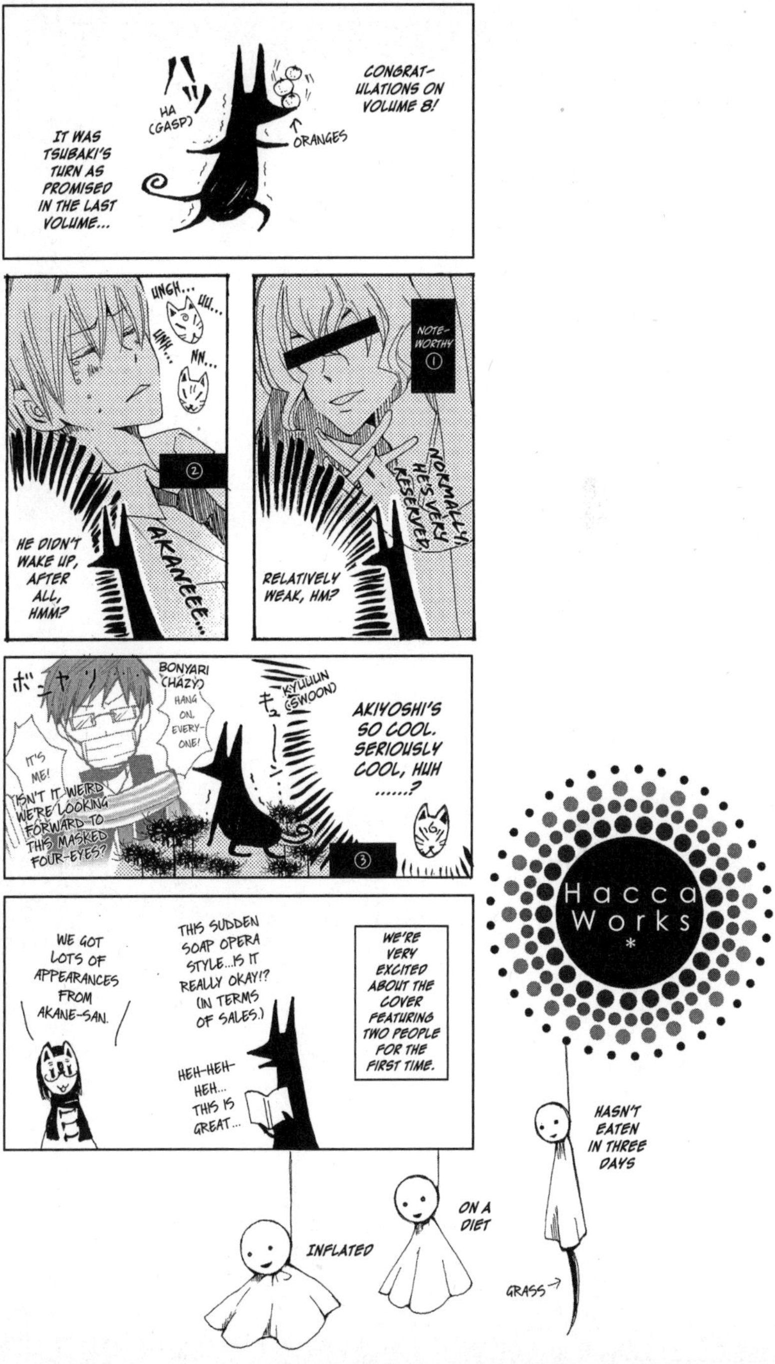
CONGRATULATIONS ON VOLUME 8!
HA (GASP)
ORANGES
IT WAS TSUBAKI'S TURN AS PROMISED IN THE LAST VOLUME...
NOTEWORTHY ①
NORMALLY, HE'S VERY RESERVED
RELATIVELY WEAK, HM?
UNGH... UU...
UNH... NN...
②
AKANEEEE...
HE DIDN'T WAKE UP, AFTER ALL, HMM?
AKIYOSHI'S SO COOL. SERIOUSLY COOL, HUH ......?
KYUUUN (SWOON)
BONYARI (HAZY)
HANG ON, EVERYONE!
IT'S ME!
ISN'T IT WEIRD WE'RE LOOKING FORWARD TO THIS MASKED FOUR-EYES?
③
WE'RE VERY EXCITED ABOUT THE COVER FEATURING TWO PEOPLE FOR THE FIRST TIME.
THIS SUDDEN SOAP OPERA STYLE...IS IT REALLY OKAY!? (IN TERMS OF SALES.)
HEH-HEH-HEH... THIS IS GREAT...
WE GOT LOTS OF APPEARANCES FROM AKANE-SAN.
Hacca Works
HASN'T EATEN IN THREE DAYS
ON A DIET
INFLATED
GRASS

Akujiki-san

SPECIAL THANKS

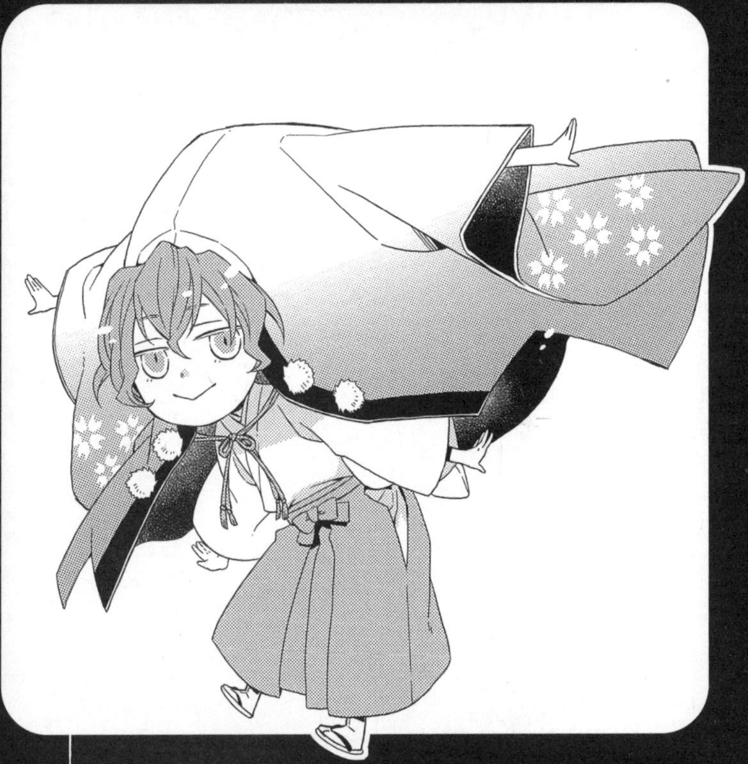

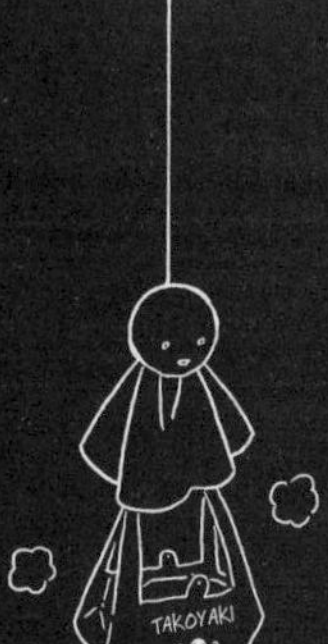
TAKOYAKI

HaccaWorks*-sama

My editor Y-san

The designer

Production assistance: S-sama, K-sama

Everyone involved in the production

Everyone reading

Thank you so much!!

nanao

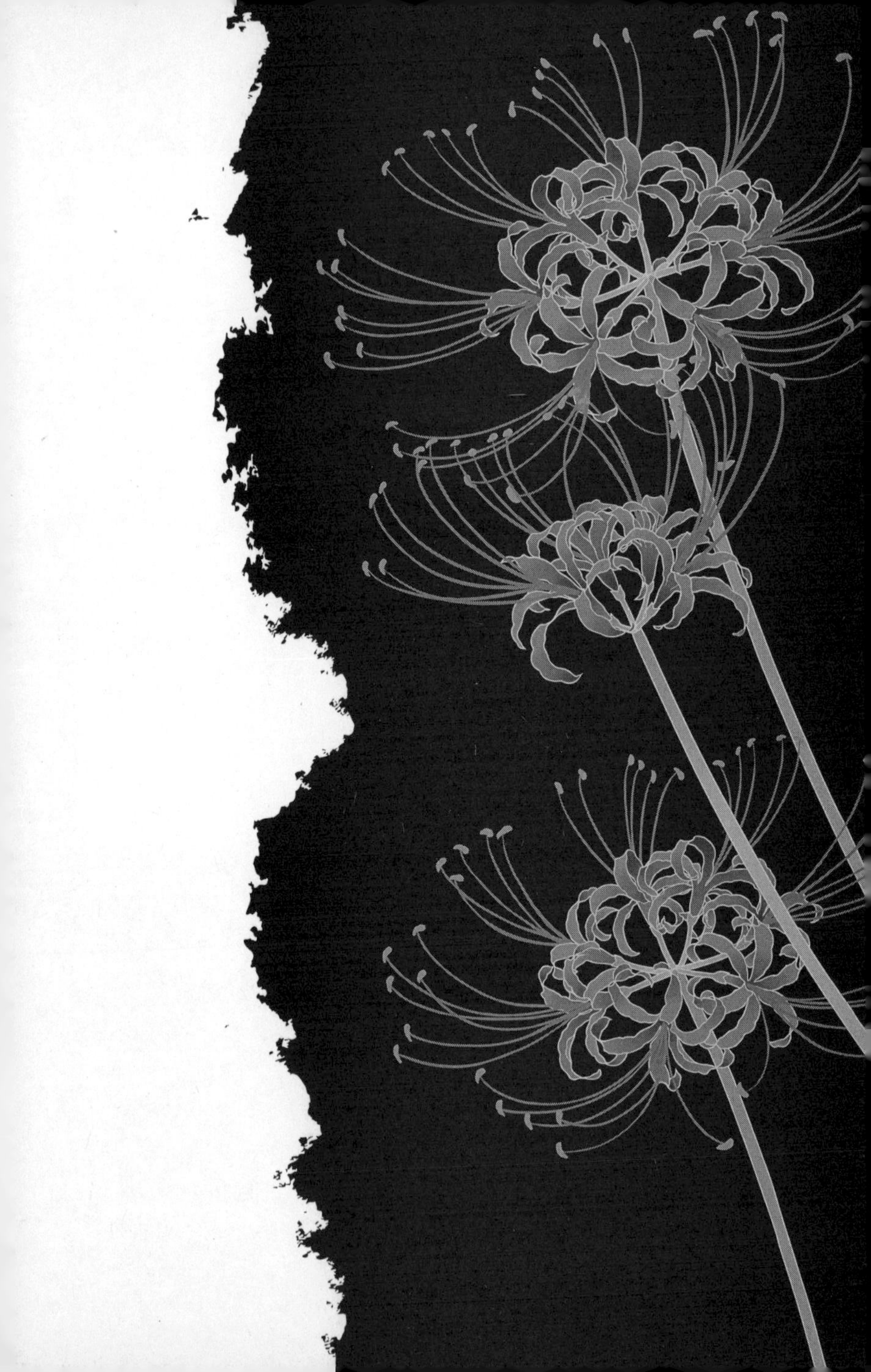

TRANSLATION NOTES

COMMON HONORIFICS

no honorific: Indicates familiarity or closeness; if used without permission or reason, addressing someone in this manner would be an insult.

-san: The Japanese equivalent of Mr./Mrs./Miss. If a situation calls for politeness, this is the fail-safe honorific.

-sama: Conveys great respect; may also indicate that the social status of the speaker is lower than that of the addressee.

-kun: Used most often when referring to boys, this indicates affection or familiarity. Occasionally used by older men among their peers, but it may also be used by anyone referring to a person of lower standing.

-chan, -tan: An affectionate honorific indicating familiarity used mostly in reference to girls; also used in reference to cute persons or animals.

Ayakashi is a general term for ghosts, monsters, haunted objects, mythical animals, and all sorts of uncanny things from Japanese folklore.

PAGE 36

Akiyoshi refers to Abe and Friends as **"the guy in two coats."** In the original, Akiyoshi uses the very apt *nininbaori* to describe him instead. *Nininbaori* is a style of Japanese comedy in which two people share a coat (*haori*), with one person playing the arms, while the other plays the head. The discord between the head and arms is where the humor comes from. The appearance of the comedy duo would be just like that of Abe and Friends.

PAGE 140

Takoyaki are fried dumplings with pieces of octopus inside, as pictured on page 141.

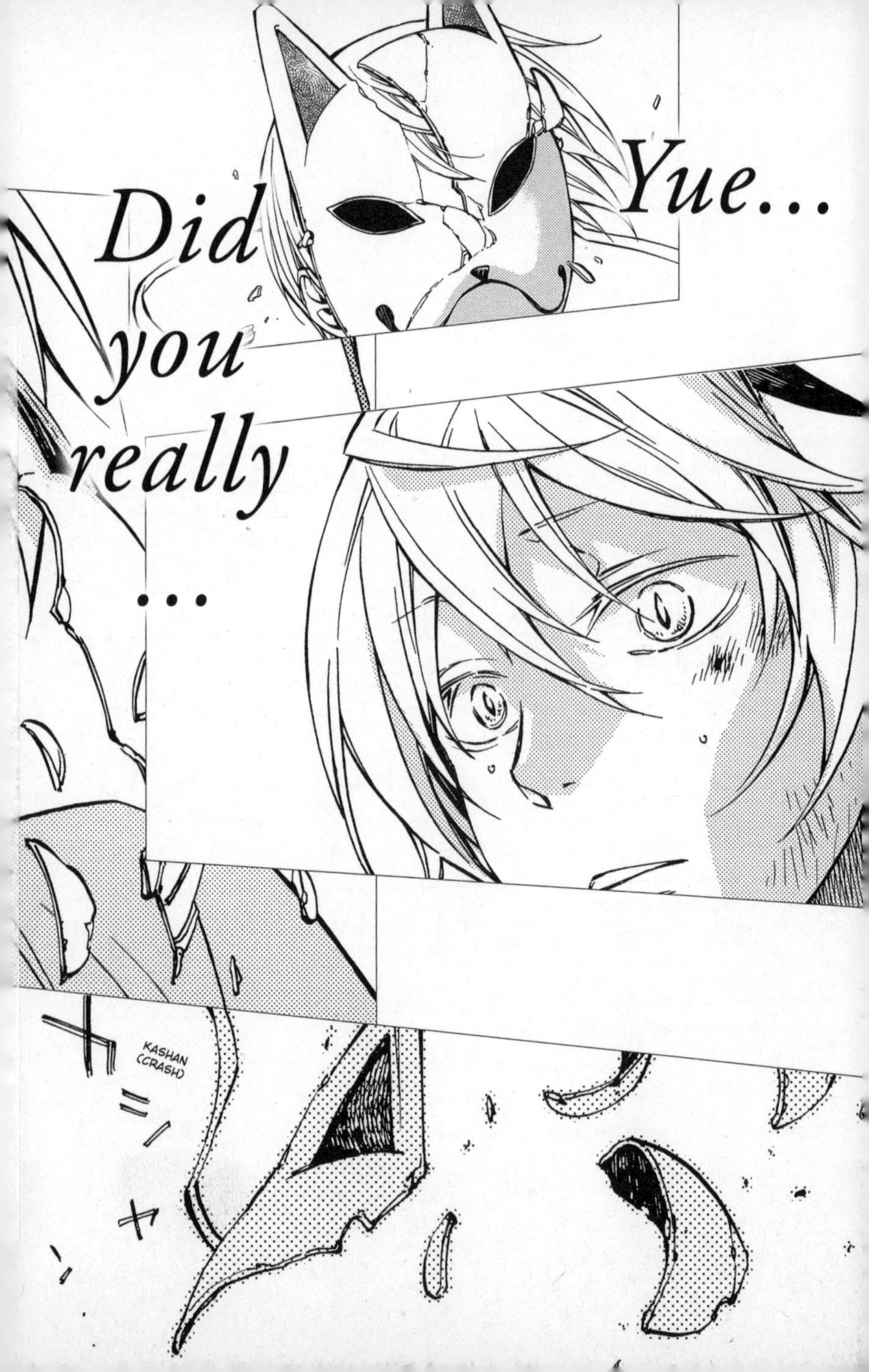
Yue...
Did you really ...
KASHAN (CRASH)

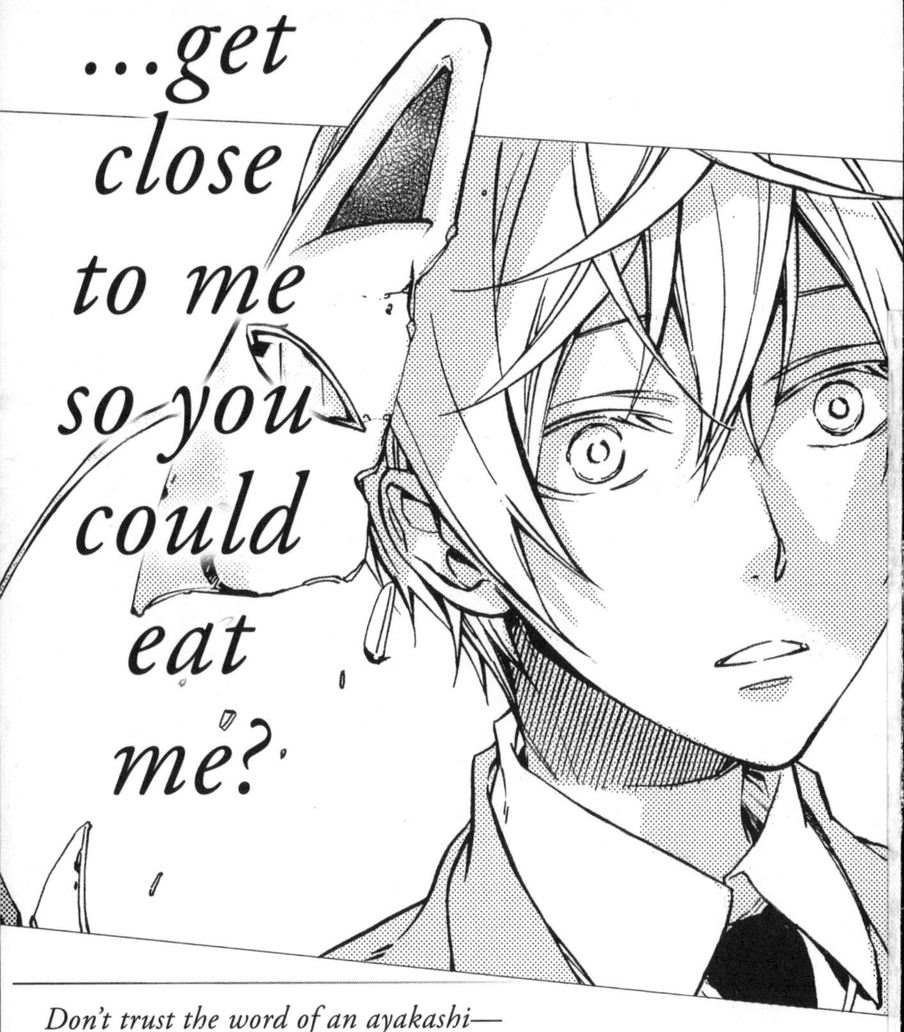
...get close to me so you could eat me?

Don't trust the word of an ayakashi—

After waking from a long dream, the story of the past unfolds before his eyes. Is it a lie? Or the truth? The climax arrives!!

Of the Red, the Light, and the Ayakashi 9

COMING IN DECEMBER 2017

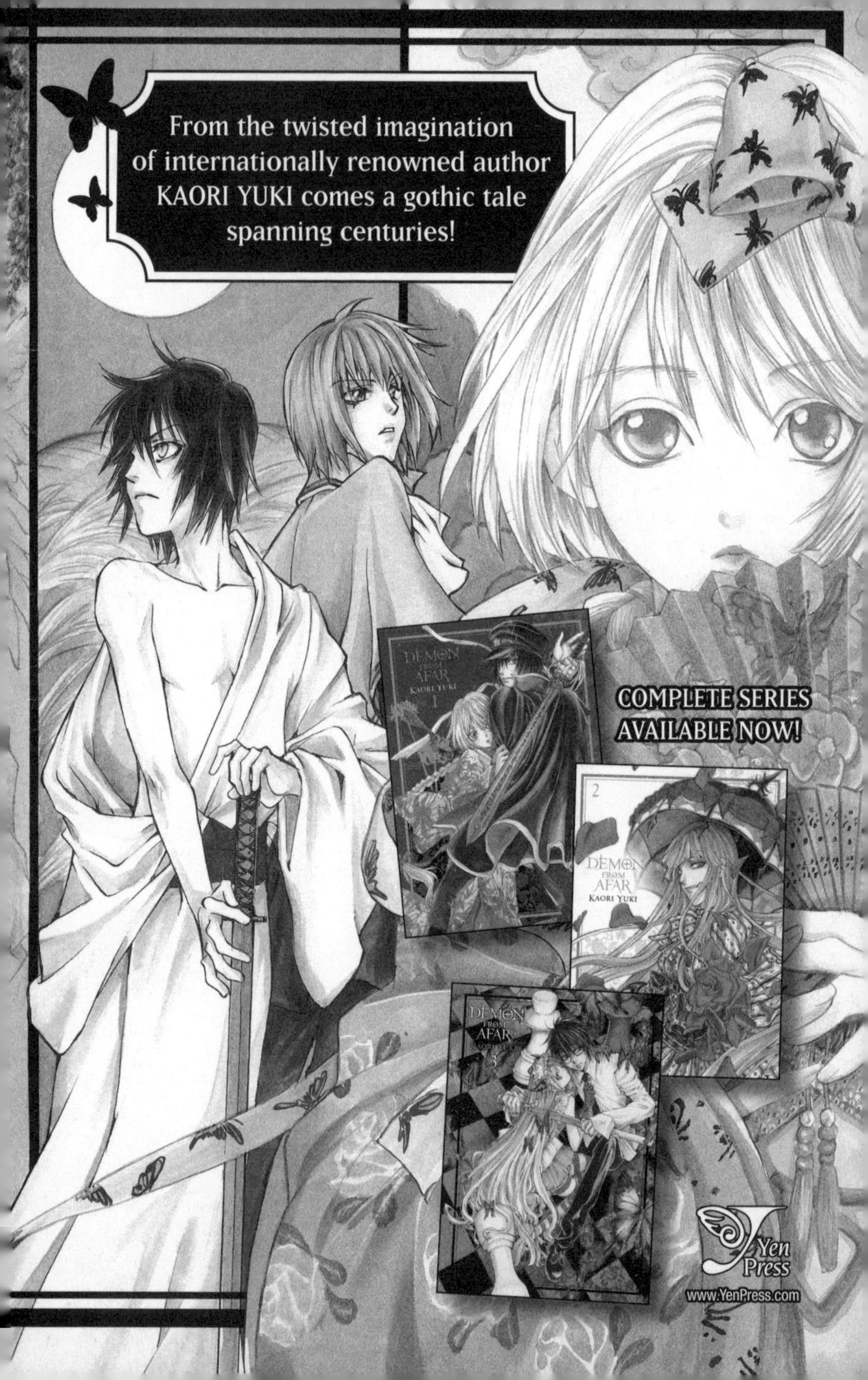
From the twisted imagination of internationally renowned author KAORI YUKI comes a gothic tale spanning centuries!
DEMON FROM AFAR
KAORI YUKI
1
2
DEMON FROM AFAR
KAORI YUKI
DEMON FROM AFAR
3
COMPLETE SERIES AVAILABLE NOW!
Yen Press
www.YenPress.com

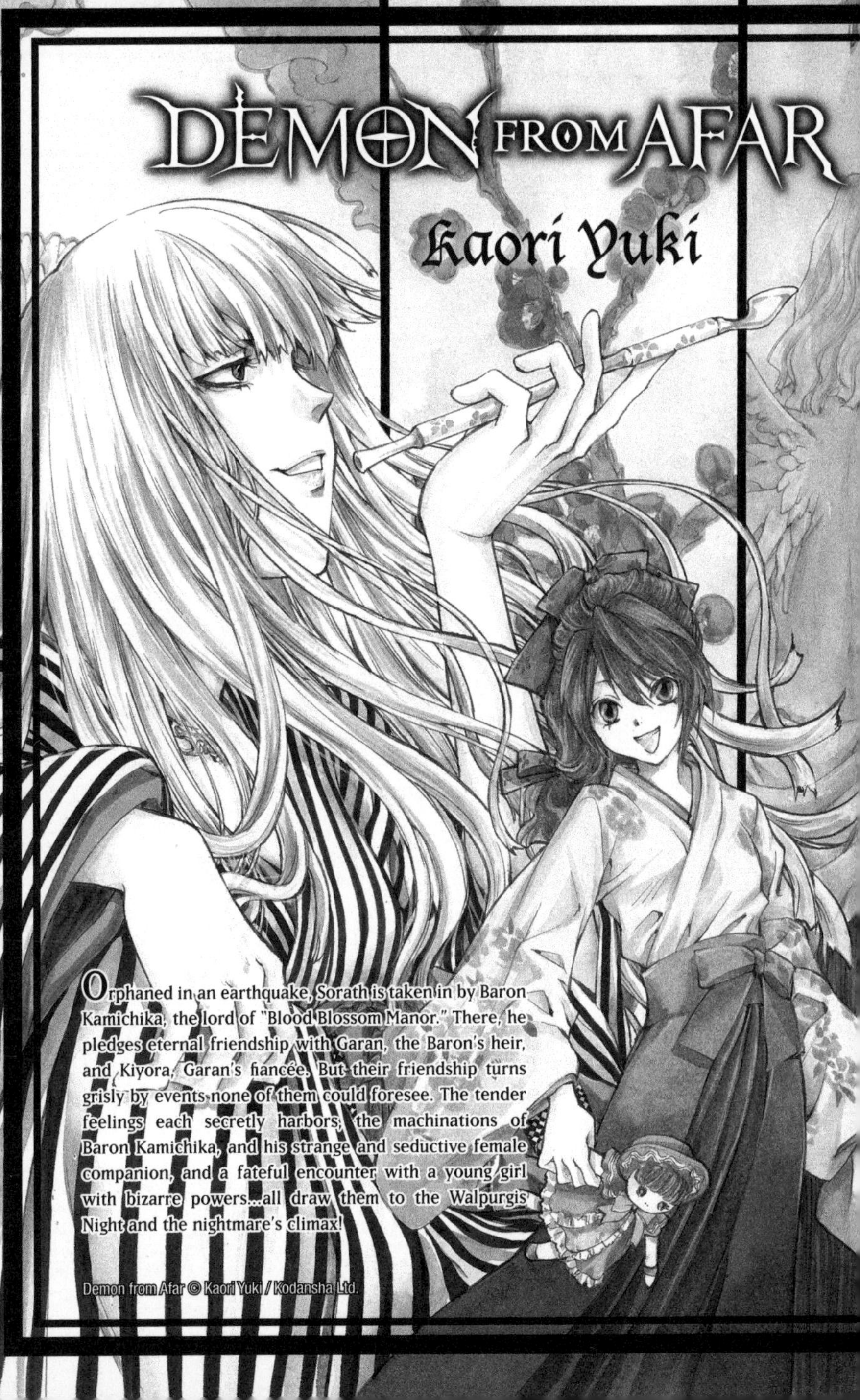
DEMON FROM AFAR
Kaori Yuki
Orphaned in an earthquake, Sorath is taken in by Baron Kamichika, the lord of "Blood Blossom Manor." There, he pledges eternal friendship with Garan, the Baron's heir, and Kiyora, Garan's fiancée. But their friendship turns grisly by events none of them could foresee. The tender feelings each secretly harbors, the machinations of Baron Kamichika, and his strange and seductive female companion, and a fateful encounter with a young girl with bizarre powers...all draw them to the Walpurgis Night and the nightmare's climax!
Demon from Afar © Kaori Yuki / Kodansha Ltd.

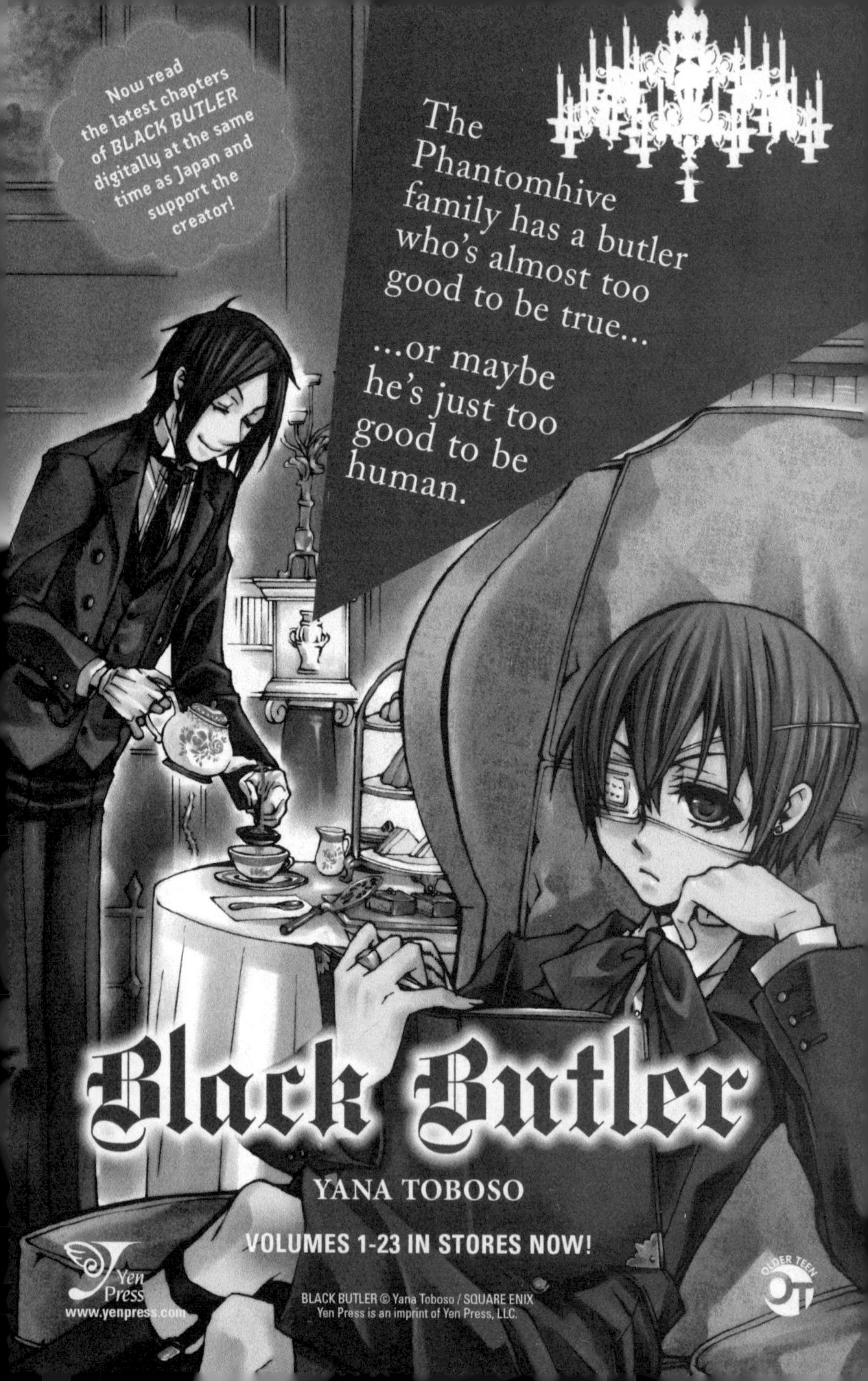

Now read the latest chapters of BLACK BUTLER digitally at the same time as Japan and support the creator!
The Phantomhive family has a butler who's almost too good to be true...
...or maybe he's just too good to be human.
Black Butler
YANA TOBOSO
VOLUMES 1-23 IN STORES NOW!
Yen Press
www.yenpress.com
BLACK BUTLER © Yana Toboso / SQUARE ENIX
Yen Press is an imprint of Yen Press, LLC.
OLDER TEEN
OT

Of the Red, the Light, and the Ayakashi

ART BY Nanao
STORY BY HaccaWorks*

Translation: Jocelyne Allen ✦ Lettering: Alexis Eckerman

AKAYA AKASHIYA AYAKASHINO
© Nanao 2016
© HaccaWorks* 2016
First published in Japan in 2016 by KADOKAWA
CORPORATION. English translation rights reserved by
YEN PRESS, LLC under the license from
KADOKAWA CORPORATION, Tokyo through
TUTTLE-MORI AGENCY, Inc., Tokyo.

English translation © 2017 by Yen Press, LLC

Yen Press
1290 Avenue of the Americas
New York, NY 10104

Visit us!
yenpress.com
facebook.com/yenpress
twitter.com/yenpress
yenpress.tumblr.com
instagram.com/yenpress

First Yen Press Edition: September 2017

Yen Press is an imprint of Yen Press, LLC.
The Yen Press name and logo are trademarks of Yen Press, LLC.

Library of Congress Control Number: 2016932691

ISBNs: 978-0-316-47235-7 (print)
978-0-316-47447-4 (ebook)

10 9 8 7 6 5 4 3 2 1

BVG

Printed in the United States of America

MARVIN REDPOST

IS HE A GIRL?

Look out for more in the
Marvin Redpost series

Kidnapped at Birth
Why Pick On Me?
Alone in His Teacher's House
Class President
A Flying Birthday Cake?
Super Fast, Out of Control!
A Magic Crystal?

and Wayside School

Sideways Stories from Wayside School
Wayside School is Falling Down
Wayside School Gets a Little Stranger
Sideways Arithmetic from Wayside School
More Sideways Arithmetic from Wayside School

Other titles by the same author

Holes
Stanley Yelnats' Survival Guide to Camp Greenlake
There's a Boy in the Girls' Bathroom
Dogs Don't Tell Jokes
The Boy Who Lost His Face

www.louissachar.co.uk